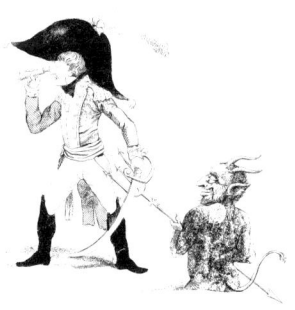

Napoleon and the Invasion of Britain

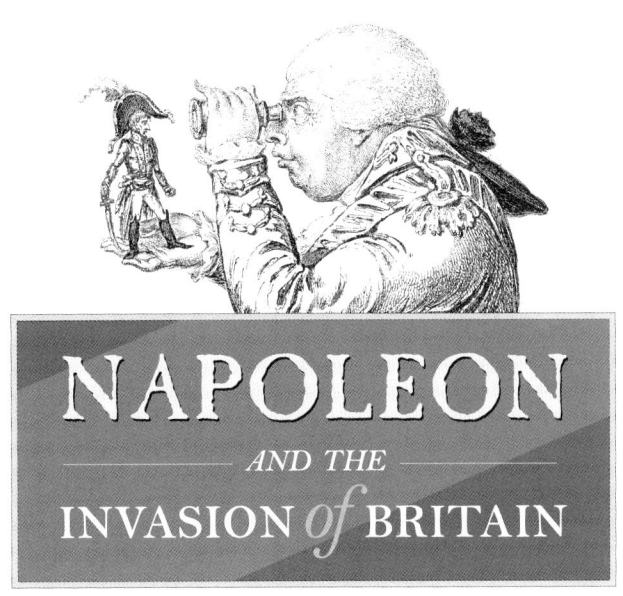

NAPOLEON
— AND THE —
INVASION *of* BRITAIN

Alexandra Franklin and **Mark Philp**
with contributions by Katrina Navickas

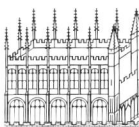

BODLEIAN LIBRARY · UNIVERSITY OF OXFORD

The exhibition at the Bodleian Library is sponsored by

Laing & Cruickshank
INVESTMENT MANAGEMENT LIMITED

This catalogue is published to accompany the exhibition at the Bodleian Library, June – October 2003

© Bodleian Library, University of Oxford 2003

Published by
The Bodleian Library
Broad Street
Oxford
OX1 3BG

ISBN 1-85124-081-0

Catalogue designed and typeset by Dot Little at the Bodleian Library
Printed by Balding + Mansell Limited, Norwich

Cover illustration: No. 59

Contents

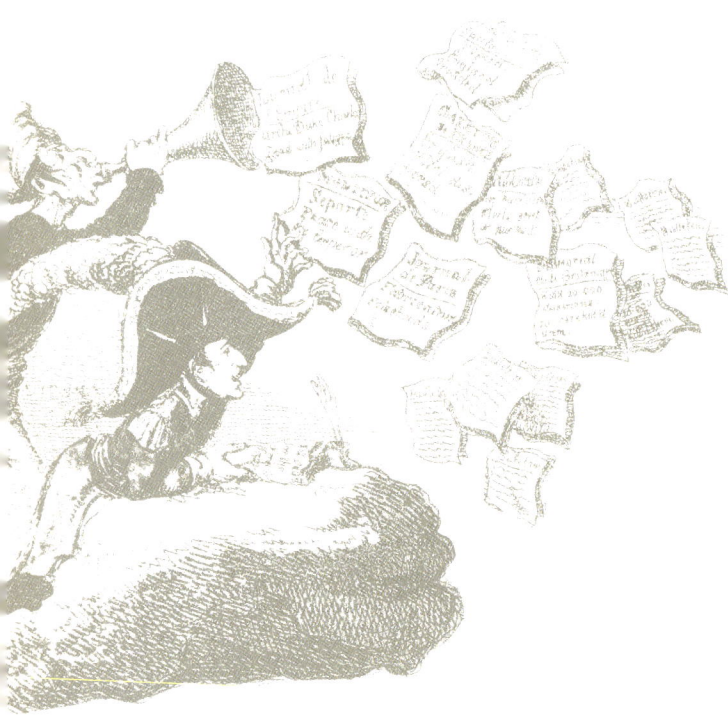

Acknowledgements

This publication complements the exhibition, *Napoleon and the Invasion of Britain*, held in the Bodleian Library from 2 June to 31 October 2003. Many thanks are due from the authors of the catalogue to the Bodleian's Exhibitions Curator, Dana Josephson and to Alison MacKay of the Conservation Section. The exhibition and catalogue have benefited from the advice and encouragement of the Keeper of Rare Books, Clive Hurst. We are grateful to Julie Anne Lambert, curator of the John Johnson Collection, for support and guidance during the preparation of the exhibition. Thanks also to the staff of the Ashmolean Museum, in the Heberden Coin Room and in the Department of Western Art, including Nick Mayhew, Jon Whiteley and Christian Rümelin. We were grateful for scholarly advice on the political prints of 1803 and on collections of political satires from Pascal Dupuy and Simon Turner. Sheila O'Connell at the British Museum and Robin Francis and Kate Jaram at the National Portrait Gallery generously shared their knowledge and expertise. A seminar series on Anglo-French relations during the wars, convened by the Maison Française and the Department of Politics and International Relations at the University of Oxford, offered many valuable insights on the period. In preparing the catalogue we were glad to be able to use the resources of the Lewis Walpole Library in Farmington, Connecticut and the Yale Center for British Art in New Haven. Finally, all errors in this publication are our own.

Many members of the Bodleian Library staff, including Alan Carter, Nick Cistone, Chris Giles, Colin Harris, Jacky Merralls and Julius Smit, contributed to the completion of this catalogue. The graphic designer Dot Little and our editor Samuel Fanous deserve special thanks for handling the publication.

Introduction

Throughout the summer of 1803, Britain prepared to defend against a French invasion masterminded by Napoleon Bonaparte, First Consul of France and an acknowledged military genius who had already provided the French Republic with a string of conquests and victories on the Continent. In May 1803, having settled his conflicts with European antagonists on the eastern front, Bonaparte was in a position to concentrate all his energies and a considerable proportion of his forces to the task of mastering his last unconquered foe. The invasion of Britain remained Bonaparte's prime objective for the two years from the early summer of 1803 to the autumn of 1805. The gravity of the situation was outlined in orders to commanders of the Eastern District:

The Brigade under your Command must be held at all times in readiness to move on the shortest notice...This constant state of preparation is the more expedient on the present occasion, from the impossibility of foreseeing the movements of the Enemy, whose extraordinary conduct in all his military enterprizes hitherto, has been noted for a degree of boldness in conception that borders on rashness, and a forcing of means in the execution, that warrants the suspicion that his arrival on our Coast may be looked for at a moment when on every ordinary principle...he might be the least expected.[1]

The prints, pamphlets and broadsides exhibited here tell the story of British fears from the beginning of the war against revolutionary France through the most intense period of national defensive mobilization in 1803. Not since 1066 had England's shores been invaded by an enemy, yet Napoleon's conquests were already legendary. The Great Admiral Lord St Vincent drily opined 'I do not say that the French cannot come– I only say that they cannot come by sea.' Yet this confidence only underlined the contrast between Britain's naval and land forces. If the Navy provided the 'wooden walls' that had protected Britain from the Spanish Armada in 1588, the relatively small army was hard pressed to conduct land warfare in Britain's colonial territories while also defending the mother nation against invasion. Now, against Napoleon's endless stream of conscripts, how strong a fighting force could Britain muster?

At the height of the invasion fear in the summer of 1803, a total of 463,134 men in Great Britain and Ireland volunteered for service in defence of the nation. Individuals in all social groups rallied to the cause. Some did so because of the fear of invasion; others were keen to share in the excitement of the struggle, as news travelled of the naval skirmishes against French ships lying in wait across the Channel in Boulogne. On a huge scale the people of Britain responded to volunteering as to a social duty, both for the local élites who took command of brigades and for the tradesmen and labourers who practised the drill.

National mobilization was accompanied by an outpouring of cartoons and broadsides in 1803. It would not be correct to call these publications the spontaneous products of 'public opinion', just as the enlistment of volunteers was not entirely spontaneous. Government propaganda efforts certainly played a part in many of the publications and expressions of loyalty and patriotism in song and print. Yet propaganda directly inspired or funded by the Government was only a small part of the total output. More significant were the broadsides and handbills produced by loyalist associations and the determination by publishers of political cartoons to capitalize on the state of excitement with new sensational images.

Loyalist publications did not simply invoke a patriotic love of king and country. Talk of the rights of Englishmen and scrutiny of Britain's constitution in light of the French Revolution had proven so divisive in the 1790s that the Government had taken drastic steps to suppress political organization on the part of the ordinary citizens it now hoped to arm as volunteers. During the invasion scare ministers felt they had no choice but to make defence of the country a popular effort.

In this respect Britain was learning from Revolutionary France, where the mobilization and management of public opinion was achieved with festivals and propaganda throughout the revolutionary period, techniques which Napoleon turned to his own use when he seized power. A bold example of his news management was the medal struck in 1803 celebrating 'La Descente en Angleterre' and marked 'Frappée a Londres – en 1804'(No. 64a).[2]

The French leader spent the summer of 1803 deploying and inspecting his troops, building up his shipping and planning his attack. British intelligence reported that by October he had a flotilla of 1,367 boats of various sizes prepared and had built up a huge army of invasion around Boulogne. When he was finally persuaded by his officers that a winter crossing would be impossible, the project was temporarily shelved until the spring of 1804. That year was spent attempting to outwit the numerically superior British Navy so as to provide cover for the invasion force, and even though he failed to do so, he remained convinced that the conquest of Britain was eminently achievable as late as June 1805:

A nation is very foolish, when it has no fortifications and no army, to lay itself open to seeing an army of 100,000 veteran troops land on its shores. This is the masterpiece of the flotilla. It costs a great deal of money, but it is necessary for us to be masters of the sea for six hours only, and England will have ceased to exist.[3]

Only late in August 1805 did Napoleon despair of his chances of securing French naval supremacy in the Channel long enough to embark the invasion troops. The Battle of Trafalgar, on 21 October, during which Nelson's ships inflicted a catastrophic defeat on the French and Spanish navies, sealed the doom of his invasion plans.

French invasion plans and attempts

Invasion by the forces of Revolutionary France was a subject of fearful speculation by Britons as soon as the two countries went to war in February 1793. These fears were first realized in December 1796 when a French force of seventeen ships of the line, ten frigates and seven transports, carrying in total 14,000 troops lead by General Hoche slipped around the British blockade of French ports and sailed for Ireland only to be immersed in fog and then dispersed by storms, much to the disgust of Irish republican Wolfe Tone, who sailed with the French fleet:

We have been now six days in Bantry Bay, within five hundred yards of the shore, without being able to effectuate a landing; we have been dispersed four times in four days and, at this moment, of forty-three sail of which the expedition consisted, we can muster of all sizes but fourteen... Notwithstanding all our blunders, it is the dreadful stormy weather and easterly winds, which have been blowing furiously and without intermission since we made Bantry Bay, that have ruined us. Well, England has not had such an escape since the Spanish Armada, and that expedition, like ours was defeated by the weather.[4]

A second attempt was made when, in February 1797, four French ships with a motley collection of disaffected troops headed for the west of England, under orders to attack and burn Bristol and then to blockade Dublin. Forced by the weather to land in Pembrokeshire, the troops ransacked the locality for food. Their leader, an American adventurer merchant captain, William Tate, quickly surrendered.

The potential for co-operation between French invaders and Irish republicans alarmed British leaders but attempted or promised French invasions were not an unqualified benefit to the republican United Irishmen. On one hand the real nature of French aims in Ireland was doubted by some in the Irish republican movement. On the other hand, reliance on the uncertain landing of a French expedition weakened the hand of the United Irishmen when a popular rebellion broke out in May 1798. By the time France mobilized to send troops, a gruesome repression of the rebels by British forces under General Cornwallis was almost over. Despite the initial success of General Humbert's landing on the West Coast in August, the groundswell of support for revolution had been broken by September and the Irish rebels and their French allies were defeated. A month later, a third wave of support for Ireland collapsed when a fleet of French ships was surrounded and defeated. On the captured flagship Wolfe Tone was arrested.

These costly and fruitless expeditions produced fierce controversy in the French Directory. They also undoubtedly intensified British fears of invasion and Britons' sense of their islands' vulnerability. One Irish correspondent loyal to the British Government commented gloomily following the Bantry Bay expedition in 1796:

The ease with which the French got into Bantry, the length of time they lay...off our coasts, and the retreat they made into their own ports, without, I may say, molestation, even in the distressed and disabled state they were in, has truly alarmed every thinking man in the nation.[5]

Could French troop ships anchor off Portsmouth or Dover? In the summer of 1797, under the direction of Hoche, France had begun to assemble an 'Armée d'Angleterre' near Brest, to complement a Dutch attack. Peace with Austria in October 1797 meant that France could turn her full attention to Britain. Napoleon Bonaparte was given command of the army of invasion and troops were transferred to northern France from Italy and Holland in preparation for a further assault. However, the defeat of the Dutch fleet at Camperdown by Admiral Lord Duncan on 11 October seems to have persuaded Bonaparte that France required, but was far from gaining, naval control of the Channel.

> Whatever efforts we make, we shall not for some years gain the naval supremacy. To invade England without that supremacy is the most difficult and daring task ever undertaken...If, having regard to the present organization of our navy, it seems impossible to gain the necessary promptness of execution, then we must really give up the expedition against England, be satisfied with keeping up the pretence of it, and concentrate all our attention and resources on the Rhine, in order to try to deprive England of Hanover and Hamburg...or else undertake an eastern expedition which would menace her trade with the Indies. And if none of these operations is practicable, I see nothing else for it but to conclude Peace with England.[6]

Instead of a direct invasion of England, Bonaparte decided to threaten British colonial interests with a daring expedition that greatly enhanced his celebrity. In May 1798 he sailed for Egypt and secured an early French victory in the Battle of the Pyramids. His ambitions were not wholly military. The Enlightenment pretensions of his expedition were signified by the employment of a number of eminent archaeologists and linguists in the study of Egyptian antiquities. But his army was marooned by the victory of the British fleet, commanded by Horatio Nelson, in the Battle of the Nile. Following a dramatic but unsuccessful attempt to conquer Syria, Bonaparte's troops became trapped in Egypt. Abandoning his army, Bonaparte escaped back to France in October 1799. As the acknowledged military genius of the French nation and having timed his return well, he orchestrated the overthrow of the Directory on the Eighteenth Brumaire (10 November) and took political power as First Consul.

William Pitt's successor as Prime Minister, Henry Addington, agreed to negotiate a peace treaty with Bonaparte in 1801, as both countries were exhausted by years of warfare. The Peace of Amiens between Britain and France lasted only one year, from 1802 to 1803. Peace with Britain enabled Bonaparte to pursue war in France's Caribbean colony of St Domingue and on the Continent, and also to consolidate troops on the coast of France for a possible invasion of England. When the Peace collapsed in May 1803, there could be no doubting Bonaparte's resolve finally to overcome his British opponents: 'Let us be masters of the Straits of Dover for six hours and we shall be masters of the world.'[7]

The prints and broadsides in this exhibition reveal a British response to Napoleon's threats in 1803 funda-

mentally different to that in the 1790s. This was partly because of the greater fear: France's military reputation had grown in the intervening years. Other reasons for the different response may be found in the changing domestic political scene. To appreciate the effect of war on British politics between 1793 and 1803, we must look back at the complex character of the British response to the French Revolution in 1789.

The 'Revolution Controversy' in Britain

In what must count as one of Prime Minister William Pitt's few massive errors of judgement, addressing the House of Commons on the budget in February 1792, he commented: 'There never was a time in the history of this country, when, from the situation in Europe, we might more reasonably expect fifteen years of peace than we may at the present moment.'[8] The ground for Pitt's optimism was the domestic conflict and confusion in France following the Revolution. Within a year, however, the conflict between French republicans and royalists – within and outside France – had led to war among the leading European powers. The months following Pitt's speech were marked by an increasing radicalism of the revolution, induced by panic at the prospect of a foreign invasion of France. Bloody scenes, including the massacre of the King's Swiss Guard in May and the September Massacres in Paris, were followed by the establishment of a new National Convention and the declaration of the Republic in September. Under General Dumouriez, the new Republic enjoyed its first military triumph with the defeat of Austrian forces in Belgium. In an ecstasy of success, the National Convention announced its willingness to aid all subject peoples wishing to 'recover their liberty'. France's defensive war aims had become a revolutionary crusade and posed an increasing threat to the crowned heads of Europe, not least to her own. Louis XVI was tried for treason and executed on 21 January 1793. Less than a year after Pitt's optimistic prediction, Britain embarked on a war that would last, with only a brief intermission, for over twenty years and that would require an unprecedented level of national mobilization.

The war against France in 1793 was not universally welcomed, either in Parliament or in the country as a whole. The French Revolution had been greeted initially with widespread enthusiasm by British observers and while some, patronizingly, saw it as evidence that France was abandoning absolutism for a liberal constitution based on the British model, many thought the changes were evidence of the rise of a new set of principles of government. Following the American Revolution (1776–83), the sweeping aside of the French feudal order seemed to foreshadow the irresistible rise of freedom and enlightenment throughout the world. In November 1789, Richard Price's sermon commemorating the Glorious Revolution of 1688 had concluded by hailing events in France as the dawn of a new era.

Behold all ye friends of freedom…behold the light you have struck out, after setting America free, reflected to France and there kindled into a blaze that lays despotism in ashes and warms and illuminates Europe. I see the ardour for liberty catching and spreading…the dominion of kings changed for the dominion of laws, and the dominion of priests giving way to the dominion of reason and conscience.⁹

Price's sermon attracted the wrath of Edmund Burke, a leading Whig increasingly uncomfortable with the reformist flirtations of his party and convinced that the Revolution was destroying the French state and that its principles threatened to spread to Britain. Burke's response, *Reflections on the Revolution in France* (1791), prophesied the destruction of civilization in France and the outbreak of a European war. The *Reflections*, now a classic of conservative thought linking the preservation of a national culture with the maintenance of political order, sparked an intense debate on fundamental questions in politics. Over 300 pamphlets were published in the subsequent controversy, including Thomas Paine's *Rights of Man*, Mary Wollstonecraft's *Vindication of the Rights of Man* and James Mackintosh's *Vindiciae Gallicae*, and the debate spilled over into novels, poetry, popular song and caricature.

The 'Revolution Controversy' gave renewed energy to metropolitan and provincial reform societies, such as the Society for Constitutional Information (SCI), and fuelled the emergence of new associations, some, such as the London Corresponding Library, organized by working people who declined the patronage and leadership of the wealthy. The reform societies sought to spread their principles more widely throughout the country through the circulation of radical literature, especially Thomas Paine's *Rights of Man* (1791–2). The Government responded with a Royal Proclamation against sedition in May 1792, instigated proceedings against Paine and encouraged the prosecution of radical writers, booksellers and publishers. Although domestic repression and the violent turn of events in France turned some liberal sympathizers against the cause of reform, many reformers retained a commitment to the ideals of the French revolutionaries.

The war against France, 1793–1801

By the time war was declared in February 1793, Britons were deeply divided in their attitudes to France and to reform at home. The reform societies grew rapidly through 1792 and were increasingly vociferous in their calls for change. Their reformist zeal was countered by loyalist associations – notably the Association for the Preservation of Liberty and Property against Republicans and Levellers, founded by John Reeves – which encouraged local magistrates and loyal subjects to be assiduous in the identification and prosecution of seditious persons. The *causes celebres* of summer and autumn, 1794, were the trials of several reform leaders for treason.

The cost of the war and the economic dislocation it caused were increasing sources of popular grievance. In the summer of 1795 there was a resurgence of radical agitation, coupled with rioting over food shortages and the expense of the war. The radical publisher and pamphleteer Thomas Spence even took advantage of a shortage of coin to strike a series of tokens with a range of pointed images, designed to convey his hostility to the status quo (Nos. 19a–g). Throughout 1795, and again in 1797–8 and 1800–01, poor harvests, food shortages and forced recruitment to the Army and Navy resulted in widespread popular rioting and demands for bread and an end to the war. In the general atmosphere of crisis and the escalating costs of war, the Government was forced to suspend the payment of specie for Bank notes.

Following the execution of the French King in 1793, devotion to George III had become a rallying cause for loyalists. In October 1795, as the King drove in the state coach to open Parliament, a window of the coach was broken by what seemed to be a pistol shot, and when it returned empty it was destroyed by a mob. The 'Two Acts' to suppress sedition and treason were passed in the wake of this apparent crisis. Whatever symbolic support the King gave to the country, the Navy was certainly Britain's bulwark against foreign invasion, and mutinies in the fleets at Nore and Spithead during 1797 raised the terrifying spectre of disloyalty in the service. Although the provocations were ostensibly pay and conditions of service, the authorities linked the mutinies to radical agitation and dealt harshly with the leaders. Finally, the Government was badly shaken by evidence of organized treason on the part of Irish republicans and fearful that parallel clandestine movements existed in England. Parliament suspended habeas corpus in April 1798, and repeatedly renewed the suspension until the Peace of Amiens. Some radical reformers were imprisoned for the duration.

The invasion threats of the late 1790s were faced by a politically divided Britain, full of mutual suspicions. To reformers, Pitt's dominance in Parliament seemed reliant on the continued war against France. In his first assessment of the capacity of the British to repulse an invasion force, General Dumouriez, the French Revolutionary general now in exile in England, portrayed the country as tottering on the brink of disorder:

The opposition to Government, revolutionary spirit, discontents of numerous workmen without work or victuals, the falling off of commerce, the distrust which the stoppage of payment and partial bankruptcies will produce in mercantile transactions, the embarrassment of the Bank, the activity of the French in fomenting discords in the three kingdoms, the necessity of keeping up a numerous army to put the coasts above insult, the dearness of this expense, the danger of arming the whole nation in the midst of the discord and innovation which agitates it: this combination of real calamities is sufficient to depress the resources and courage of the nation, which derives all its strength from its riches and commerce, though the French should not even employ more decisive measures against it. What will be the consequence, if the French, turning all their strength and industry towards their navy, obstinately determine the execution of a descent?[10]

War machines

A frequent subject of prints was new technology, such as the telegraph, used to fight the war. The new machines of war created by both sides were the subjects of serious and satirical prints. Communications were vital to the rapid movements of troops and ships desired by both army and naval commanders. Following the development of a telegraph system by the French early in the Revolutionary War, the British installed telegraphs to convey news of attack as rapidly as possible to London and to troops stationed around the coast. Caricaturists must have seen a parallel between this visual signalling of coded messages and their own coded representations of political figures, and the telegraph appeared in several cartoons, such as 'The budget or John Bull frightened out of his wits' (No. 20).

Techniques of invasion were also imagined in many British and French prints during the two major threats of

1798 and 1803. French caricatures in 1803 showed invasion forces travelling by tunnel to England. Some French contraptions, Jean-Charles Thilorier's proposal of a giant balloon, with a platform for 3,000 soldiers and Pierre Forfeit's suggestion of floating fortresses, were copied and parodied in English prints. A more significant development, for future warfare, was the American Robert Fulton's proposal for a submarine, unmanned torpedoes and steam-powered vessels to carry troops across the Channel regardless of the weather. But Fulton was increasingly disappointed in the French response and after the Peace of Amiens was enticed to England with the prospect of his plans being developed by the British. A cartoon anticipating the help of his invention is in the Curzon collection, entitled 'A salute for Boney from the impregnable battery'. The contribution of such inventions to the conflict was minimal, but they played a role in the collective imagination of the period, and perhaps in the climate of fear, although it is notable that caricatures and prints of such inventions were much more the staple of 1798 than they were of the invasion fear of 1803–05. In that conflict, caricaturists had another object upon which to focus.

One indication of how seriously the British Government treated the threat of invasion, even after 1803, was the investment made in fortifying the coast of England. Between 1803 and 1810 the British coastline was subjected to earthworks on a scale not seen since the reign of Henry VIII. Defensive Martello towers around the south coast were proposed in 1803, and although the first was not finished until 1806, the chain was complete by 1808. In addition, a 'grand shaft' was created to allow soldiers to descend the cliffs around Dover under cover, the Dover Citadel fortress was substantially reinforced and a canal was built across the Romney Marsh as a 'wet-ditch'.[11] Although these fortifications and bulwarks against invasion were completed only after 1805, they testify to the recognition of the need to adapt to the prospect of armed conflict on England's soil and to the difficulty of designing and executing major fortifications with any speed. Moreover, given how extensive the preparations were, it is remarkable how little public criticism they elicited, and how minor a role they play in the prints of the period.

The Peace of Amiens 1801–03

Pitt resigned from office in 1801 over George III's refusal to grant civil rights to Catholics after the Act of

Union between Great Britain and Ireland. Under Addington, the Government ratified the Treaty of Amiens in March 1802. Popular relief was palpable. Eight years of war, domestic conflict, financial hardship and military imposition had left the country exhausted. A good harvest, reductions in taxation (including an ending of income tax) and the release from prison of reform agitators held on suspicion of sedition seemed to promise that the war against republican France was truly over. The Peace allowed a spate of continental visiting, with Fox and many others (whether or not in sympathy with France) keen to see Bonaparte in person and to catch up on the latest French fashions. Seeing the First Consul and his regime at first hand aroused doubts in some of these visitors as to whether Bonaparte was really the rightful successor to the Revolution. Already a prescient attack had been made on Bonaparte by a French émigré, Jean Peltier, in the French anti-republican paper, *L'Ambigu*, published in London. Peltier represented Bonaparte as a would-be emperor and was prosecuted in the English courts for libel against the First Consul. The French ambassador denied Bonaparte's involvement, but fulminated against the liberties taken by the English press.

Bonaparte's sensitivity to propaganda and scandal mongering, the stock in trade of parts of the English press, did not help to ease his relationship with Britain. Moreover, serious conflicts over the treaty were quick to emerge. To Bonaparte's fury, Britain refused to cede Alexandria and Malta as agreed. Britain objected that France had broken the treaty by her annexation of Piedmont and the imposition of a new constitution on Switzerland – matters Bonaparte considered entirely domestic in character. As tension grew, misinformation and misunderstanding spread. In part response to what he saw as scurrilous accounts of his campaign in Egypt, Bonaparte used *Le Moniteur*, the official publication of the French Government, to publish a report by the French Colonel Sebastiani suggesting that the British would be unlikely to hold Egypt for long – a thinly veiled indication of his continuing ambitions to attack British colonial interests. By early 1803 Britain recognized that the Peace was unlikely to last, and as tension escalated it seemed more prudent to accept the inevitable than to surrender territory to France or to give the French further time to prepare for hostilities. On 18 May Britain declared war. Among the causes cited was a libel against George III in a Hamburg newspaper, by order of the French minister, and a French demand for the restriction of the British press. The question of

press freedom and accurate reporting thus played a visible role in the deterioration of relations between Britain and Napoleon's France in 1803.

The 'Patriotic War', 1803–05

When Britain declared war in May 1803 the country responded in a dramatically different manner than it had ten years earlier. In large part this was because the dangers were defined clearly as threats to the British population. Invasion by Bonaparte seemed all too possible, after his successes elsewhere. Moreover the war would clearly affect the population at home, through dislocation of trade and the possible loss of colonies, if French power continued to increase. A rebellious spirit remained; there had been a late attempt by United Irishmen to spread insurrection simultaneously in Ireland, England and Scotland in 1802–03, but the movement was broken by the arrest, trial and execution of Colonel Despard in February 1803, and subsequently by the suppression of Robert Emmet's attempted rising in Dublin in July 1803. In neither case was the scale of preparations and support comparable to 1798. Instead, large numbers of Britons demonstrated in visible and practical forms their commitment to resisting French invasion, even if their loyalty to the Crown and commitment to Britain's war aims might have been more complex and more conditional than the Government would have liked.[12]

The loyalism of 1803 was in part a result of the Government's new strategies for mobilization. In the early 1790s, radical reformist agitation and the popularity of Tom Paine's *Rights of Man* suggested to Parliament that it would be folly to arm a mass of volunteers to defend a staunchly anti-reformist king and administration. By the end of that decade, it had become accepted that it was necessary to do so. The regular army was seriously depleted by its losses in the West Indies and the threat of invasion required that these troops be supplemented in some way, either by militia or by volunteers.

Conscription into the militia was unpopular, whether by the press-gang forms or in the form of balloting, which required an area to deliver up a certain number of men. In contrast, volunteering, organized by local lords lieutenant, was widely popular. Volunteers remained in their locality, contributing to the war effort without coercion and volunteering was a wonderful opportunity for dressing up, parading round, inventing coats of arms and songs for the unit and being seen by one's neighbours to be doing work of consequence. It was the popularity of volunteering, especially compared to other means of augmenting forces, that convinced ministers such as Henry Dundas in 1798 that it was the only solution to mass mobilization. 'I know of no other way of doing it but in the way it is now going on, nor do I conceive it either prudent or practicable in any other way.'[13]

The Militia and Volunteers Acts of 1798 and 1799 marked a change in the Government's position and a recognition that the ever more formidable French Army would have to be met on its own terms: 'a nation which attacks en mass can only be repelled by a defence en mass'.[14]

As Captain James Burney wrote: 'Dislike to an administration, dislike to a government, and dislike to the country itself are three different things,' and while there may have been fears on the first front there were fewer on the second, and fewer still on the third. He added,

whatever suspicions there may be of disaffection, any danger to be apprehended from arming, is obviated by the people being divided and exercised by parishes; and where the parishioners are numerous, they may be exercised by portions, on different days, so that shall be out one forenoon in the week.[15]

Yet volunteering also exposed the qualifications to loyalism hinted at by Captain Burney. Many volunteers were reluctant to serve outside their county and the corps remained largely local bodies with no formal subordination to the regular forces. People's motives clearly differed: many men enjoyed what was effectively an expression of a local patriotism, coupled with the chance to wear uniform; some saw the importance of resisting invasion but demonstrated little respect for the existing political order; and many others were resolutely committed to defending their homes and communities, but often refused outright to serve more widely. It remained entirely unclear how these troops would cope when faced with battle-hardened French regiments.

The Government's turn to the voluntary principle as its best chance of domestic defence, under the leadership of Dundas and Pitt, was indicated in its decision in 1799 to allow those volunteering (and subsequently whole counties who met a volunteer quota) to avoid conscription into the Army or militia. The first large-scale volunteering activity early in 1798 indicated the

potential for the emergence of a mass army of the nation. In the first three months of that year, when invasion seemingly loomed, the number of volunteers doubled from 25,000 to 50,000, and their numbers then doubled again in the following three months. They quickly provided an essential supplement to the official forces both in 1798 and again in 1801 when Bonaparte once more threatened invasion. There were attempts to reduce the reliance on volunteers and to reverse the relief from conscription during the period of peace, but these were not pressed hard. In fact, the Government's growing confidence in the volunteers was far from a case of blind faith: considerable resources had been devoted to the task of assessing the loyalty of the people and their willingness to serve. Under the Defence of the Realm Acts of 1798 and 1803, returns were sought from local lords lieutenant and lesser office holders and magistrates throughout the country estimating the likelihood of ordinary people volunteering, their grounds for refusing and whether or not they would, as volunteers, accept posting outside their localities.

With the resumption of war in 1803, the Government was faced with a tide of volunteering that they could neither ignore nor, seemingly, control. Returns to Parliament in 1804 recorded a total of 480,000 volunteers in uniform. Added to those in the regular forces and the militia this meant that close to one in five able-bodied men were in uniform. The Government was impressed and relieved, but the large numbers brought new problems as well. While in 1798–9 most units were led by men of consequence and their commands replicated the traditional social hierarchy, in 1803–04 the numbers involved meant that many units were being led by men who could not claim to be persons of quality – a fact that re-awakened fears in some quarters that the levee en masse could undermine the traditional social order. While in the first part of the revolutionary wars the strategy for national defence had rested on an elite officer corps, with a conscripted army and militia, from 1798 there was an unambiguous turn to national popular mobilization and, by 1803, mass volunteering and arming was increasingly seen as a way of generating and sustaining a loyal and patriotic spirit among the ordinary people of Britain.[16]

Boney: Napoleon as England's enemy

One component of the popular patriotism in 1803 was that much of its rhetoric was directed against Bonaparte rather than against 'French principles' as in the earlier phase of the war. As First Consul, and still more so as Emperor, he was portrayed as an autocratic, domineering and utterly ruthless tyrant, acquiring by 1803 the nickname 'Boney'. Although he had earlier commanded wide respect, even in Britain, as a military leader of daring and ability he was increasingly feared as a ruthless butcher.

Charges of cruelty emerged in accounts of Bonaparte's Egyptian and Syrian campaigns in 1798. By 1803 a number of books, both scurrilous and respectable, contained the story of a massacre following Napoleon's victory at Jaffa. The inhabitants of the besieged city had accepted the word of an officer that if they surrendered they would be spared. Once inside the city, Napoleon ordered the men, women and children massacred, alongside 1,400 captives taken at Gaza. Modern sources add to the horror by reporting that the troops were ordered either to drown or bayonet the victims so as to save valuable ammunition.[17] Napoleon felt his actions were justified, but his British critics were unequivocal in their condemnation. Another component of the 'Black Legend' concerned the collapse of the French siege of Acre, shortly afterwards. Forced to retreat across the desert with over 2,000 wounded men, fearful of delay in the face of the advancing Turkish forces and convinced that if the sick were left they would be summarily slaughtered, Bonaparte suggested that the worst cases be administered an overdose of opium. This was given to 30 plague victims, and the rest were carried back to Jaffa, where he again ordered the poisoning of, according to Sir Robert Wilson, 580 of the sick and wounded troops.[18]

Accounts of Jaffa were partly contested during the Peace of Amiens. D. P. B. Eccleston's 'Sketch of the Character of General Bonaparte in Letters to the Editor of the Lancaster Gazeteer' (1802) (No. 77) drew attention to inconsistencies in the accounts and suggested that they were driven by malicious intent, though he failed to produce much evidence directly refuting the stories. However, once war broke out, Eccleston withdrew his pamphlet from sale. 'When Nappy became our enemy again, I called them in from the shops and suppressed their sale,' reads an inscription by the author of the Bodleian Library copy. Both events remained a central part of histories of the Egyptian campaign.

Bonaparte felt personally frustrated over his failure in Egypt and over the reporting of the Jaffa incident. He had seen the campaign as an opportunity for scientific exploration and discovery, and took with him leading members of French scientific circles. Many reports testified to his own bravery in visiting the sick and wounded, despite the risk of contagion. In the campaign, he faced appalling logistic and tactical problems to avoid the massacre of his troops by the Turks. But propaganda wars are not the best context for making sophisticated judgements. The Black Legend became a shorthand for charges of inhumanity against Napoleon. In British publications this was contrasted with an idealized character of British soldiers and sailors, who were portrayed as showing a humane concern for comrades and defeated foes.

British representations of Bonaparte during and after the Egyptian expedition, much like the contemporary French images, linked him to republican principles while recognizing his attractiveness as a military hero. From 1803, though, the focus was on his character and ambition – an ambition interpreted as personal rather than ideological. The many cartoons and prints converged on a single portrayal of Napoleon, both dangerous and romantic – diminutive, autocratic, haunted by his misdeeds and assassination threats and aspiring to power beyond measure. The trend was enhanced when he crowned himself Napoleon I in Notre Dame in December 1804. For those who had lauded his republicanism this was seen as conclusive evidence that Britain was being threatened not by French political principles but by a despot seeking world domination. As a result, resisting Boney could be seen as essential, regardless of one's sympathies for the principles of the French Revolution. The choice was offered in stark terms: 'You must immediately choose which you will have: a Corsican master, with rapes, pillage, confiscations, imprisonments, tortures, and scornful slavery, or George III with Old England, proud Freedom and Prosperity.'[19]

Popular prints and propaganda, 1789–1805

The number of cartoons devoted to Napoleon in 1803 highlights the changing role of this form of print. Political cartoons became a regular feature in printsellers' shops during the eighteenth century as part of an expanding market for prints of all kinds. The attention of the political world was riveted on the cartoons in print-shop windows. Politicans feared (or hoped) to find their likenesses in the cartoons. Caricatures from the skilled pens of Thomas

Rowlandson, James Gillray and Isaac Cruikshank were not only amusing and shocking, but also captured in images the rising tide of voices expressing public opinion on political events. By 1803, the average print run was perhaps 500 copies, not as large a circulation as some newspapers and pamphlets. At a price of one shilling, coloured etchings were too expensive for most working people, but affordable for the middle class and established tradesmen. A cheaper way to enjoy a range of images is suggested by advertisements on some prints offering 'folios of caricatures lent for the evening'. These clues to the way cartoons were viewed suggests that audiences might have followed the caricatures as they appeared, responding to each new cartoon.

The French Revolution in 1789 promised much material for the cartoonists, and the political issues it raised directly concerned the question of public opinion and popular political power. From this time forward, the number of political cartoons published every week was consistently higher than the number of social satires. British cartoonists had to invent a new iconography of politics to describe controversies which were no longer simply partisan duelling but incorporated radical admiration for revolutionary principles, loyalist recognition of the 'vulgar', as in Hannah More's 'Village Politics', and the terrifying example of French regicide.[20] Cartoons after 1789 were addressed to a wider public whose allegiances were seriously courted by publications and images of all kinds. To reflect the political experiences of this audience, cartoonists developed a new political imagery, blending popular visual themes with titillating glimpses of famous political figures.

Throughout the eighteenth century, the notion of a 'balanced' constitution had provided cartoonists with a useful set of visual metaphors.[21] On the three constitutional elements of King, Lords and Commons sometimes represented as a tripod or a temple, rested the authority of the Church and the Crown. In partisan satires, Tories or Whigs were shown upsetting the balance or pulling down the pillars of the temple. The 1790s presented constitutional questions in a new context, with radical demands for popular representation questioning whether either party in the House of Commons could pretend to represent the popular element of the constitution. The political controversies of the 1790s, taking inspiration from events in France, increasingly betrayed a widening gulf between the people and Parliament, and even between the people and their King.

Loyalist groups hoped that British audiences would reflect on the happiness of their constitution compared to the disorder in France. This sentiment was best expressed in Thomas Rowlandson's 'The Contrast – Which is best?' (No. 1), publication of which was sponsored by the Association for Preserving Liberty and Property against Republicans and Levellers. Rowlandson's design, and James Gillray's 'French liberty/English slavery' (No. 4) following it, inspired many copies and a craze for 'contrast' which was used to illustrate not only political but social and cultural confrontations. Richard Newton's 'Contrasted Drummers' (1795) (Fig. 1 *illus. p. 17*) were French and English, but he continued the theme into humorous observations on domestic social stereotypes, producing 'Contrasted Lovers', 'Contrasted Husbands' and 'Contrasted Walkers'.[22] These show what cartoonists liked about contrast – it provided a perfect platform for caricaturing, as each side provided a foil for the other.

Gillray's strange 'Britannia between Scylla and Charybdis' (1793) (No. 2), stands as a transitional image, using both the balance and contrast themes, expressing the eighteenth-century view that a moderate course was the route to political stability and emphasizing the dangerous extremes of democratic sharks and the regal whirlpool. But this design also hints at the disturbing ambiguity of the contrast theme as employed during the 1790s. Humorous contrasts like Newton's social satires invited the viewer to reject both extremes. But to refuse to take sides in the war between Britain and revolutionary France suggested not moderation but a radical political stance. Serious contrasts, as presented by Rowlandson or in the broadside *A King or a Consul?* (No. 7), attempted to force a choice between two extremes. Yet these stark oppositions in cartoons tended to replicate and exacerbate, rather than conceal or heal, the political divisions within Britain. Moreover, the invitation to choose opened the possibility of viewers of different political opinions identifying with the 'wrong' figures in the cartoons. In some of Gillray's caricatures of blood-thirsty French revolutionaries, there is a positive frisson for the viewer in the anarchy he portrays.

Suspicion of popular crowds, heightened by the French Revolution, influenced the portrayal of the English everyman, John Bull. His image proliferated in the 1790s, appearing an estimated six times more often than in earlier decades.[23] But he had changed from the citizen sometimes shown in the mid-eighteenth century as a staunch defender of the rights of Englishmen. Instead, the cartoons of the 1790s purveyed an image of the ordinary Englishman as suspicious of politicians and political ideas, passive and bemused, more concerned with food and drink than with political ideas.[24]

During the invasion scares of 1798 and 1803, a weak John Bull was no longer appropriate as the country mobilized against a possible invasion. In a return to some of his earlier stout-hearted strength, John Bull in 1803 was more often shown as a citizen (well-informed about public affairs) than as a farmer or labourer. These prints show John Bull armed with a sword, rather than with a knife and fork, in recognition of the recruiting of volunteer regiments.

But John Bull in these years also served another purpose, representing the nation as a whole in a single body. This quality became especially important during the 1790s, as social divisions were increasingly written of, by radicals and loyalists, in political tones. Although cartoonists were keen to include the 'ordinary man' in their designs, John Bull had a shifting social identity, as farmer, citizen, sailor and volunteer soldier in turn. By appearing in all of these occupations, he lessened the distinctions between them. The social dramas of scorn and resent-ment which can be seen in William Hogarth's satires of the mid-eighteenth century (for instance, in 'The Good and Bad Apprentice', 'Marriage a la Mode' and 'The Rake's Progress') were absent from political cartoons of 1793–1803.[25] An exception proves the rule that John Bull rarely appeared within a hierarchy of social ranks. In 1798 Sir John Dalrymple's elaborate designs for 'Consequences of a French invasion' (BM 9182, etched by Gilray) placed John Bull as a farmer beside other representative figures (manufacturer, sailor, curate).[26] What Dalrymple's amateurish suggestions ignored was that political cartoons had turned away from the use of emblematic figures in this way, towards personal caricature. Audiences hoped to recognize individuals. Even John Bull, an invented figure, might appear as a disguised caricature of a real person.

In an extension of the notion that the King was the father of his people, John Bull was frequently identified with George III. Paradoxically, this device also prevented any explicit representation of the relationship between the people and their King as separate entities. Although John Bull was often shown with ministers (usually being bled for tax revenues), he rarely met George III in these cartoons. Perhaps this was because the satirical mode was so volatile that solemn, quasi-

religious emotions such as loyal deference were nearly impossible to represent. Again, an exception, Richard Newton's 'Treason!' of 1798, proves the rule that a meeting could have disastrous consequences, as in that design John Bull displays his flatulent contempt for the King's portrait.[27]

Most of all, John Bull was a national symbol, and in 1803 the majority of cartoons showed him confronting Napoleon Bonaparte.

The depiction of historical persons also changed between the 1790s and 1803. The Whigs, and their leader Charles James Fox in particular, were no longer so easily identified as liberty-capped revolutionaries in 1803.

The enemy, from a generalized figure of 'the French', was by 1803 identified as an individual – Napoleon. Increasingly in British cartoons over the period 1798 to 1803, Napoleon Bonaparte had become the national symbol of France. In compositions in the 1790s based on a theme of contrast, the objects of attack included such revolutionary values as liberty and equality. While the French pretensions were caricatured and ridiculed, a tension in the prints remained because the ideals themselves were still valued in Britain. The prints of 1803 dispensed with national contrasts and focused on the singular figure of 'Little Boney'. Alarmingly, he appeared anywhere and everywhere, his small size both a sign of the caricaturists' contempt and a warning that he might creep unnoticed past any sleeping John Bull. Nor was this fascination confined to satirical prints – the daring of Bonaparte's Egyptian expedition had fired the imagination of the English as well as the French, and even the 'Black Legend' of atrocities in Egypt and the Middle East served in some ways to enhance interest in the French general. But the efforts of English print-makers were also only a reflection of the proliferation of the Bonapartist image in France, where a sustained campaign by his supporters ensured that Napoleon's face was reproduced in print, oils and marble, as the military hero and redeemer of France.[28] British caricatures capitalized on the fame not only of Napoleon's name but of his looks. Behind this attention to appearance lay a conviction among many in the audience that the face was an expression of an inner individuality.

The historian Dorothy George saw the British prints of 1803 as expressive of 'simple-minded patriotism', and pointed out that they emerged during 'an upsurge of national ardour in which propaganda might seem

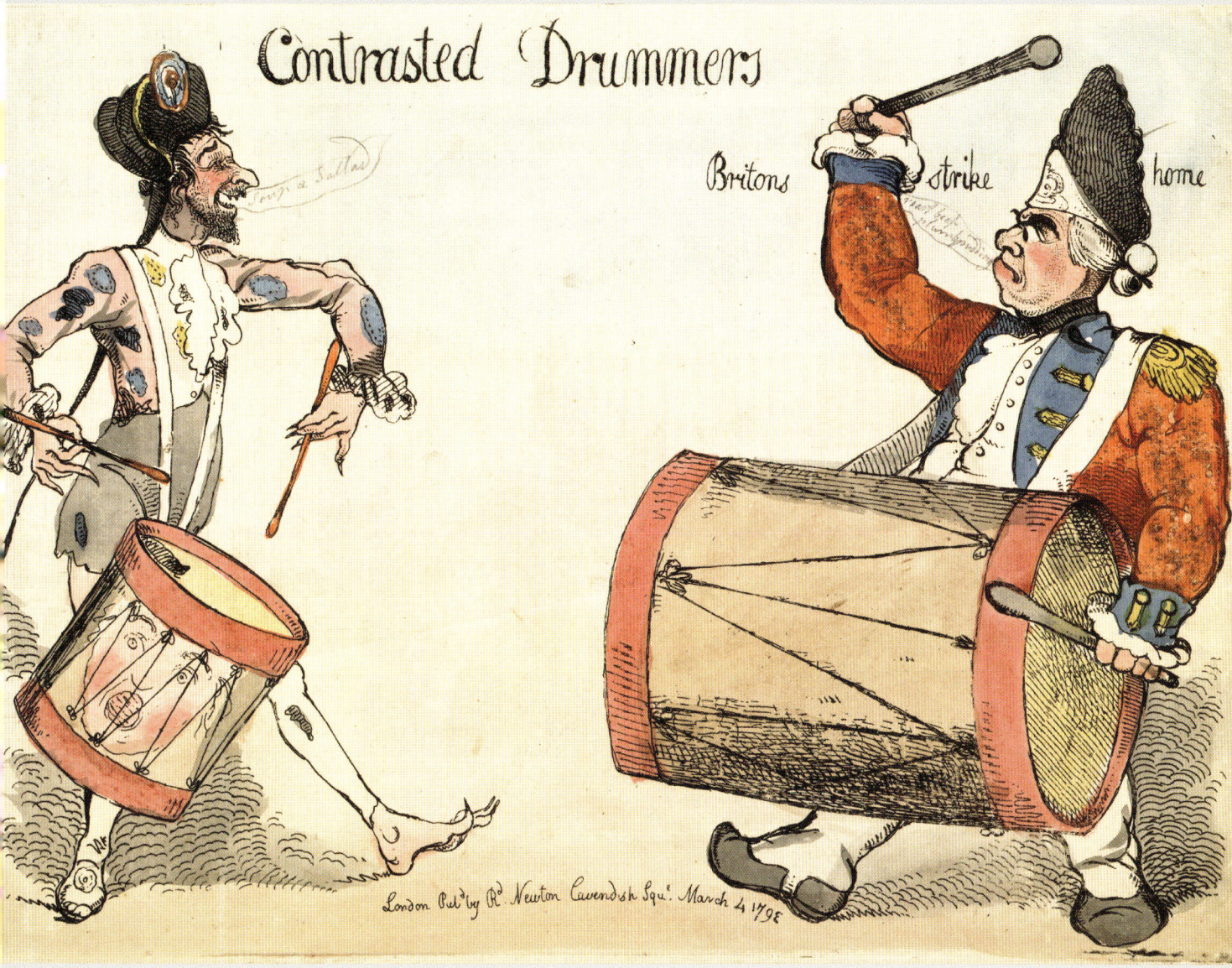

Figure 1
Richard Newton (1777–98)
Contrasted drummers
Hand-coloured etching 25.7 x 35.6 cm (sheet); 25 x 35 cm
(platemark)
Published 5 March 1793 by Richard Newton
Curzon b.2(62)

This print was published during the imprisonment of
Newton's employer, William Holland, for selling a
pamphlet by Tom Paine. Someone has added speeches
in pencil: the French drummer says 'Soup or sallad'; the
English drummer replies 'Roast beef, plumb pudding'.
Newton published several prints under his own name
during Holland's imprisonment. Like this one, they
lacked long captions, suggesting Holland himself
might have customarily done the lettering on the
plates. Timely in its reference to the war, this cartoon
was also part of the fashion for contrasts. Newton
produced 'Contrasted Walkers', 'Contrasted Husbands'
and 'Contrasted Lovers' in June, July and August 1795.
George M. Woodward and Isaac Cruikshank
caricatured contrasted Oxonians in 1796 (BMC 8975).

unnecessary'.[29] Between three and five cartoons were published each week in 1803. Pascal Dupuy's work on a complete index has already shown that the rate of production was impressive and that the focus of the prints was extremely narrow. From May 1803 to the end of 1804, more than 140 extant prints depicted the conflict between Britain and 'Boney'. In contrast, fewer than twenty focused on domestic political affairs until the sudden explosion following the Melville corruption scandal in 1805.

The cartoons were just part of a much larger campaign of loyalist print. The invasion scare encouraged printers to mount a campaign of loyalist publishing, in the form of broadsides and handbills, calling on Britons to resist Napoleon and to reject French political ideas.[30] Those most active in producing such handbills were not the print-sellers, but the government publishers Asperne, Hatchard and Ginger, who advertised bulk purchases cheap, with a note encouraging 'Noblemen, Magistrates and Gentlemen' to 'cause them to be posted up in public places'. These broadsides emphasized the contribution ordinary subjects might make to the defence of the realm, and spelled out the terms on which loyal patriotism would be received: as a free choice of submission to the Crown and constitution.

And while an occasional pro-French squib or comment can be found in collections of political pamphlets, ballads, and broadsides, the material is almost entirely anti-Bonaparte in character. This impression is confirmed by Stella Cottrell's analysis of broadsides between 1789 and 1815, showing that the prose publications of 1803–05 were also dominated by diatribes against Bonaparte.[31] Most made reference to the Jaffa massacre and the 'enslaving' of French citizens. Nor is it necessary to believe that this was systematic government propaganda, and that alternative radical voices had been stifled. A handful of prosecutions for sedition can be found, and the Government clearly did provide financial support for publications such as Cobbett's *Important Considerations*. Also, John Reeves' loyalist Association for the Preservation of Liberty and Property Against Republicans and Levellers returned briefly to life. But these centralized initiatives account for only a very small proportion of the abundant material attacking Bonaparte. Publications were also financed by local communities with money raised by public subscription to support the war effort. Many pamphlets represent the entrepreneurial instincts of printers and publishers who saw a ready market in people's fears and their need for

reassurance and a sense of common endeavour. The varied origins of the prints, ballads and broadsides and the richness of local collections does suggest that they were capturing a broadly shared sense of commitment and of national unity; in turn they generated the evidence of patriotism which ministers and the King were so eager to find.

British propaganda about the invasion threat was not limited to prints, broadsides and the popular press. Local volunteer corps commissioned tunes for marching and ballads for singing; theatres put on productions of Henry V and loyal concerts; military bands played across the country and contributed to the entertainments and dances of local communities; Charles Dibdin with his son Thomas achieved national recognition as composers of popular ditties and musicals, singing the praises of Jack Tar and hymning Britain as a 'tight little island'. The tunes and many of the songs borrowed extensively from earlier ballads, carrying with them resonances from earlier traditions, and many pieces stayed in the national consciousness for generations. They shaped the way contemporaries would have read and viewed the political cartoons.

We must wish we knew more about the audience for political cartoons when we consider that while ostensibly reflecting 'simple-minded patriotism', the caricatures often seem to express a sceptical, perhaps self-deprecating, assessment of the contribution ordinary people might make to public life and to defence of the realm. The contrast between the image of John Bull as a volunteer, hot and bothered on his little horse, and the proud, cool young men modelling uniforms in Rowlandson's plates for *Volunteers of London and Environs* makes the point.

Why was there such a proliferation of publications if the determination to fight a French invasion was already so strong? Obviously there was a fear at some level that Napoleon might take advantage of any weakness in Britain's defensive spirit. A further answer may lie in domestic politics before and after 1803, and in particular the desire of loyalists to capture the high ground of patriotism. The tracts and broadsides added to an insistence on military service a patriotic tone which was distinctly royalist and loyalist, while at the same time acknowledging, in many asides, the concerns expressed throughout the 1790s about freedom of speech, standards of living and the limits of social deference. The invasion fear of 1803 reinvigorated loyalist and Government efforts to capture public opinion on behalf of the 'mild and legitimate sovereign', George III. A word picture was presented in a song significantly titled *The Choice*, published by Hatchard and offered for sale at three pence per dozen.[32] The final verse imagined British volunteers fighting Napoleon's invading army on the beaches, singing, 'Then Britons guard their ancient fame/ Assert their empire o'er the sea/ And to the envying world proclaim/ One Nation still is brave and free.'

A changed political culture

At the level of parliamentary politics, opinion was no longer so dramatically polarized in 1803 as in 1793. The determined opposition to war that had been shown by the Whig opposition died away after 1802, and Pitt on his return to government sought to build a broader government coalition, even, at one point, attempting to include Fox. This unity between parties reflected the feeling that the war was now a basic struggle against Napoleon's personal ambitions for power and empire. In 1803 patriotism overlay, though it did not entirely erase, sectarian political differences.

A broader definition of 'the people' now seemed possible, to include those Mr. and Mrs. Bulls who would be relied upon to stop a French advance. The British liberties that they defended were carefully distinguished from French Revolutionary principles of equality and fraternity. The levee en masse and the unprecedented militarization of the country exalted the subject's military duty. A 'nation in arms' might not be the nightmare of anarchy it had once seemed, but a loyal hierarchy under the rule of George III. This form of patriotism was often demonstrated in local pride and particular practices. One example was the determination of volunteer regiments to wear distinctive uniforms, in the teeth of Government attempts to impose standard military dress. The rich diversity of uniforms continued, painstakingly recorded by artists employed by local worthies.

Patriotism and reform after 1803

Popular patriotism itself offered a language and an intellectual framework that provided a new generation of political opposition with a critical political lexicon and rhetoric, centred around the corruption of the state. The single most important domestic controversy during 1803–05 was not the change of administration from Addington to Pitt, but the accusations of corruption in

supplying the Navy that ultimately forced the resignation of Lord Melville (Henry Dundas) as First Lord of the Admiralty in the spring of 1805.

Melville's resignation was the first of a series of corruption scandals that dogged governments for the rest of the war. Twelve years of war created financial and administrative problems leaving ministers open to charges of mismanagement or worse. After the Melville scandal, Pitt's political situation deteriorated. When he died in January 1806, the immediate invasion threat was over, but so too was support for his leadership and the broader political unity that had marked the height of the invasion scare.

After 1805, parliamentary reform as a method for curing the evils of government, returned to the political agenda, on the basis of a popular patriotism united not only against Napoleon but against City profiteers and corrupt ministers whose activities endangered British interests at home and abroad. The arch publicist of this new popular politics was William Cobbett, who travelled politically from staunch supporter of the war to fierce critic of the British Army. In June 1803 Cobbett sent his pamphlet *Important Considerations for the people of this Kingdom* to Prime Minister Addington to make such use as he saw fit. Recognizing its power as a patriotic rallying call, the Government had thousands of copies printed and distributed throughout the country – with every minister of every parish enjoined to distribute copies to every pew, and to spread others through the aisles where the poorer sort sat. Over the next few years, Cobbett's support for the war and his patriotism increasingly parted company. He came to see the war as a device for the enrichment of a few at the expense of the many. As the threat of invasion and violation at the hands of the Corsican upstart diminished, so too did Cobbett's willingness to defend the war. His criticism of those who persevered with it, profited from it and managed it incompetently, became increasingly bitter. In 1810, Cobbett was jailed for sedition, after a violent outburst against the flogging of 'mutinying' English soldiers by German troops in British pay. In the same year, Francis Burdett, the new hope of British radicalism, was imprisoned in the Tower of London for a libel of the House of Commons which arose from his defence of the right of the public to attend an Inquiry into an affair involving corruption in the military. Using the distinctions Captain Burney raised between disliking one's administration, disliking one's government and disliking one's country, the patriot concerns with corruption suggested to reformers that faults in the administration could be remedied only by reform in the structures and institutions of government.

Napoleon's reputation

When Napoleon was defeated at Waterloo there remained a possibility that he could regroup and continue the war. He decided, however, to abdicate in favour of his son, the King of Rome, and determined to live in the United States of America. As English ships were blockading the French ports, Napoleon negotiated with Captain Maitland of HMS *Bellerophon* for safe passage to England. Maitland suggested that Napoleon might even be offered asylum in England. As the ship arrived at Torbay it attracted boatloads of sightseers and crowds thronged the coast. English perfidy, or the right of the victor, resulted in the rejection of his request for asylum. Instead, the former Emperor was to be treated as a prisoner of war. In a final irony, Napoleon tried to use the power of public opinion and English law in his favour, preparing a writ of habeas corpus against the Government. To avoid this legal action, the *Bellerophon* was instructed to take to sea – leaving the jurisdiction of the English courts. Once suitably distant, Napoleon was transferred to HMS *Northumberland* for the long run to St Helena. The sense that this was unworthy treatment was widely spread. No longer the enemy, Napoleon became a source of fascination among those who had fought or prepared to resist him. Moreover, he was gradually re-admitted to the pantheon of heroes. Propaganda songs of the invasion period, excoriating the monster Bonaparte, are commonplace in libraries and in private collections from the period, but some of those that have survived in the oral tradition are of a different cast, offering a more nuanced assessment of the man and his qualities and anticipating the continuing fascination of his history as a man and as a symbol.

It was over that wild beaten track, a friend of bold Bonaparte,
Did pace the sands and lofty rocks of St Helena's shore.
The wind it blew a hurricane, the lightning's flash around did dart,
The sea gulls were shrieking, and waves around did roar,
Ah! hush, rude winds the stranger cried awhile I range the dreary spot,
Where last a gallant hero his envied eyes did close.
But while his valiant limbs do rot, his name will never be forgot.
This grand conversation on Napoleon arose.

That conversation continues.

The Curzon Collection and its Creators

The Curzon Collection

George Nathaniel Curzon, Marquess Curzon of Kedleston (1859–1925) bought the extra-illustrated volumes of A. M. Broadley's *Napoleon in Caricature* (1911), J. H. Rose's *The Life of Napoleon* (1901) and Lord Rosebery's *Napoleon (the last phase)* (1900), at the sale of Broadley's library in 1916. At that time he was Chancellor of Oxford University, and his bequest of Napoleon-related books and prints, including the political cartoons, came to the Library in 1926.

The cartoons relating to Napoleon held in the Curzon collection number at least 1,200. They are both British and Continental European in origin, and reflect the range of artistic styles used in political caricature – with notable national differences – as well as the changing view of France and Napoleon in British publications during the period 1789 to 1815. In addition to the cartoons, the Curzon volumes contain original drawings by the caricature artists Gillray and Rowlandson and printed broadsides from the period.

In addition to the prints, the Curzon collection contains books relating to Napoleon's life, and especially to his captivity on St Helena. These are catalogued in the general book catalogue of the Bodleian Library.

Authors and Illustrators

'Grangerization' and A. M. Broadley's collection of political cartoons

Grangerization, or the practice of extra-illustrating books with original prints and documents of all kinds, is so called after the Rev. James Granger (1723–76), the vicar of Shiplake, Oxfordshire. Rev. Granger composed a *Biographical History of England* expressly for the purpose of enabling his contemporaries to pursue the popular hobby of collecting engraved and mezzotint portraits. The invitation to arrange a collection of pictures within an existing book was irresistible to a certain type of collector, in Granger's own century and later, who chose items by theme or subject. Alexander Meyrick Broadley (1847–1916) was one of these. His vast collection of letters, prints and books relating to French history,

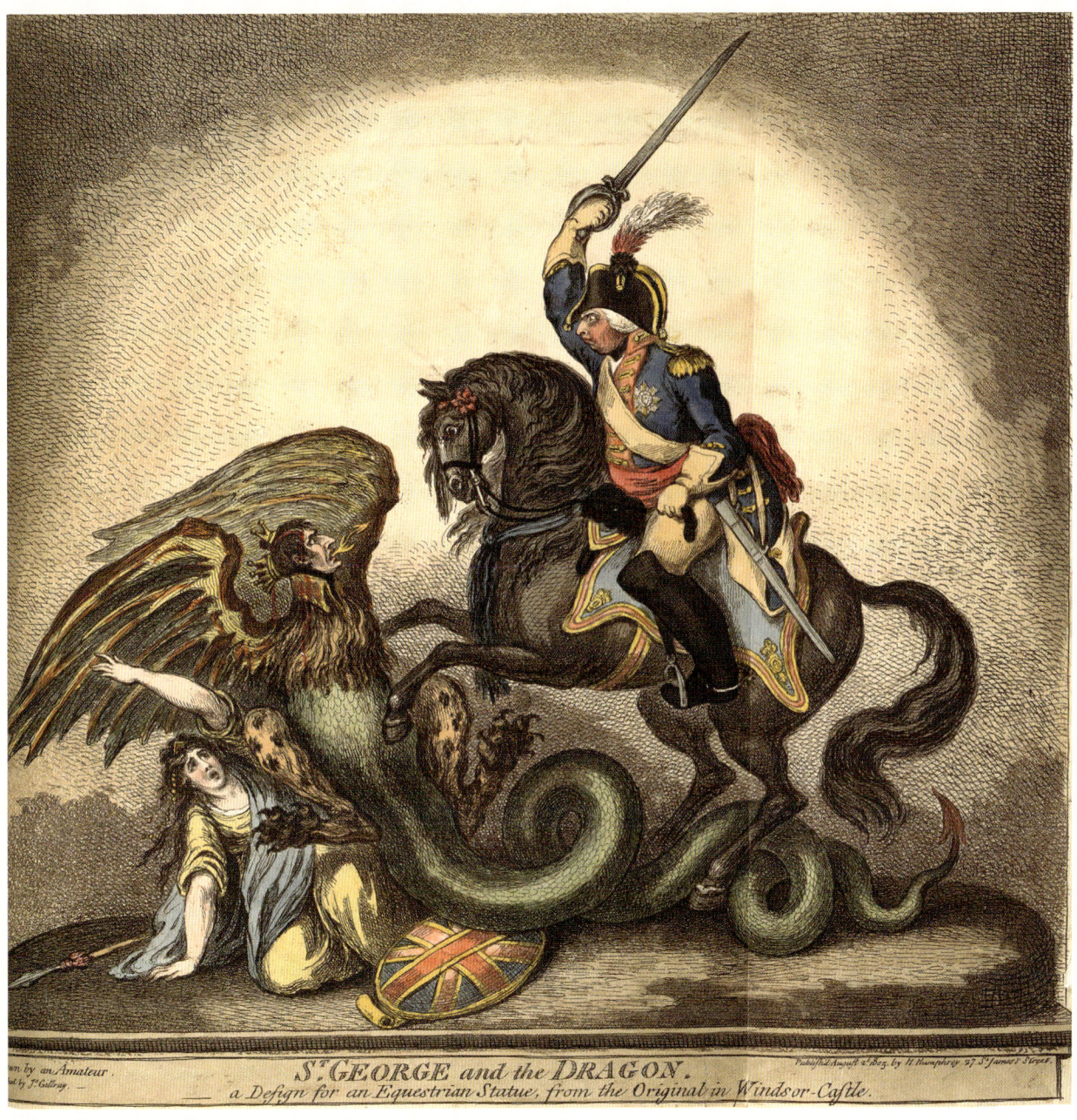

St. GEORGE and the DRAGON.
a Design for an Equestrian Statue, from the Original in Windsor-Castle.

Figure 2
Designed by Col. James Bradyll; etched by James
Gillray (1756–1815)

**St. George and the dragon – a design for an
equestrian statue, from the original in Windsor
Castle**

Hand-coloured etching and aquatint
Published 2 August 1805 by Hannah Humphrey
Curzon b.23(253)
BMC 10424

This dramatic composition conceals Gillray's typically
ambiguous message: George III draws his sword to slay
the dragon, Napoleon, but in doing so threatens also to
trample Britannia. The nation mobilizing for
aggression against an enemy power risks damaging
part of its own nature.

British naval history and the life of Napoleon is only partially represented in the current exhibition. The Bodleian Library is fortunate to have one of Broadley's own works, *Napoleon in Caricature*, extra-illustrated with the cartoons and drawings he used in composing the book, many of which are on display in this exhibition.

A. M. Broadley

Alexander Meyrick Broadley (1847–1916) was a journalist and historian who used his collections of prints and autograph letters both to extra-illustrate books by other authors and to write his own works on the Napoleonic wars and British social life during the eighteenth and nineteenth centuries. Examples of books extra-illustrated by Broadley can be found in several libraries and archives in the US and UK, and include the lives of celebrated literary figures as well as military leaders. Broadley's library was sold in 1916 but several items are reunited in the Bodleian Library and shown in this exhibition, including the prints now in the Curzon collection and the manuscript of Dumouriez's *Memoirs on the defences of Great Britain and Ireland* from the Lyell collection.

London Caricaturists During the French Revolutionary Wars

James Gillray (1756–1815)

Gillray was widely admired for the complexity and detail of his designs, which were collected by the Prince of Wales, among others. Gillray's ferocious caricatures parodied all politicians regardless of party, but his fundamental attachment to the Pitt Government during the wars against revolutionary France was enhanced by a government pension in 1797. From 1791 his publisher was Hannah Humphrey, with whom he lodged at her addresses first in Old Bond Street and then at 27 St James's Street, London.

Thomas Rowlandson (1756–1827)

A sweetness of tone and delicacy of line characterized Rowlandson's illustrations (as seen in the *Volunteers of London and Environs*) and even his social satires of London amusements. His political cartoons were often etched from designs by amateurs.

Isaac Cruikshank (1764–1811?)

The Edinburgh-born Cruikshank began his career as a cartoonist in 1784. His talent was more uneven than Gillray's, but he was especially prolific in etching many of his own and other artists' designs. His cartoon 'Buonaparte at Rome giving audience in state' (1797) was one of the first British caricatures of the French General. Isaac's son, George Cruikshank, helped in his father's workshop and became the leading caricaturist and illustrator of the next generation.

Richard Newton (1777–98)

A youthful prodigy, Newton had a remarkable but short career. He worked for the publisher William Holland while still in his teens, and then published on his own account for a year or so just before his death. Newton's political cartoons were radical in tone, notably 'Treason!!!' (1798), against the 'Two Acts'. Newton's publisher, William Holland, who also published many of the prints in this exhibition, was convicted of sedition in 1792 and imprisoned for a year in Newgate for selling Tom Paine's pamphlet, *Address to the Addressers*. His arrest and conviction illustrate the point that prose was more likely to be judged seditious than even the most virulent pictorial satire.

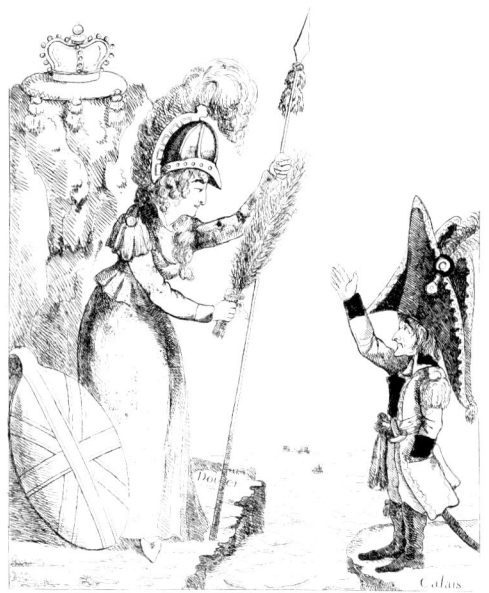

Right and p.24: Item 14 (detail)

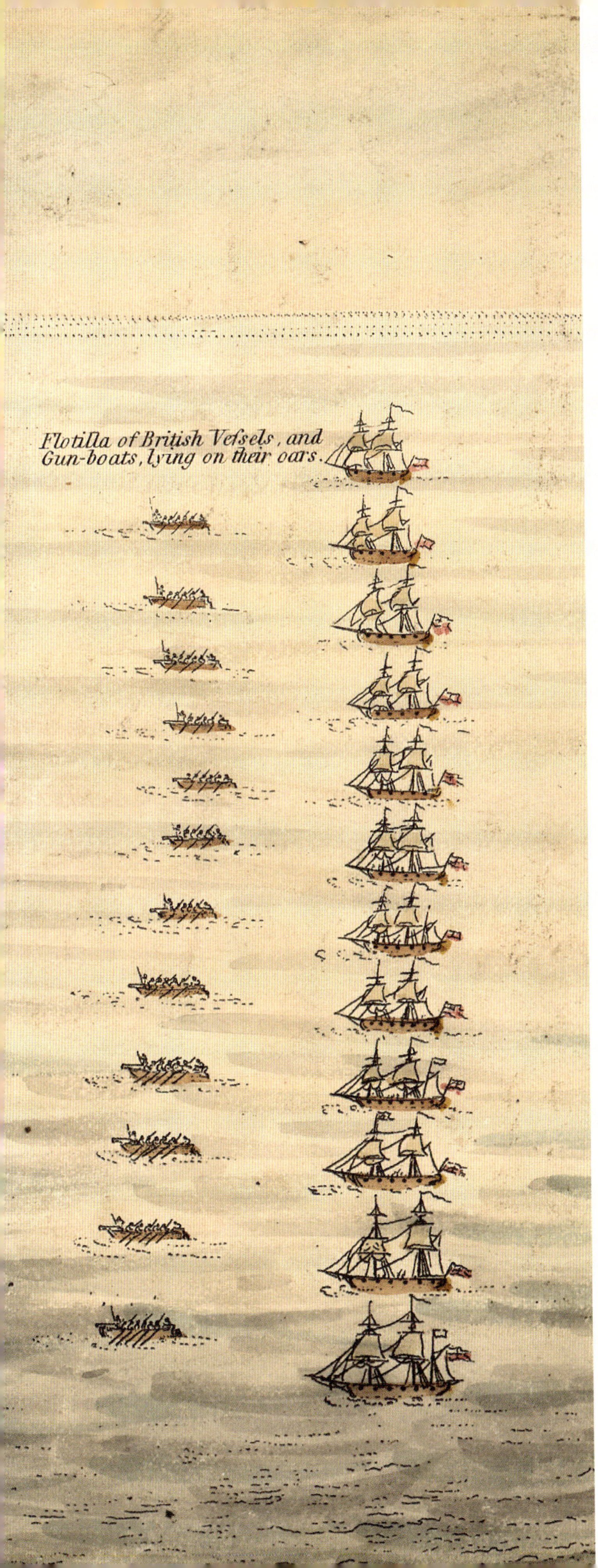

Flotilla of British Vessels, and Gun-boats, lying on their oars.

❊

The Catalogue

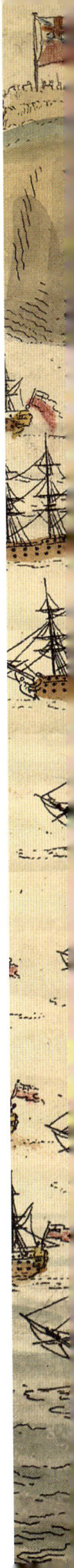

❊

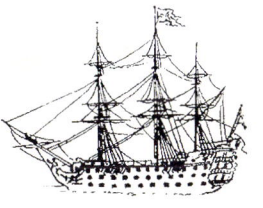

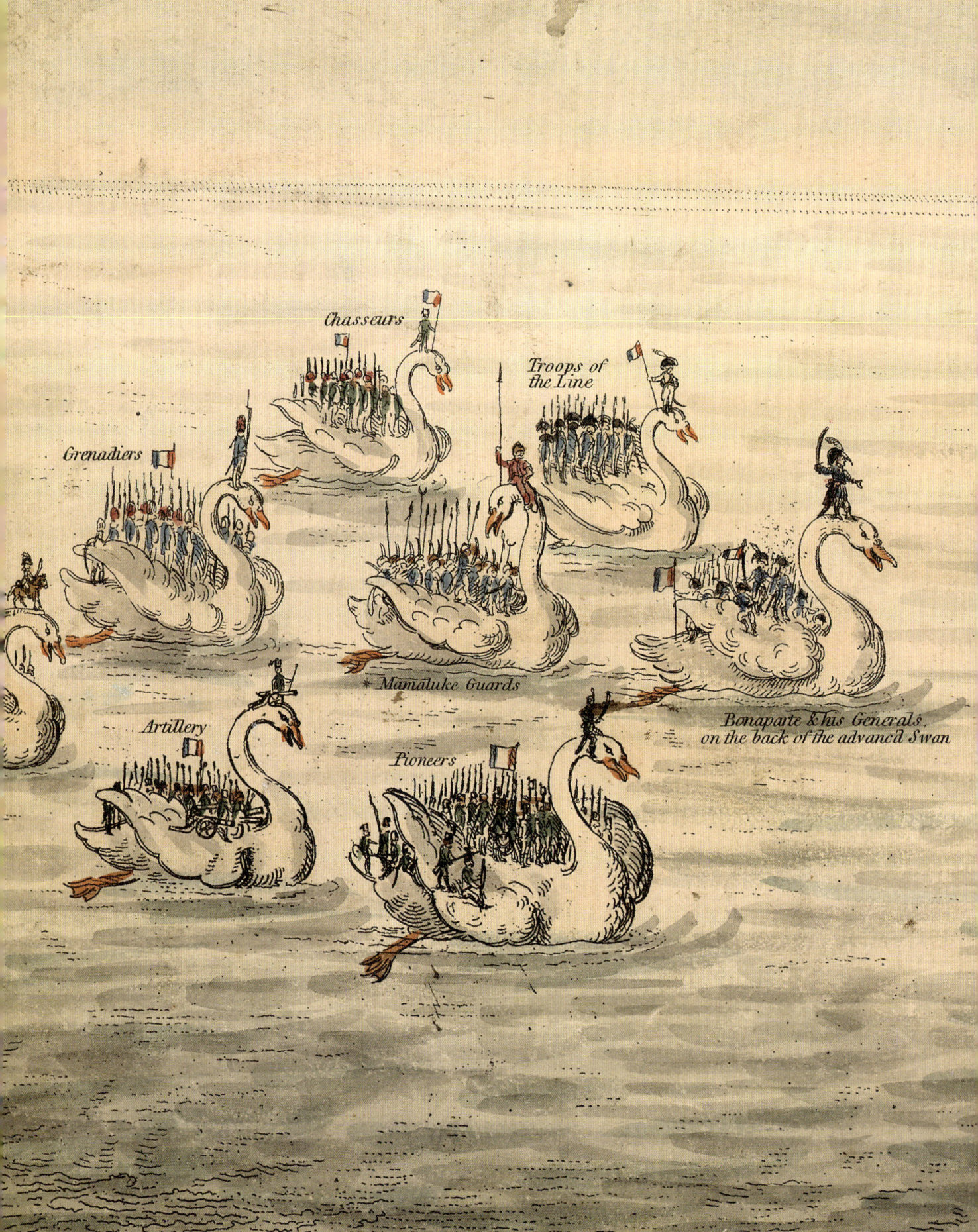

Chasseurs

Troops of
the Line

Grenadiers

* Mamaluke Guards

Bonaparte & his Generals
on the back of the advanc'd Swan

Artillery

Pioneers

The Contrast

Visual contrast is an ancient form of
humour and was a favourite device of
caricaturists in the 1790s. The
oppositions they drew between Britain
and France continued a long history
of English Francophobia, given a new
edge by the French Revolution of
1789. But as a visual and literary
device, contrast could be a double-
edged sword. Most obviously, in
graphic terms, it required that France
and the Revolution occupy an equal
space in the print opposite Britain and
her constitution.

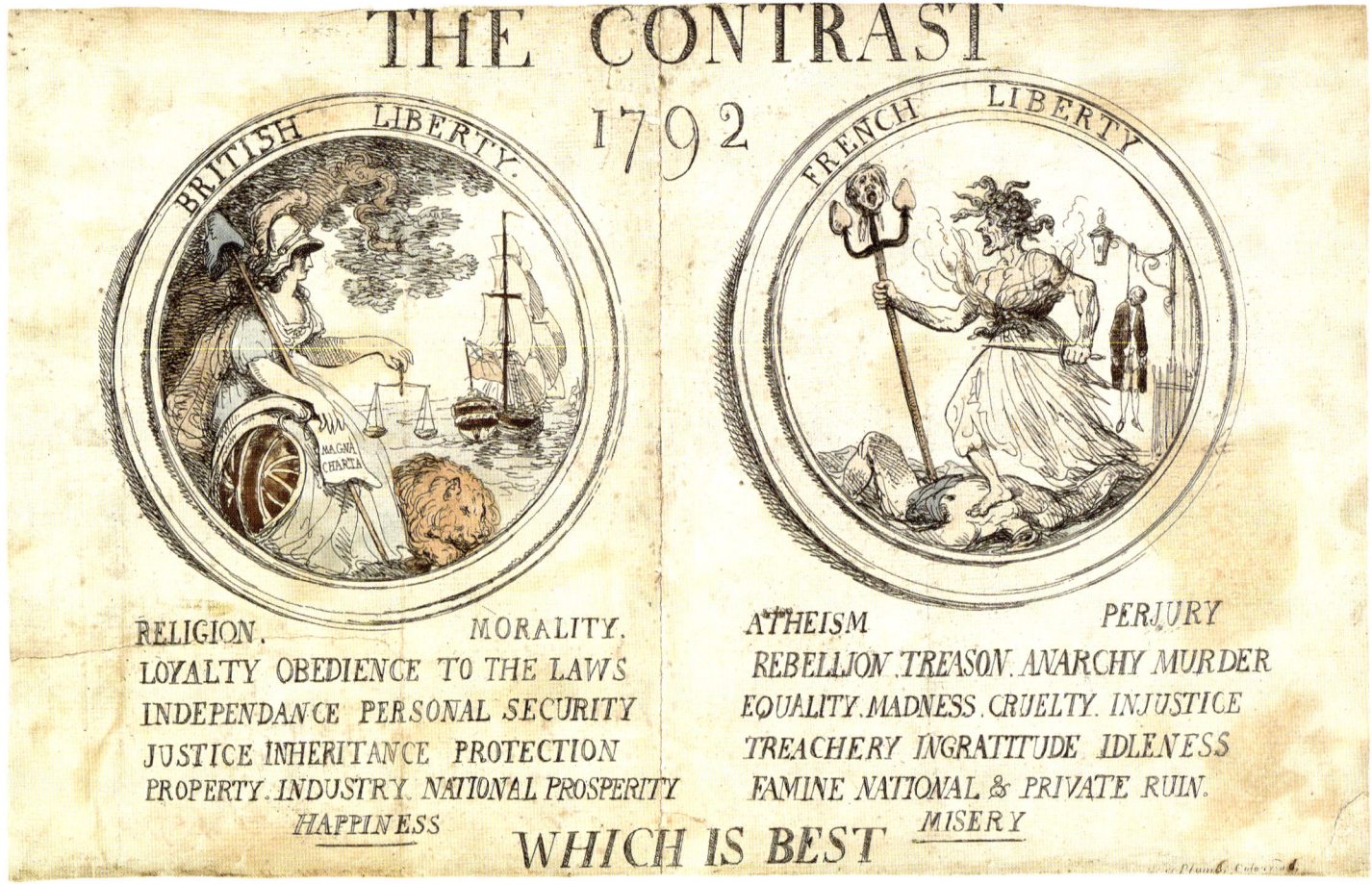

1

Thomas Rowlandson (1756–1827)
The contrast 1792
Hand-coloured etching 26 x 41.8 cm (sheet); diameters of medallions
16 cm
Published [1792]
John Johnson Collection: French Wars and Revolutions folder 4 (28)
BMC 8149

The year 1792 was a period of bloody political conflict
in France, which culminated in the trial and execution
of the King, Louis XVI, in January 1793. Here Great
Britain is represented by Britannia, associated with
naval power and commercial strength. The red liberty
cap atop her spear suggests that the weapon is to be
used only in defence of British freedom – but the cap of
liberty would become a more controversial symbol in
later years, as it became associated with republicanism.
This print was distributed cheaply as part of the
loyalist campaign in 1792 aimed at counteracting the
rhetoric of French revolutionaries and British
reformers.

2

James Gillray (1756–1815)

**Britannia between Scylla and Charybdis, or –
the vessel of the Constitution steered clear of
the Rock of Democracy, and the whirlpool of
Arbitrary Power**

Hand-coloured etching 30.3 x 36 cm (platemark)
Published 8 April 1793 by Hannah Humphrey
Douce Prints W.1.2 (406)
BMC 8320

Prime Minister William Pitt (1759–1806) steers the
boat carrying a young and pretty Britannia to safety,
the castle of Albion. The republican sharks swimming
around the rock of Democracy are caricatured as
opposition Whigs, from the top Joseph Priestley,
Charles James Fox and Richard Brinsley Sheridan. The
whirlpool of Arbitrary Power is represented by an
upturned crown.

Gillray has invested a political argument familiar to his
British audience with new significance in the light of
events in 1792 and 1793. Most immediately, the sharks
with their liberty caps and tricolour rosettes represent
French Revolutionaries and the sinking crown signifies
the collapsed Bourbon monarchy, potentially dragging
Europe into chaos. Britain had entered the war against
revolutionary France after almost a year of fighting
between the great powers on the Continent. In this
sense, the theme of this print
anticipates the song praising Pitt in
1802 as 'the pilot who weathered
the storm' – a wartime leader who
brought the country through the
European-wide struggle between
republicanism and royalism.

But there is also a domestic
dimension to the print.
Throughout the eighteenth century
the strength of the English
constitution was thought to be its
perfect balance between popular
and royal power, or as it was
sometimes expressed, its
democratic and monarchical
elements. The belief of Pitt and his
ministers in 1793 was that
Parliament continued to represent
all members of the nation

adequately, preserving this balance. The Whig
opposition, on the other hand, expressed more
sympathy with reformers who sought to broaden the
franchise. This is the significance of the Whig faces
given to the republican sharks.

In this context the identity of the sinking crown must
also be considered. For his own part, Gillray had
participated in a popular anti-royalism current in the
decade before the revolution, producing several prints
in the early 1790s ridiculing the monarchy and the
Royal Family. These appeared in the aftermath of the
crisis over the King's health in 1788, when he was
believed insane, and also reflected disgust at the lavish
and dissolute lifestyle of the Prince of Wales. The 1788
episode provoked partisan conflict between the Tories,
led by Pitt, and the opposition Whigs who could not
disguise their hopes for a Regency under the Prince. In
1791, Gillray caricatured Pitt, George III's favourite
minister, as 'An excrescence; a fungus – alias – a
toadstool upon a dunghill' (BMC 7936), the 'dunghill'
being the Crown itself. 'Britannia between Scylla and
Charybdis' tells a different story; seen in the context of
the French Revolution, Pitt is credited with an
independence from extreme principles. As a whole,
Gillray's design emphasizes the threat which the
French Revolution posed to Britain, not only through
the wars against France but through domestic radical
agitation in sympathy with revolutionary principles.

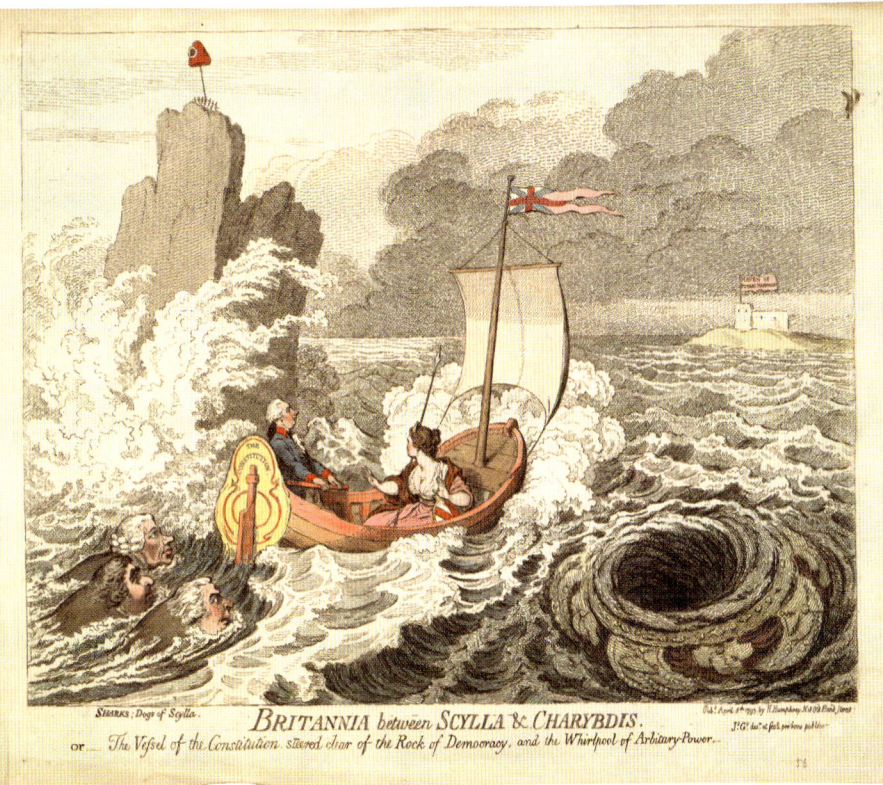

SHARKS; Dogs of Scylla.

BRITANNIA between SCYLLA & CHARYBDIS.
or ... *The Vessel of the Constitution steered clear of the Rock of Democracy, and the Whirlpool of Arbitrary Power.*

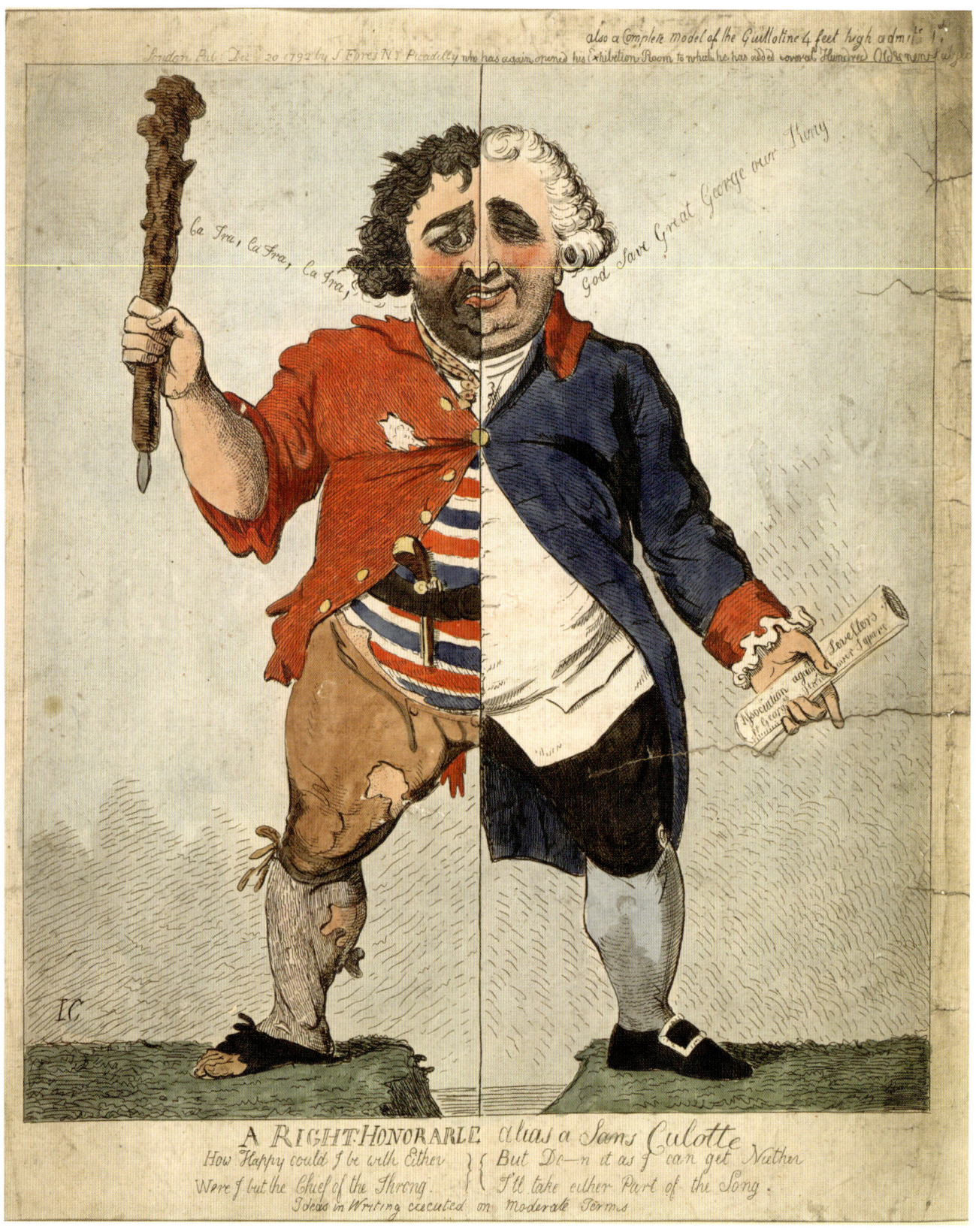

3

Isaac Cruikshank (1764–1811?)
A right honora[b]le alias a sans culotte
Hand-coloured etching 37.8 x 31.6 cm (sheet)
Published 20 December 1792 by S. W. Fores
John Johnson Collection: Political Cartoons 1 (93)
BMC 8142

The subject is Charles James Fox (1749–1806),
leader of the Whig opposition in Parliament and a
self-proclaimed admirer of French revolutionary
principles. The Whigs opposed war against
republican France and continued to support some
measure of parliamentary reform in Britain.

4

James Gillray (1756–1815)
French liberty. British slavery
Hand-coloured etching 24 x 34.4 cm (sheet)
Published 21 December 1792 by Hannah Humphrey
Curzon b.2(51)
BMC 8145

On the left, an emaciated Frenchman eats onions in
front of an open fire, seated on a wooden stool on the
bare floor of his kitchen. He sings the praises of
'liberté...No more Tax!...all Free Citizen!...by Gar how
ve live!'. Worthless paper *assignats* protrude from his
pocket. More heartening than his food may be a 'Map
of the French Conquests' hanging over the fireplace.
Facing him, a fat Englishman, as comfortably
upholstered as his red plush dining chair, carves an
enormous roast beef, grumbling, 'Ah! this cursed
Ministry! they'll ruin us with their damn'd Taxes'.
Unlike Rowlandson's print, this cartoon satirizes both
figures, mainly for their inability to see beyond their
desire for lower taxes.

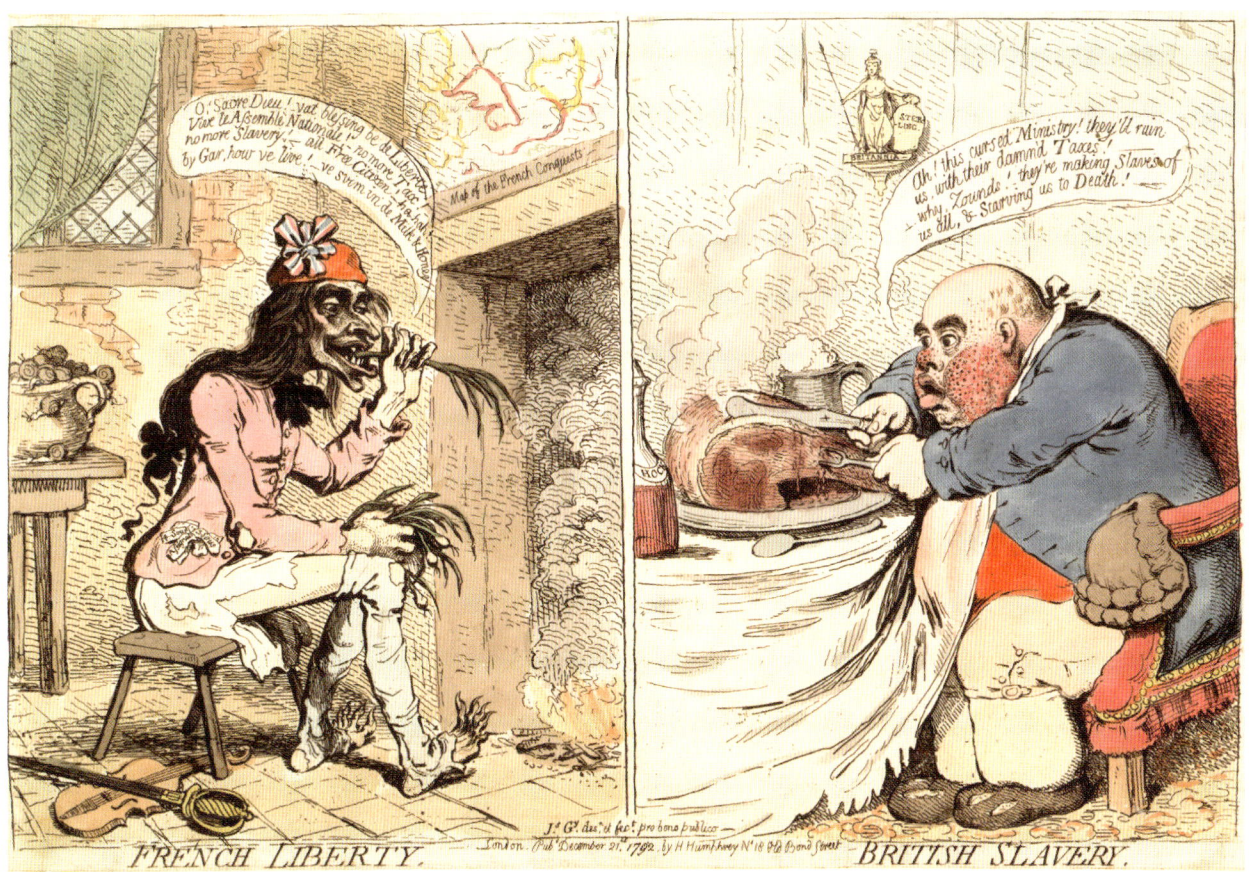

Invasion!

As soon as war was declared in February 1793, Britons speculated on the possibility of a French invasion. There were several attempts in the early years of the war: in 1796, when a fleet sailing for Ireland was dispersed by storms; in 1797, when a small force actually landed at Fishguard and was captured; and most notably in 1798, when French troops arrived in Ireland to support a nationalist rebellion. The memories of these earlier attempts heightened the alarm of 1803. To this was added the knowledge that France's most daring military commander, Napoleon Bonaparte, had taken command of the project to invade Britain.

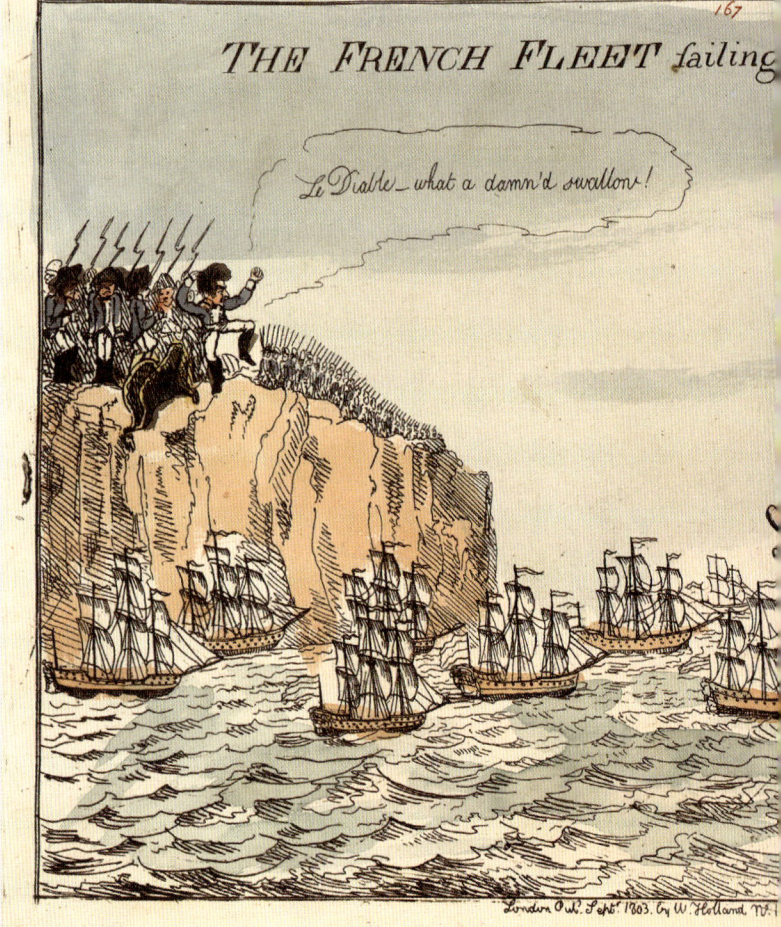

5

The French fleet sailing into the mouth of the Thames!!!

Hand-coloured etching 23 x 40.4 cm (subject)
Published September 1803 by William Holland
Curzon b.12(10)

The figure of Jack Tar, the typical British sailor, embodies the Thames mouth in this fantasy of a French invasion attempt met by overwhelming naval power.

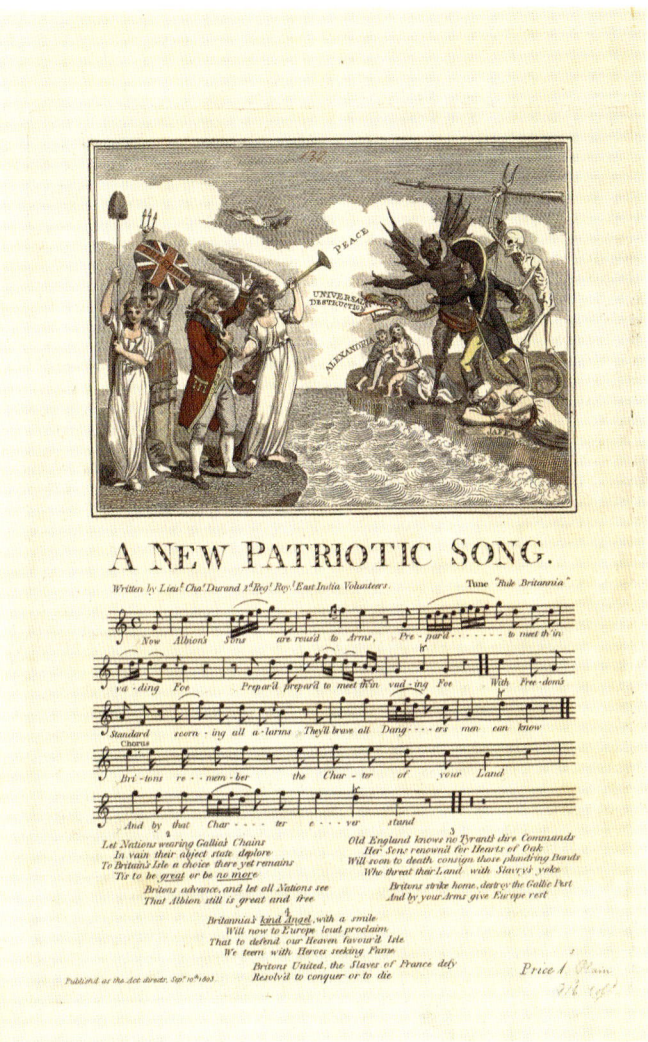

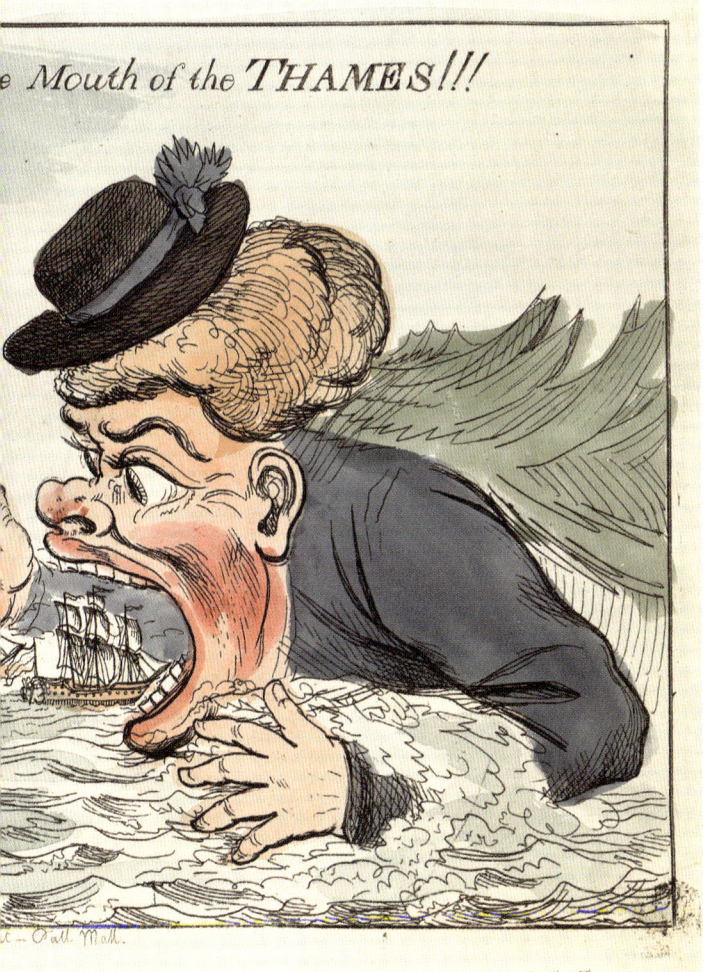

6

A new patriotic song

Written by Lieut. Charles Durand, 2nd Regiment Royal East India Volunteers

Illustrated broadside: engraving of illustration 34.5 x 24.4 cm (platemark)
Published 10 September 1803
Curzon b.12(3)
BMC 10094

The song and the illustration both refer to Napoleon's alleged cruelties during the Egyptian campaign of 1798–9, including the slaughter of civilians at the capture of Alexandria and the killing of prisoners at Jaffa. On the English shore, George III is represented in a heroic stance opposing invasion. The author was a member of one of the volunteer corps raised by the East India Company.

7

[Hannah More (1745–1833)]
A king or a consul?
Broadside, 37.7 x 25.5 cm
Printed and sold by S. Hazard; sold also by Messrs. Rivingtons, St
Paul's Church-Yard; Hatchard, Piccadilly, London; James, Wine-
street, Bristol
John Johnson Collection: French Wars and Revolutions folder 4 (63)

This broadside ballad was sold by the publishers of the
Cheap Repository Tracts, a series of loyalist songs and
stories produced by the evangelical educator Hannah
More and her friends, mostly between 1794 and 1799,
for the moral improvement of working people. This
song was written in response to the 1803 invasion
threat. It was offered for sale at one halfpenny or, to aid
free distribution, at three shillings and sixpence per 100.

The contrast between Britain and France is here
presented as a choice between George III and Napoleon
Bonaparte – suggesting a subliminal fear that British
readers of popular tracts might be considering the
merits of Napoleon's leadership. *The Choice* is the title

of another broadside of 1803, in which the choice of
French conquest or death is rejected by British soldiers
who make clear their choice – to support their King and
constitution.

Like other loyal papers, this song refers to the stories
of atrocities committed under Bonaparte's command in
Egypt and Syria, and Napoleon's fury at the reports of
these in British newspapers.

And lest we should publish his horrible tricks
With our freedom of printing a quarrel he picks
But we keep no secrets, each newspaper shews it
And while we act fairly we care not who knows it.

8

**Let Englishmen keep a
watchful eye**
Broadside, 23.2 x 28.7 cm
London, Nichols and Son, [1803]
John Johnson Collection: French
Wars and Revolutions folder 4 (66)

Let ENGLISHMEN
keep a watchful Eye upon
FRENCH SPIES,
who are employed to pull down or deface
all Loyal and Patriotic Papers.

NICHOLS and SON, Printers, Red Lion Paſſage, Fleet Street.

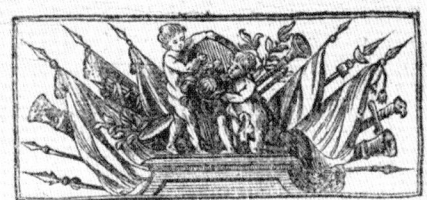

A KING or a CONSUL?

A NEW SONG to the Tune of *Derry down*.

COME all ye brave Englishmen, list' to my story,
You who love peace and freedom, and honor and
    glory!
No foreign usurper they hither shall bring,
We'll be rul'd by a *native*, our Father and King.
        Derry down, down, down, derry down!

No Corsican Despot in England shall rule,
No Disciple avow'd of the Mussulman school;
A Papist at Rome, and at Cairo a Turk,
Now this thing, now that thing, as best helps his
    work.   Derry down,

Shall Atheists rule Britons? O never, no never,
Forbid it Religion for ever and ever;
Their heathenish Consuls then let them not bring,
Our Country is Christian, and Christian our King!
        Derry down,

In England when wounds are the sailor's sad lot,
Their wounds and their sufferings are never forgot;
To a Palace far nobler our Vet'rans we bring,
Than is kept for himself by our merciful King.
        Derry down,

Let any compare, if my saying he blames,
The splendors of Greenwich* with those of St. James.
—Once *Buoni* trepann'd his poor troops to the East,
O'er deserts too sultry for man or for beast;
        Derry down,

When the battle was over, and hundreds were found,
By the fortune of war gash'd with many a wound;
Diseas'd and afflicted---now what do you think
This tender Commander oblig'd them to drink?
        Derry down,

You fancy 'twas grog, or good flip, or good ale;
No, 'twas *poison*, alas! was the soldiers' regale;
See *Jaffa*†—see *Haslar*‡—the diff'rence to prove,
There poison, *here* kindness, *there* murder, *here*
    love.   Derry down,

---

* A magnificent Hospital for Sailors.
† Where French Soldiers were *poisoned* in the Hospital.
‡ The Royal Portsmouth Hospital where English Sailors are
treated like Princes.

And lest we should publish his horrible tricks,
With our freedom of printing a quarrel he picks;
But *we* keep no secrets, each newspaper shews it,
And while we act fairly we care not who knows it.
        Derry down,

To Frenchmen, O Britons, we never will trust;
Who murder their Monarch can never be just;
That freedom we boast of, the French never saw,
'Tis guarded by order and bounded by law.
        Derry down,

That *Buoni*'s invincible, Frenchmen may cry,
Let Sidney the brave give each boaster the lie;
Tho' the arrows of Europe against us are hurl'd,
Be true to yourselves and you'll conquer the world.
        Derry down,

Tho' some struggles we make, let us never repine,
While we sit underneath our own fig-tree and vine;
Our Fig-tree is Freedom, our Vine is Content,
Two blessings, by nature for Frenchmen not meant.
        Derry down,

French liberty Englishmen never will suit,
They have planted the tree, but *we* feed on the fruit;
Then rail not at taxes, altho' they cut deep,
'Tis a heavy Insurance to save the brave Ship.
        Derry down,

Let narrow-soul'd *party* be banish'd the land,
And let Englishmen join with one heart and one
    hand;
Let each fight for his Wife, for *we* marry but *one*,
The French wed so many, they oft care for none.
        Derry down,

One King did not suit them, three Tyrants they
    chose,
And their God they renounce while their King they
    depose;
Then we ne'er will submit to the Corsican's rod,
Britons want but one Wife, and one King, and one
    GOD.
        Derry down, down, down, derry down!

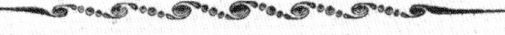

BATH: Printed and sold by S. HAZARD:

Sold also by Messrs. RIVINGTONS, St. Paul's Church-Yard; HATCHARD, Piccadilly, London;
JAMES, Wine-street, Bristol; and by all the Booksellers in the UNITED KINGDOM.

Price One Half-Penny, or 3s. 6d. per Hundred.

9

Plain answers to plain questions in a dialogue between John Bull and Bonaparte, met half seas over between Dover and Calais

Broadside, 55.2 x 44.4 cm
London, John Hatchard , [1803]
Printed by J. Brettell, 54,Great Windmill Street, Haymarket
John Johnson Collection: French Wars and Revolutions folder 4 (92)

Quizzed by John Bull, Bonaparte states confidently that he expects to be in London, 'About the end of September; or October at latest'. He attempts to explain away the stories of atrocities during the Egyptian expedition, but vows to conquer Britain with dire consequences for the people.

John Bull: ...What do you most depend upon?
Bonaparte: On foggy weather – long nights – a want of discipline in your troops – a want of spirit and of union in your people.

This broadside, like many others, presents freedom of the press as a British liberty which is also a weapon in Britain's arsenal against Napoleon.

John Bull: Why are you such an Enemy to our LIBERTY OF THE PRESS?
Bonaparte: Because it exposes all my deep designs. Because it makes me odious amongst my own subjects...Because it recommends love, loyalty, and support to a king whom I mean to depose; and unanimity to a country, which I mean to conquer.

Hatchard offered these loyal papers for sale at sixpence per dozen, hoping that 'Noblemen, Magistrates, and Gentlemen' would distribute them free and have them posted in public places.

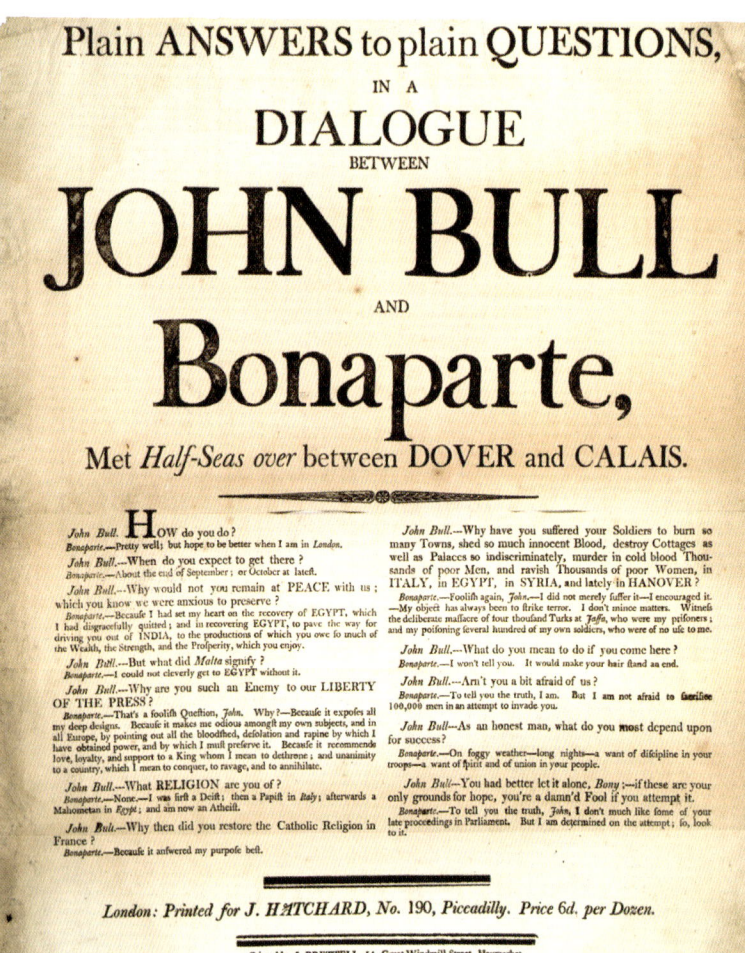

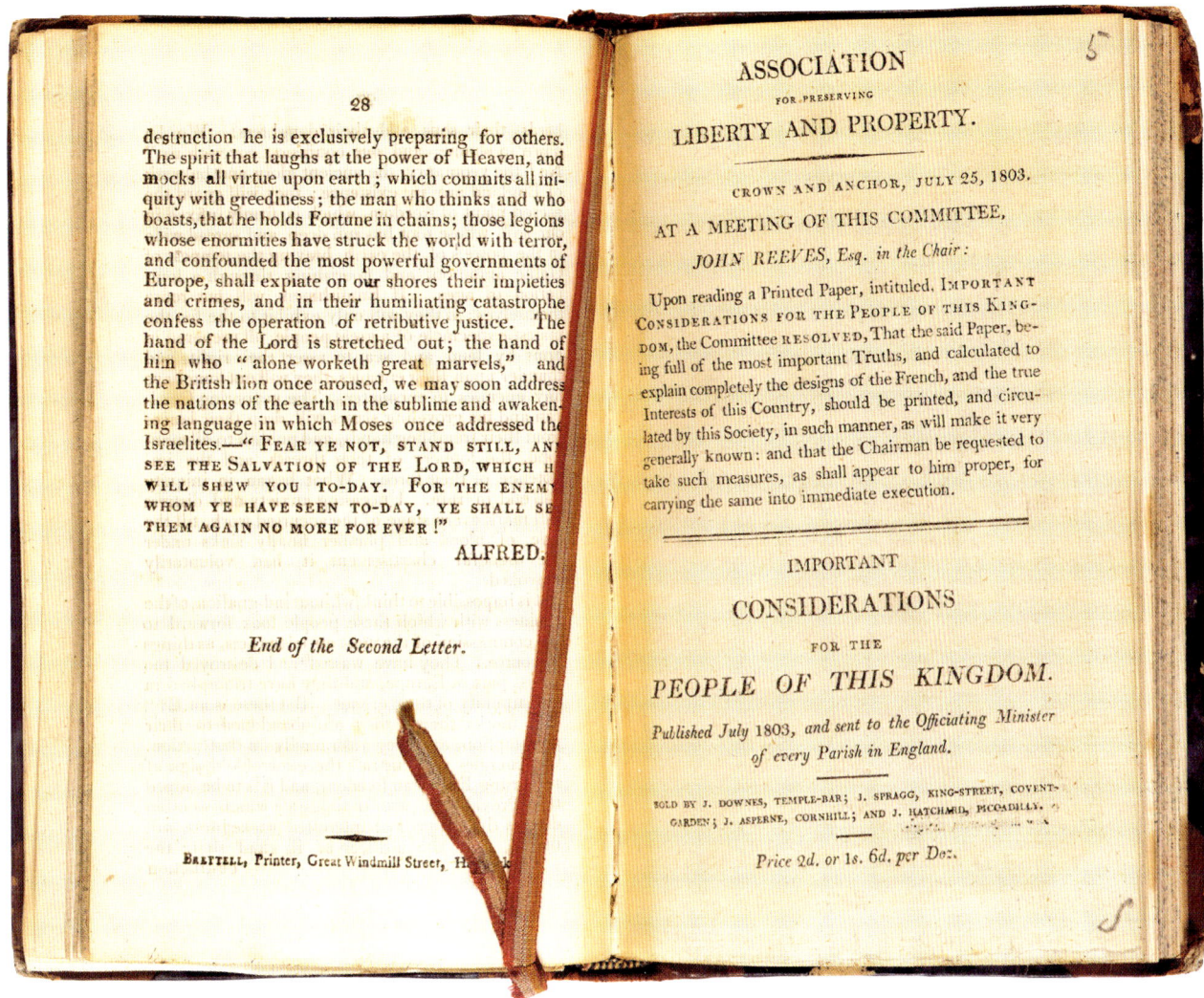

10

William Cobbett (1762–1835)

Important considerations for the people of Great Britain

London, J. Downes, J. Spragg, J. Asperne and J. Hatchard, 1803
22871 f. 63(5).

In Cobbett's view, Napoleon's motive was more than the ambition to conquer Britain. 'The First Consul has a reason, peculiar to himself, for wishing to reduce us to a state of poverty, weakness, submission, and silence.' This was fear of the example set by English liberties and the constitutional monarchy. During his long career by turns a Tory and a Radical, Cobbett cherished a loyalty to the constitution which held governments to a high standard of probity and respect for individual liberties. He railed at corruption in his journal, the *Political Register*, and in the 1830s became a prominent advocate of parliamentary reform.

Publication of this pamphlet was sponsored by the Association for Preserving Liberty and Property, a group originally formed in 1792 by John Reeves (1753?–1829) to oppose the spread of French revolutionary ideas in Britain. The cover price of '2d or 1s 6d per dozen' confirms the intention that this pamphlet should be as widely distributed as possible.

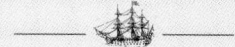

Invasion Machines

The London Chronicle of January 2 1798 printed a report by an English sailor recently returned from Brest, who claimed to have seen in progress the construction of an immense raft. 'It is to be 700 yards by 350, and to be worked by machines, windmills, horsemills, &c.; a grand citadel is to be built in the centre.' Printmakers seized on this description and caricaturists imagined numerous fantastical designs of the rafts.

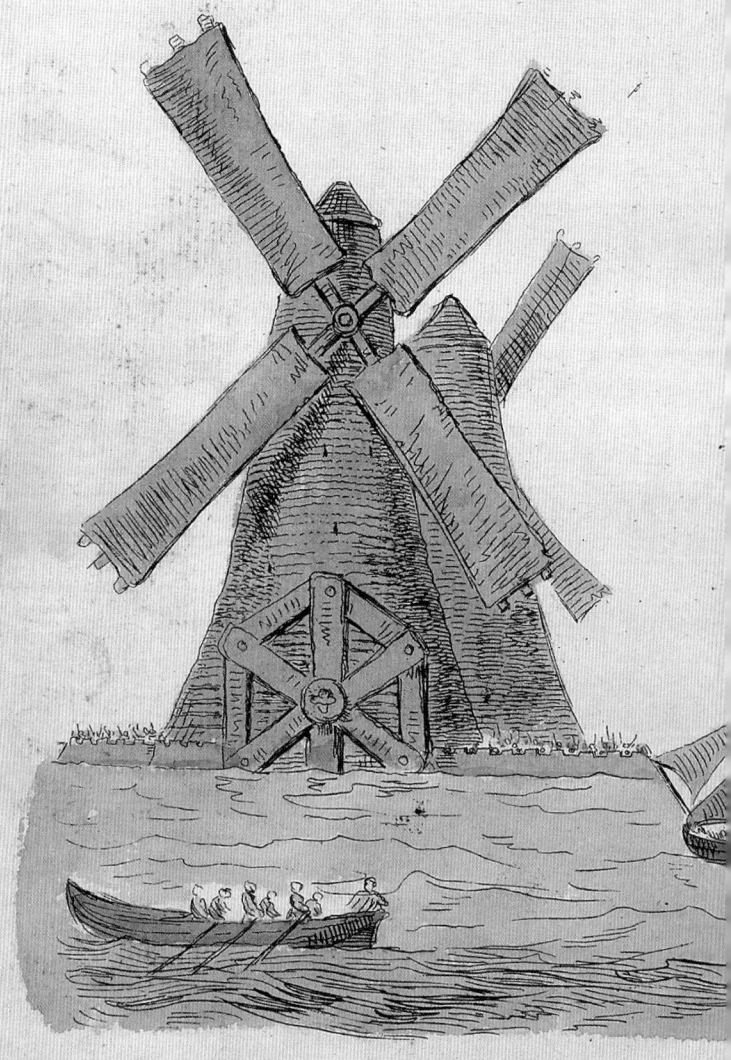

This tremendous Machine extends 2,500 feet in length, and
facility, from whatever point it may blow.   In the mid
on each fide, and at the e
Publifhed b

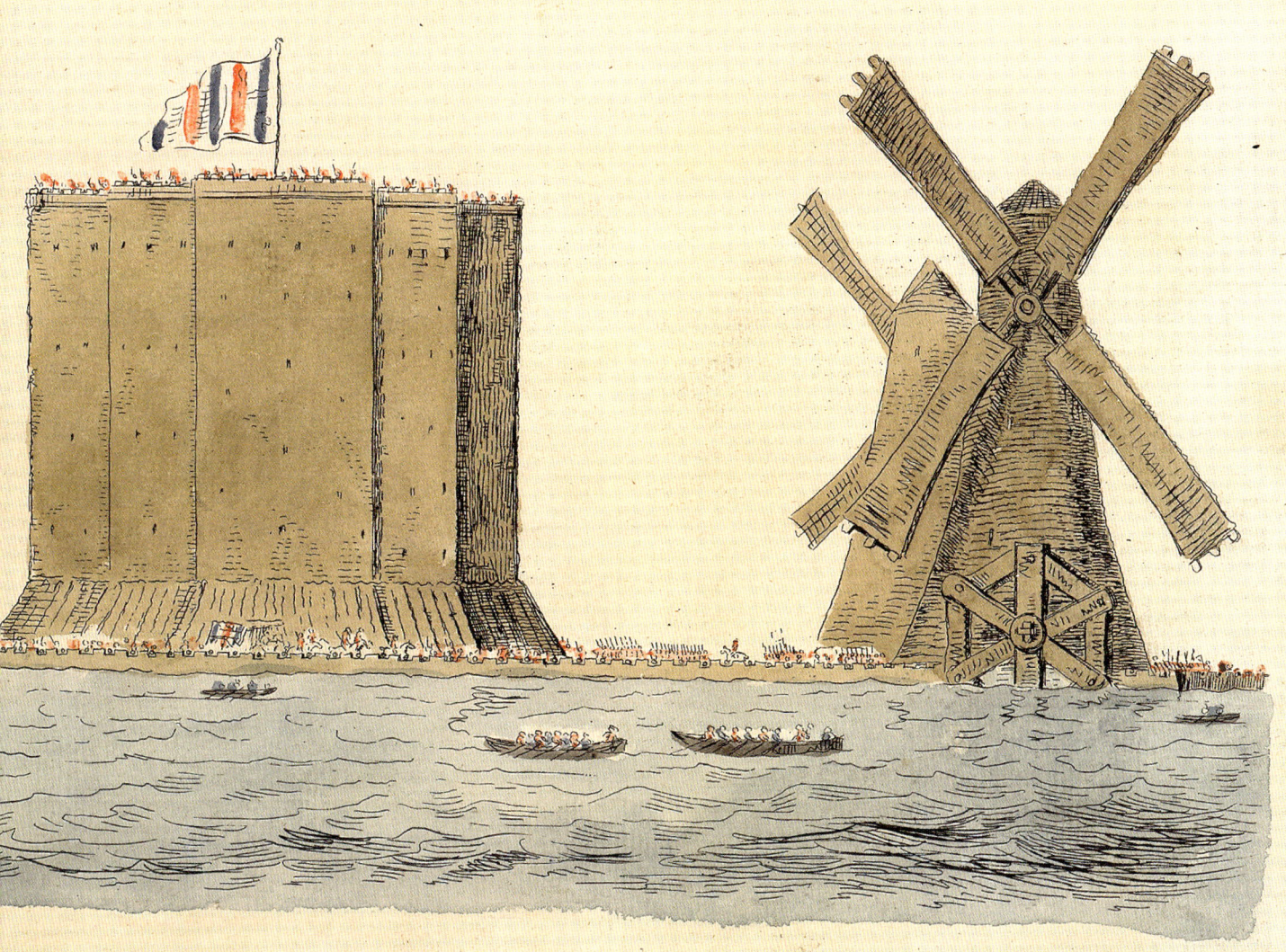

FT, and its APPARATUS, as invented by the FRENCH for their proposed

INVASION OF ENGLAND

(Drawing of a Prisoner who has made his Escape from France.)

et in breadth, is to be navigated by four wheels, turned in the water by the action of the wind, and moving with equal
ort, which enclofes mortars and perriers, for the defence of the troops in their difembarkation. The Raft is armed
36 and 48 pounders, to the amount of 500 pieces, and is intended to carry 50,000 men.
KIN, the Corner of Caftle Street, Leicefter Square, January, 1798.

PRICE ONE SHILLING.

11

An exact representation of a raft, and its apparatus, as invented by the French for their proposed invasion of England

Hand-coloured etching, 25 x 36.7 cm (sheet)
Published January 1798 by J. Aitkin
Curzon b.3(83)

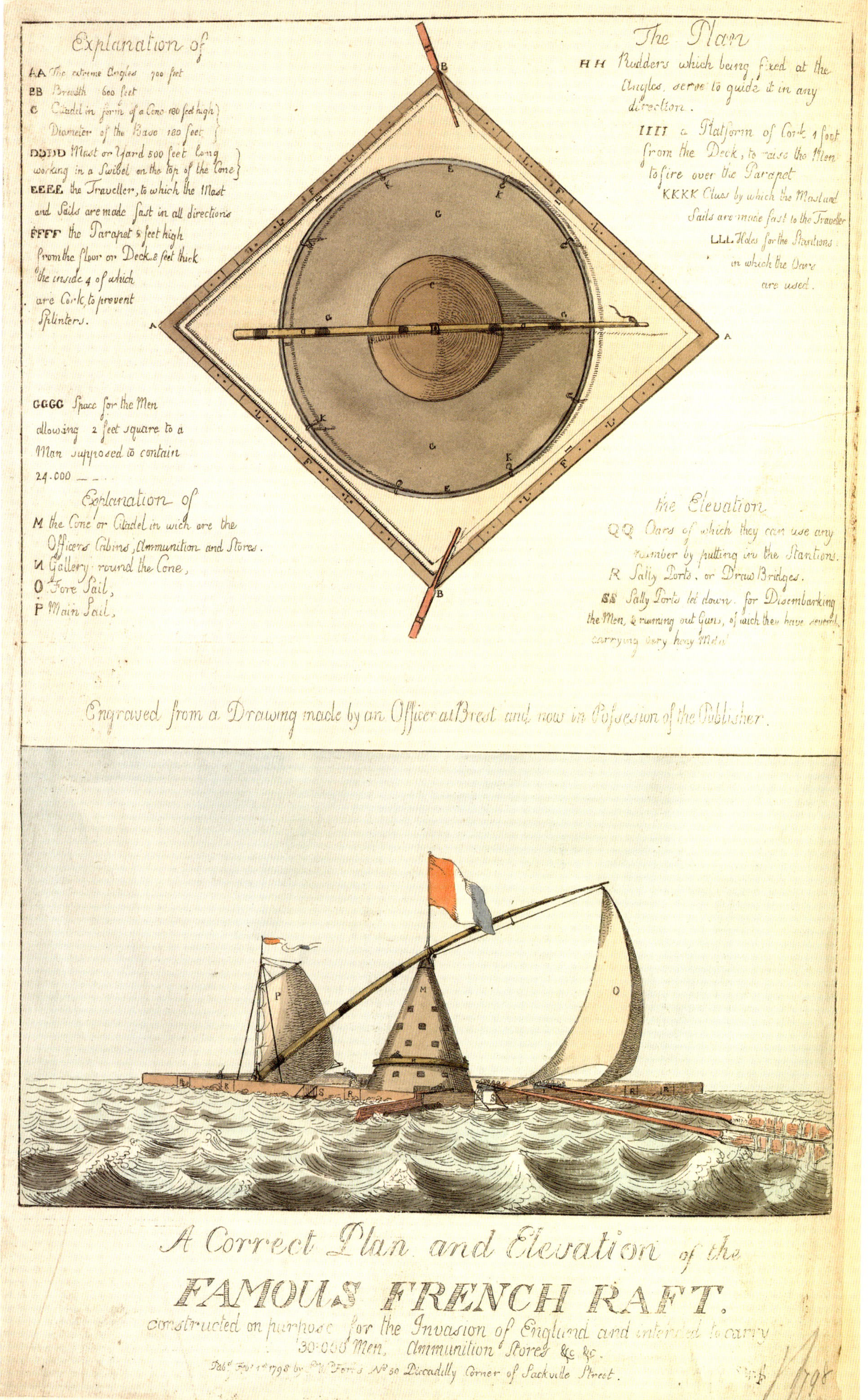

Explanation of

AA The extreme Angles 700 feet

BB Breadth 600 feet

C Citadel in form of a Cone 180 feet high }
Diameter of the Base 180 feet }

DDDD Mast or Yard 500 feet long }
working in a Swivel on the top of the Cone }

EEEE the Traveller, to which the Mast
and Sails are made fast in all directions

FFFF the Parapet 5 feet high
from the floor or Deck, 2 feet thick
the inside 4 of which
are Cork to prevent
Splinters.

GGGG Space for the Men
allowing 2 feet square to a
Man supposed to contain
24.000 ____

The Plan

HH Rudders which being fixed at the
Angles, serve to guide it in any
direction.

IIII a Platform of Cork 1 foot
from the Deck, to raise the Men
to fire over the Parapet

KKKK Clues by which the Mast and
Sails are made fast to the Traveller

LLL Holes for the Stantions
in which the Oars
are used.

Explanation of

M the Cone or Citadel in wich are the
Officers Cabins, Ammunition and Stores.

N Gallery round the Cone,

O Fore Sail,

P Main Sail,

the Elevation

QQ Oars of which they can use any
number by putting in the Stantions.

R Sally Ports. or Draw Bridges.

SS Sally Ports let down for Disembarking
the Men, & running out Guns, of wich they have several,
carrying very heavy Metal

Engraved from a Drawing made by an Officer at Brest, and now in Possession of the Publisher.

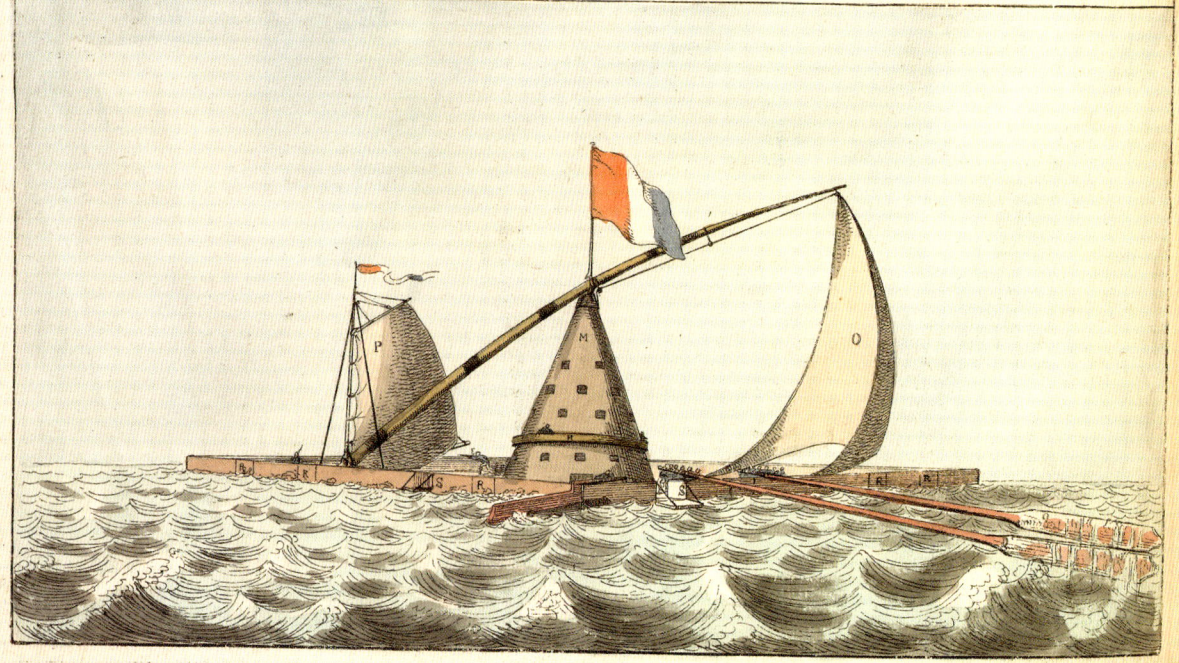

A Correct Plan and Elevation of the
FAMOUS FRENCH RAFT.
constructed on purpose for the Invasion of England and intended to carry
30.000 Men, Ammunition Stores &c &c.

Pub.d Nov.r 1.st 1798 by W.m Fores N.o 50 Piccadilly Corner of Sackville Street.

1798

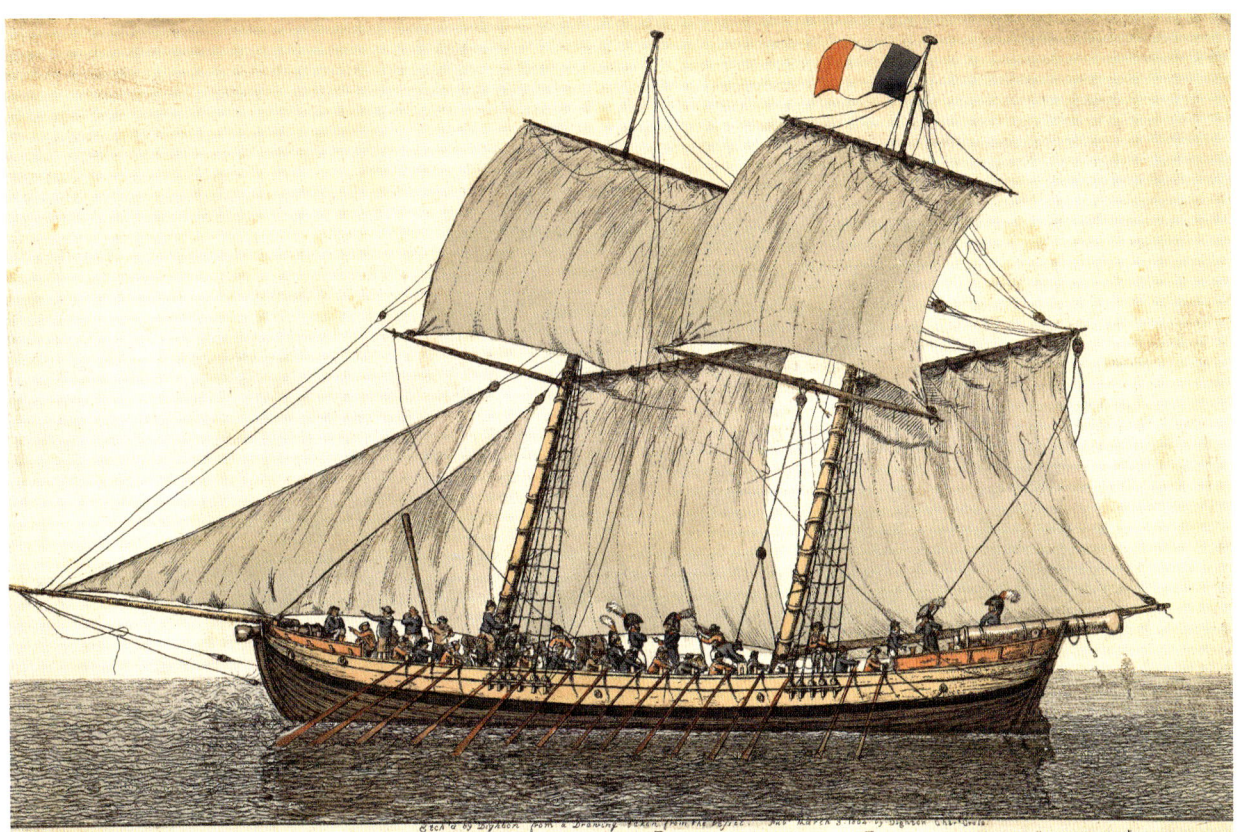

A CORRECT VIEW of the FRENCH GUN BOAT [LA GRASHE FEU] Taken by Capt Sr Richd STRAHAN
1st Clafs Rowing from 36 to 40 OARS.   DIMENSIONS { Length of the DECK 79 Feet.   Breadth 19 Feet.   Depth in the HOLD 5 Feet 9 Inches.

12

A correct plan and elevation of the famous French raft, constructed on purpose for the invasion of England and intended to carry 30,000 men, ammunition stores &c. &c.

Engraved from a drawing made by an officer at Brest
Hand-coloured etching, 32.3 x 23.7 cm (subject)
Published 1 February 1798 by S. W. Fores
Curzon b.23(197)

13

Robert Dighton (1752–1814)

A correct view of the French gun boat [La Grashe Feu] taken by Capt. Sr. Richd. Strahan

Hand-coloured etching, 21.5 x 31.8 cm (sheet)
Published 3 March 1804 by Dighton
Curzon b.4(35)

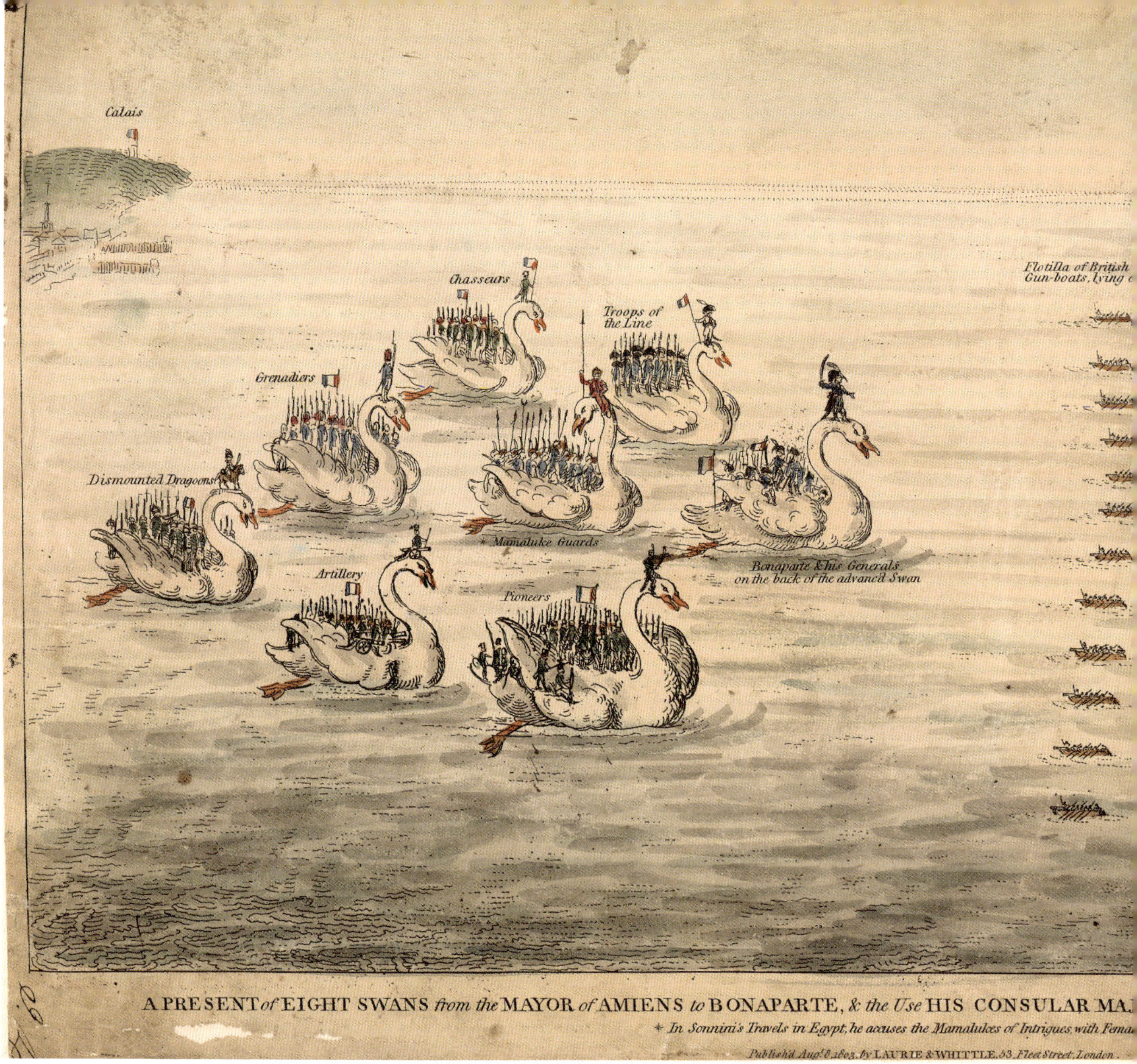

14

More rafts – or, a new plan for invading England. A present of eight swans from the mayor of Amiens
Hand-coloured etching, 23.3 x 42.5 cm (subject)
Published 8 August 1803 by Laurie & Whittle
Curzon b.23(190)

15

[?West]
John Bull viewing the preparations on the French coast!
Hand-coloured etching, 22 x 32.4 cm (subject)
Published 13 October 1803 by William Holland
Curzon b.11(54)
BMC 10110

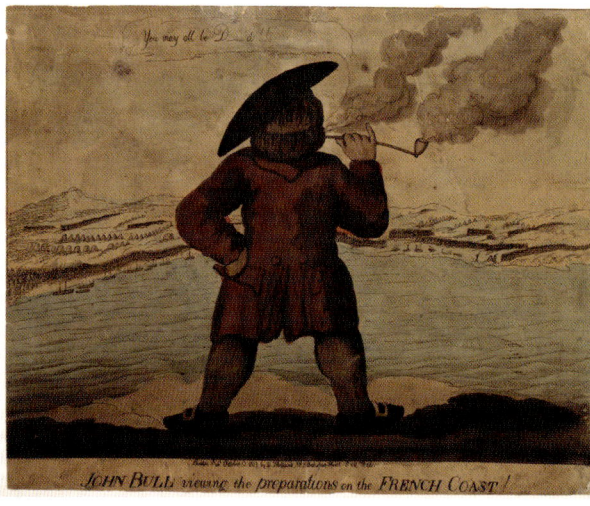

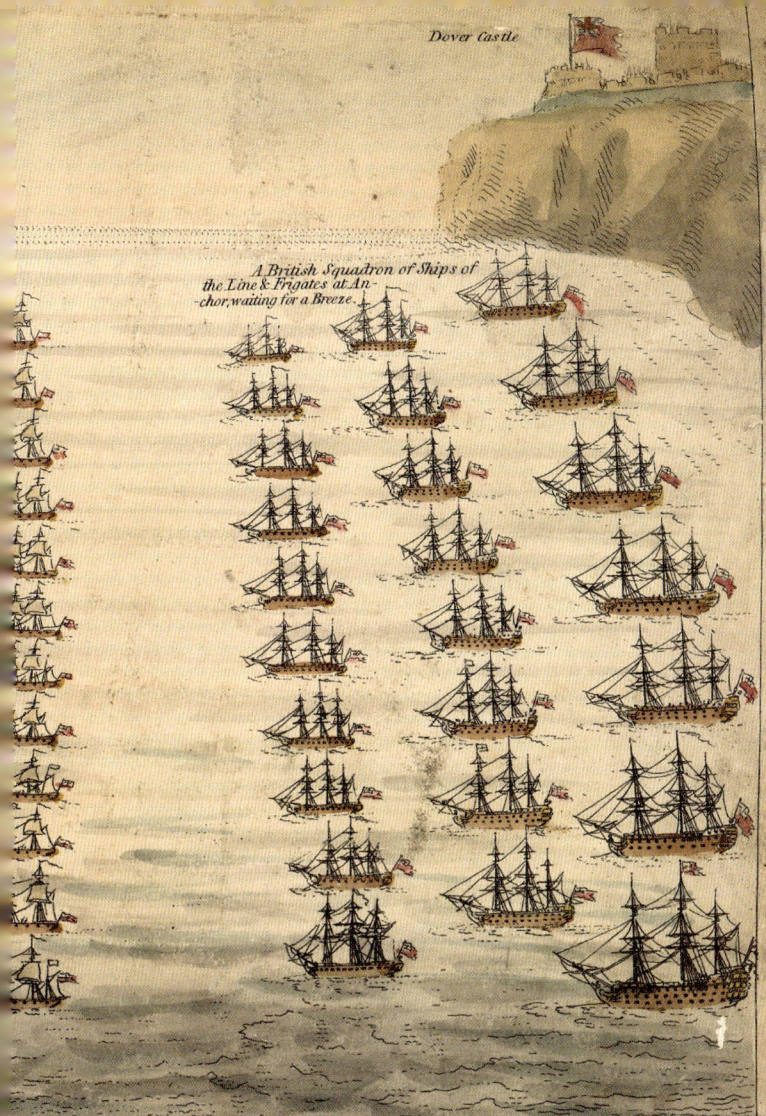

Dover Castle

A British Squadron of Ships of the Line & Frigates at An-chor, waiting for a Breeze.

...ds making of them, in CROSSING the BRITISH CHANNEL.

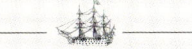

Divisions in Wartime

During the 1790s Government ministers, alarmed at the thought that British radical reformers might take inspiration from French revolutionary principles, initiated a series of measures to suppress political dissent. Three reform leaders were found guilty of sedition by a Scottish court and sentenced to transportation in 1794. Twelve others, arraigned for treason in London during the same year, were acquitted and escaped the death penalty. In the following year the 'Two Acts' were passed to prevent seditious meetings and publications, effectively driving the reform movement underground. Mutinies in the spring of 1797 on troop ships stationed at Spithead and the Nore prompted widespread fears of radical subversion, which were not wholly misplaced. In wartime more than ever, the safety of the nation depended on the loyalty and obedience of ordinary sailors and soldiers, some of whom had been impressed into the services. The Irish rebellion of 1798 further intensified fears of deep-rooted social unrest.

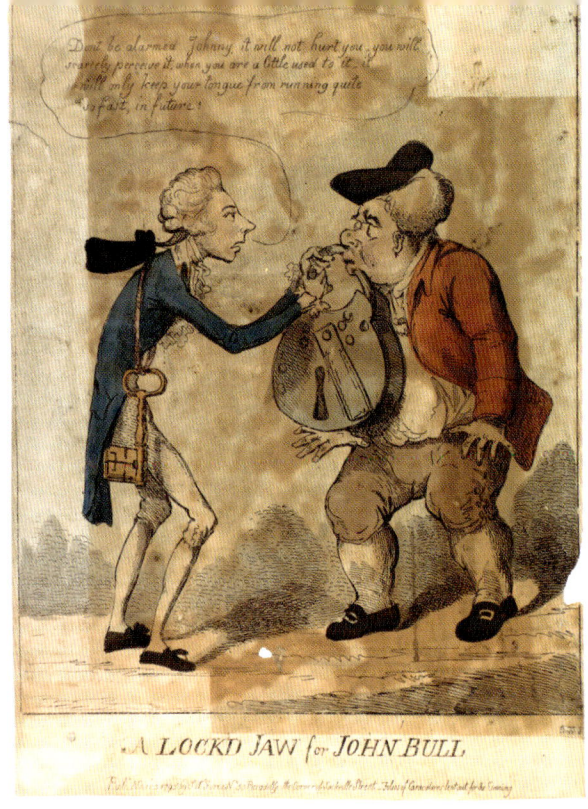

16

[?West]

A lock'd jaw for John Bull

Hand-coloured etching 33.8 x 23.7 cm (sheet)
Published 23 November 1795 by S. W. Fores
John Johnson Collection: Political Cartoons 1 (108)
BMC 8693

William Pitt, the Prime Minister, is the figure fixing a padlock on the lips of John Bull in this satire on the Acts against Treason and Seditious Meetings – the 'Two Acts'.

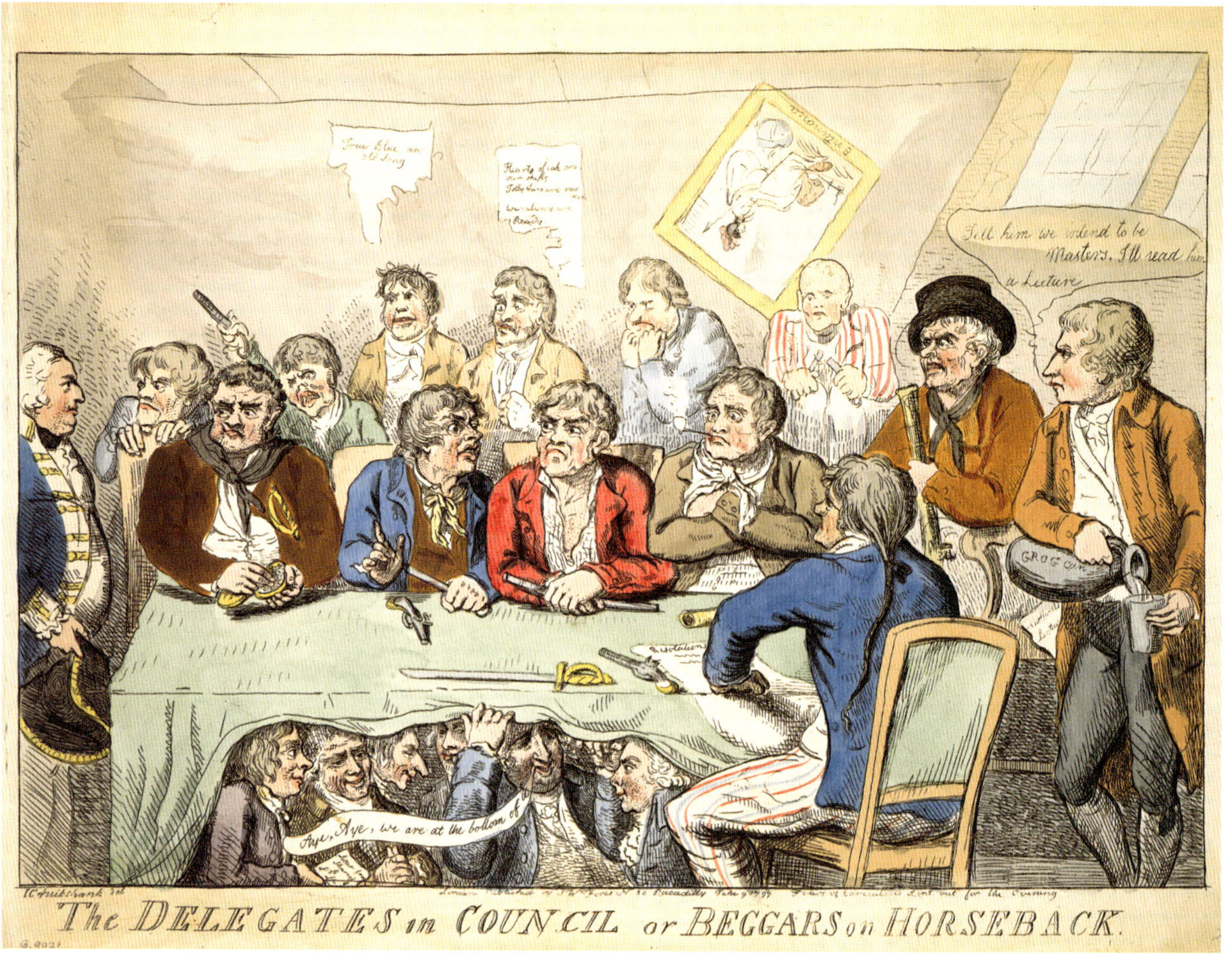

17

Isaac Cruikshank (1764–1811?)

The delegates in council or beggars on horseback

Hand-coloured etching, 25.5 x 35 cm (subject)
Published 9 June 1797 by S. W. Fores
Ashmolean Museum
BMC 9021

In April and May of 1797, naval mutinies in the British fleets stationed off Spithead and the Nore shocked the country. This print depicts the meeting between Admiral Buckner and the leader of the mutineers, Richard Parker, aboard HMS Sandwich on 20 May 1797. Parker is seated at the head of the table with his hat on. Standing beside him is the radical reformer John Thelwall, one of the reformers tried and acquitted of treason in 1794. Thelwall advises Parker, 'Tell him we intend to be masters.' On the wall, a picture of Britannia is upside-down, indicating the damage done by the mutiny to Britain's naval strength. Secret Whig support for the mutineers is implied by the politicians Charles James Fox and Richard Brinsley Sheridan hiding under the table. Parker was executed for his role in the mutiny.

18

The History of Two Acts, entitled An act for the safety and preservation of his majesty's person and government against treasonable and seditious practices and attempts and An act for the more effectually preventing seditious meetings and assemblies

London, G. G. and J. Robinson, 1796
8o Z 600 Jur.

This volume contained the parliamentary debates on the 'Two Acts', as well as the petitions submitted to Parliament and resolutions of public meetings concerning the Acts. Passage of the Acts followed Government alarm – whether real or pretended – at the jostling of the King's coach and an apparent attempt to assassinate George III in November 1795. Several of the petitions and resolutions expressed a wish to protect the King from harm. However many also went on to complain that the Acts threatened to damage the constitution, by allowing prosecutions for sedition against a large range of publications and by limiting the right of subjects peaceably to assemble.

At a meeting of inhabitants of London's Cheap Ward on 19 November 1795, the publisher and printseller John Boydell was in the chair. That meeting resolved:

That the Bills now opening in Parliament will, if carried into effect, be...a direct violation of the Bill of Rights, and, by subverting the liberty of the Press, and the Freedom of Public Discussion, must tend to alienate the attachment of the people from the constitution of the country, and shake their heretofore acknowledged loyalty to their sovereign (p. 328).

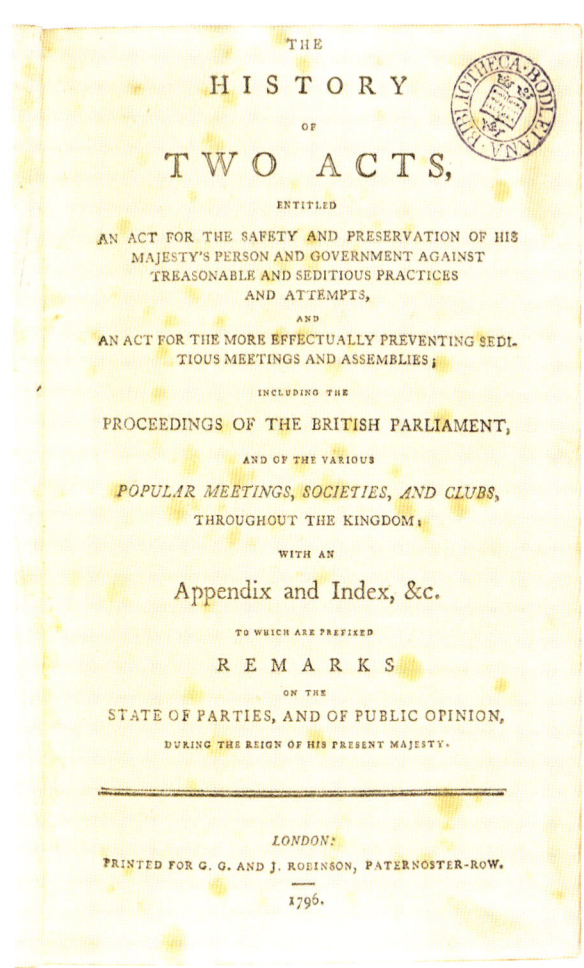

THE
HISTORY
OF
TWO ACTS,
ENTITLED
AN ACT FOR THE SAFETY AND PRESERVATION OF HIS
MAJESTY'S PERSON AND GOVERNMENT AGAINST
TREASONABLE AND SEDITIOUS PRACTICES
AND ATTEMPTS,
AND
AN ACT FOR THE MORE EFFECTUALLY PREVENTING SEDI-
TIOUS MEETINGS AND ASSEMBLIES;
INCLUDING THE
PROCEEDINGS OF THE BRITISH PARLIAMENT,
AND OF THE VARIOUS
POPULAR MEETINGS, SOCIETIES, AND CLUBS,
THROUGHOUT THE KINGDOM;
WITH AN
Appendix and Index, &c.
TO WHICH ARE PREFIXED
REMARKS
ON THE
STATE OF PARTIES, AND OF PUBLIC OPINION,
DURING THE REIGN OF HIS PRESENT MAJESTY.

LONDON:
PRINTED FOR G. G. AND J. ROBINSON, PATERNOSTER-ROW.
1796.

19
Political tokens

In the 1790s Britain suffered an acute shortage of specie, which was finally resolved by a new minting of coin. Meanwhile, to fill the need for coins of small value, token makers produced substitutes of their own design. One of the most innovative token producers was the pamphleteer, parliamentary reformer and proponent of land reform, Thomas Spence. Spence was not the first to use the tokens to reflect issues of the day, but he was one of the most popular of token producers and his satirical images served to insinuate radical messages into the pockets of a considerable portion of the country. His own interest in tokens and their significance is signalled in his book, *The Coin Collector's Companion, Being a Descriptive Alphabetical List of the Modern Provincial Political and other Token Coinage* (1795). Spence's coins are sometimes directly polemical, and sometimes merely puzzling. In one stamp he combined the head of an ass looking right with the head of a man looking left. The similarity between the man's face and caricatured representations of George III is striking, but nothing else on the coin identifies the King, so the image remains ambiguous. This kind of allusive imagery became a common ploy to avoid prosecution in print as well as on these tokens. If the oppositional message appeared only on a close reading, it could be claimed to be 'all in the eye of the beholder'– and the publisher would evade conviction.

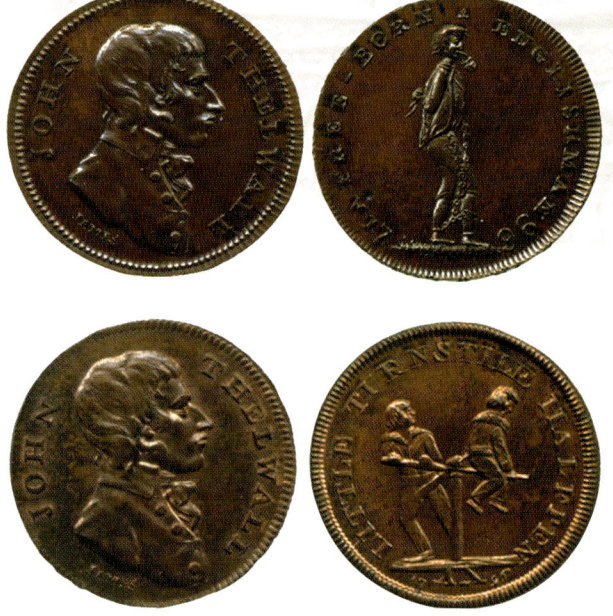

19a

Obverse: Profile of John Thelwall facing right: JOHN THELWALL, signed James
Reverse: Shackled figure standing, r. profile, mouth padlocked: A FREE-BORN ENGLISHMAN 1796
29mm

19b

Obverse: Profile of John Thelwall
Reverse: Two boys at a turnstile: LITTLE TURN-STILE HALFPENNY
(A reference to Spence's address in Little Turnstile)
29mm

19c

Obverse: Bust of John Horne Tooke, signed Jacobs
Reverse: Facade of courthouse. Above, SESSIONS
HOUSE; below, OLD BAILY

29mm

19d

Obverse: Britannia seated facing right: ROUSE
BRITANNIA
Reverse: An ass bearing two pairs of panniers, labelled
'RENTS' and 'TAX'S'; encircling motto: I WAS AN
ASS TO BEAR THE FIRST PAIR

29mm

19e

Obverse: Head of a man conjoined to head of an ass. At
top: 1795; below: ODDFELLOWS, left-side A
MILLION HOGG; right side a GUINEA PIG. The left-
facing bust bears a strong resemblance to George III.
Reverse: Four men dancing around a pole, surmounted
with a head radiant: TREE OF LIBERTY

29mm

19f

Obverse: A prisoner gnawing on a bone: BEFORE THE
REVOLUTION
Reverse: Britannia seated facing right: ROUSE
BRITANNIA

29mm

19g

Obverse: Three men dancing and one eating at a table
under a tree: AFTER THE REVOLUTION
Reverse: An ass bears two pairs of panniers, labelled
'RENTS' and 'TAX'S'; encircling motto: I WAS AN
ASS TO BEAR THE FIRST PAIR

29mm

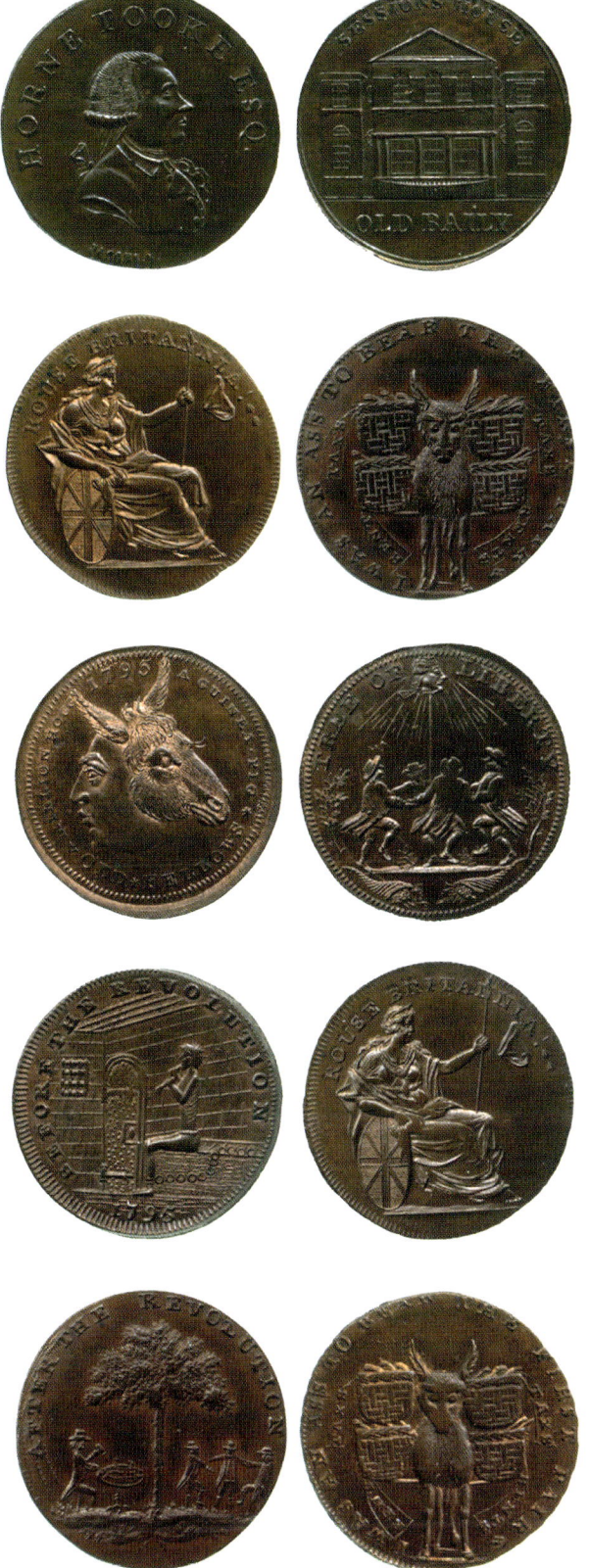

The Great Fear in 1798

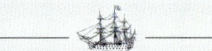

During 1798, the massing of a French 'Army of England' moved Samuel Taylor Coleridge to write a poem entitled 'Fears in solitude'. Not everyone was so convinced of the danger, and many satires, continuing their focus on domestic and partisan politics, portrayed the threat as a convenient excuse for Pitt's Government to raise taxes.

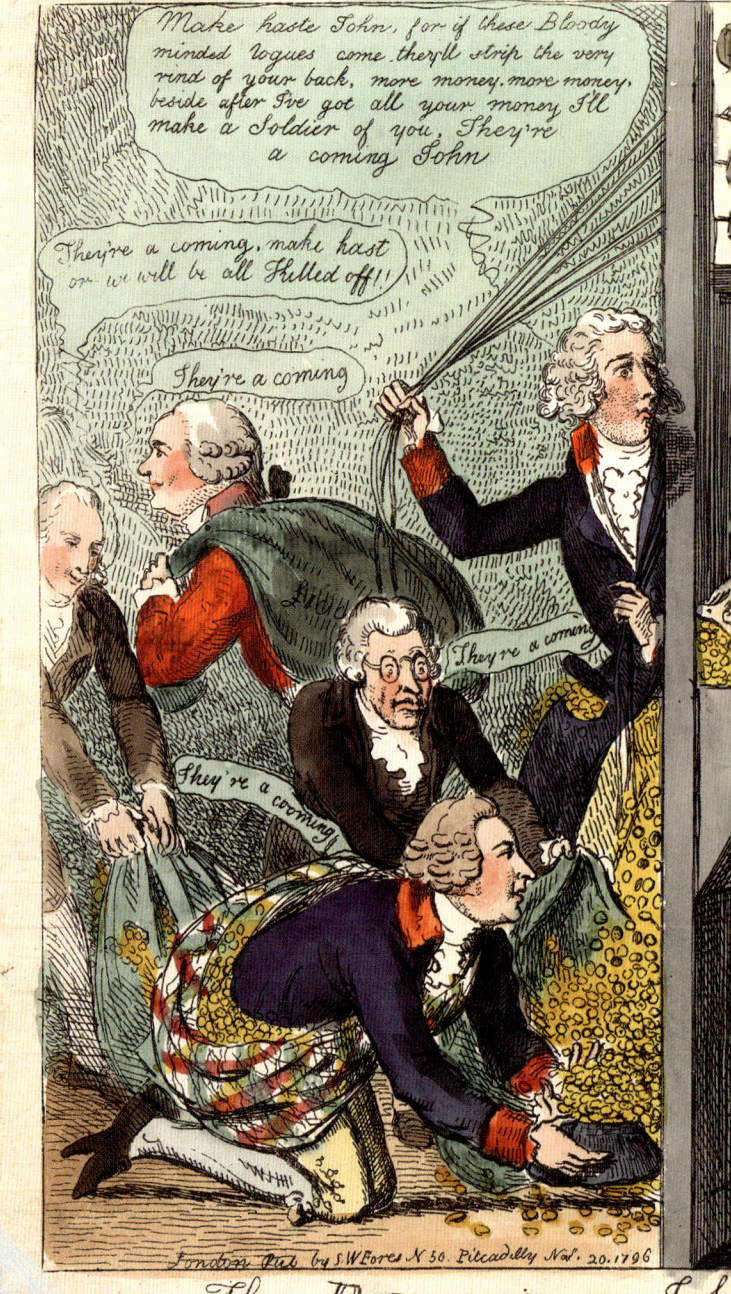

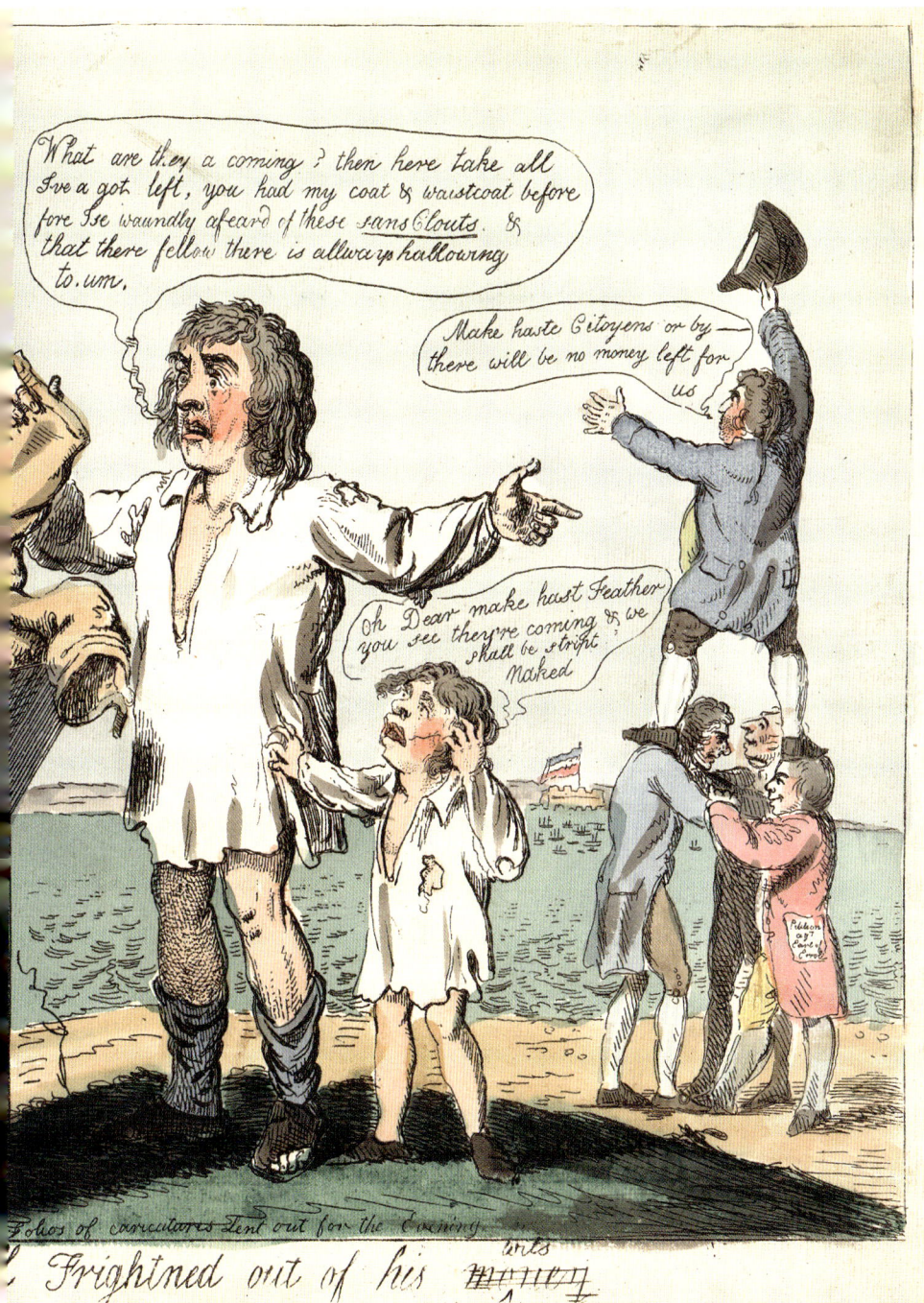

20

[Isaac Cruikshank (1764–1811?)]

The budget or John Bull frightened out of his ~~money~~ wits

Hand-coloured etching, 24.4 x 35.2 cm (subject)
Published 20 November 1796 by S. W. Fores
Curzon b.3(66)
BMC 8837

In 1796 a telegraph, using a series of panels which could be set open or closed, was erected on the top of the Admiralty building in London, part of a communications system linking London and the coasts, intended to speed naval reports and orders to the fleet and to warn of any attempted invasion from across the Channel. Here Pitt manipulates the telegraph to spell out 'They are coming'. Behind him raking in the tax revenues are members of the Cabinet and political supporters: Henry Dundas (Secretary of War), Edmund Burke, William Wyndham Grenville (Foreign Secretary) and William Windham. The opposition Whigs, led by Charles James Fox, encourage the French invasion force.

Even the usually pro-Pitt Cruikshank reacted to the financial policies of the war years with this complaint that the Government's war policy was to be supported by higher taxes and the imputation that invasion scares were invented by ministers.

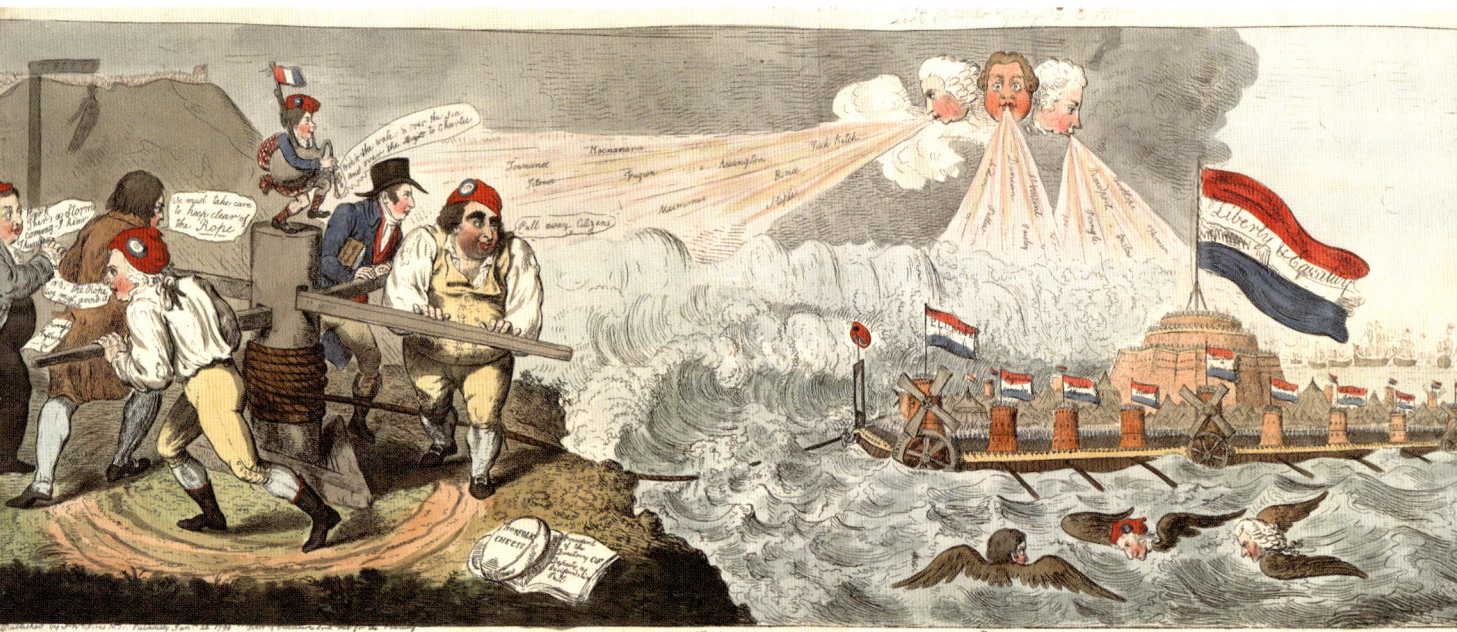

THE RAFT IN DANGER or the REPUBLICAN CREW DISAPPOINTED.

21

[Isaac Cruikshank (1764–1811?)]

The raft in danger or the Republican crew disappointed

Hand-coloured etching, 23.7 x 67.3 cm (subject)
Published 28 January 1798 by S. W. Fores
Curzon b.3(84)
BMC 9160

In this cartoon Whig sympathies with reform are again satirized and combined with a reference to the invasion rafts supposedly under construction on the French coast. The politicians assisting the raft are, clockwise around the windlass from the right, Charles James Fox, Richard Brinsley Sheridan, Lord Norfolk, George Tierney and Lord Bedford. The Scotsman with bagpipes is the Earl of Lauderdale. In the sky the heads of Dundas, Pitt and George III blow the vessel back to France. By this time the Whigs in Parliament were a tiny minority, a portion of the party having joined Pitt's majority in 1794. The raft is copied from other designs incorporating a windmill and gun-turrets. It brings a guillotine, topped with a liberty cap.

22

Isaac Cruikshank (1764–1811?)

Voluntary subscriptions

Hand-coloured etching, 23.5 x 34.6 cm (subject)
Published 16 January 1798 by S. W. Fores
Ashmolean Museum
BMC 9157

New wartime taxation included the tripling of assessed taxes on property values in 1797. Here Pitt and Dundas (Secretary of War) are in a counting house, awaiting payments to a proposed source of revenue, a voluntary subscription fund. George III is satirized for his initial reluctance to contribute to the fund. By convention, and especially as this print is critical of him, he is partly concealed behind the door. In the doorway is George Tierney, a political opponent of Pitt who later fought a duel with him. Above the door is a bust of George III as 'King of Corsica', referring to his acceptance of the Crown when Britain occupied Corsica between 1794 and 1796.

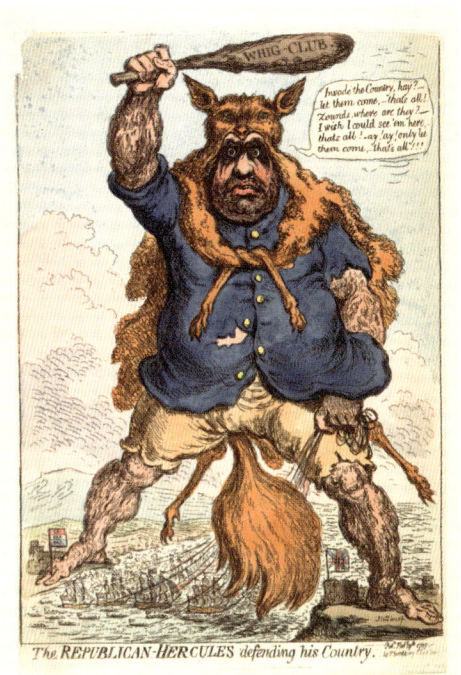

The REPUBLICAN-HERCULES defending his Country.

23

James Gillray (1756–1815)

The republican – hercules defending his country

Hand-coloured etching, 34.7 x 24.9 cm (subject)
Published 19 February 1797 by Hannah Humphrey
Curzon b.16(222)
BMC 8987

Charles James Fox is satirized for professing loyalty to Britain while maintaining his sympathy for French revolutionary principles. Though he publicly vowed to fight any invasion himself, Fox doubted the seriousness of the invasion threat in 1797 and questioned the Government's demands for more army funds. Like the earlier 'Right Honorable, alias a Sans Culotte' (No. 3) this print ridicules Fox's attempted straddling of the divide between Britain and France.

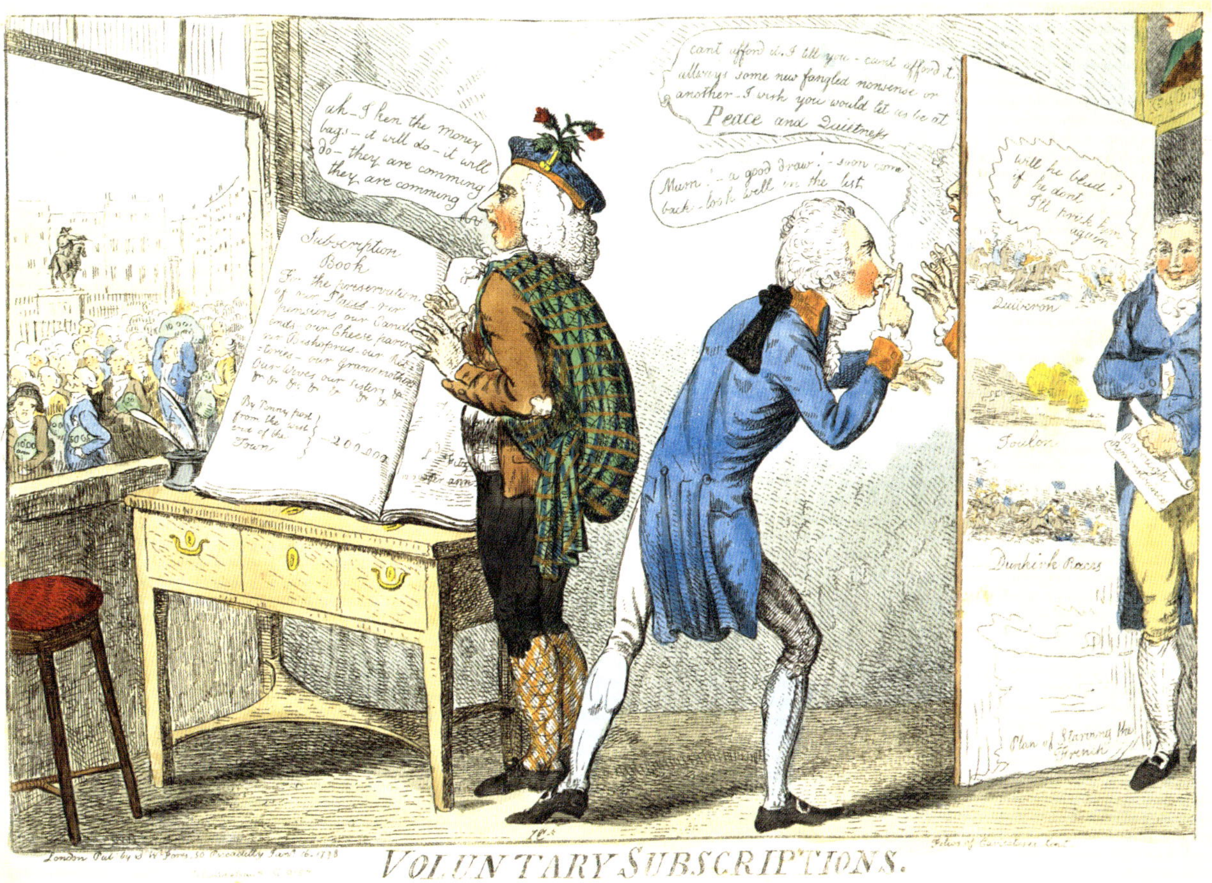

VOLUNTARY SUBSCRIPTIONS.

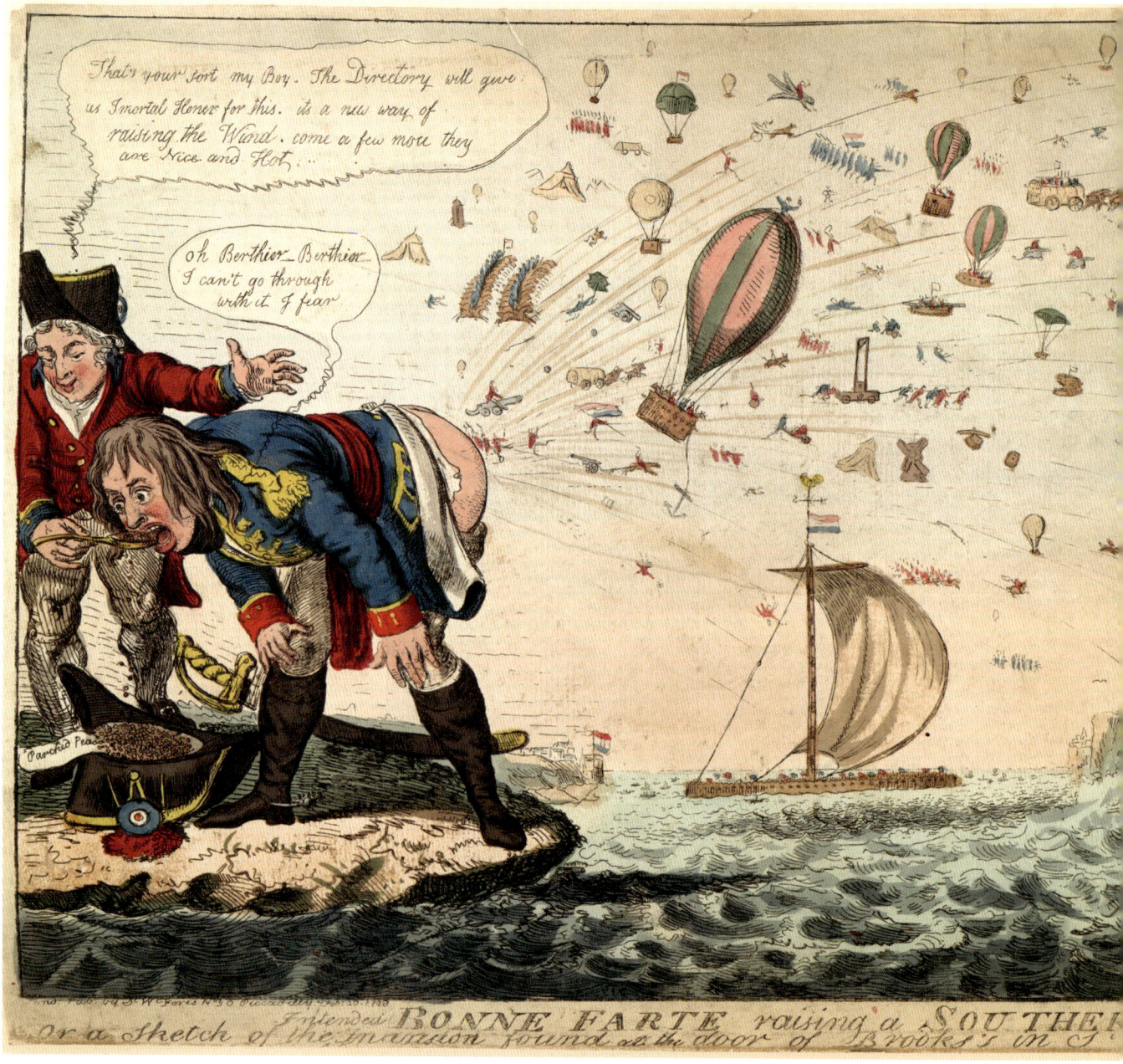

24

[Isaac Cruikshank (1764–1811?)]

Intended bonne-farte raising a southerly wind

Hand-coloured etching, 24.5 x 36.1 cm (subject)
Published 20 February 1798 by S. W. Fores
Curzon b.17(190)
BMC 9172

Napoleon first appeared in a British political cartoon (also by Isaac Cruikshank) in March 1797, at the time of his victory over the papacy. Following his success in Italy, he was appointed to lead the so-called 'Army of England', the French force designated to conquer Britain. This began the identification of Napoleon with invasion plans, though here he is portrayed as a reluctant participant.

On the English shore, the Whig leaders Fox and Sheridan greet the invasion force, joined by John Horne Tooke, the radical pamphleteer.

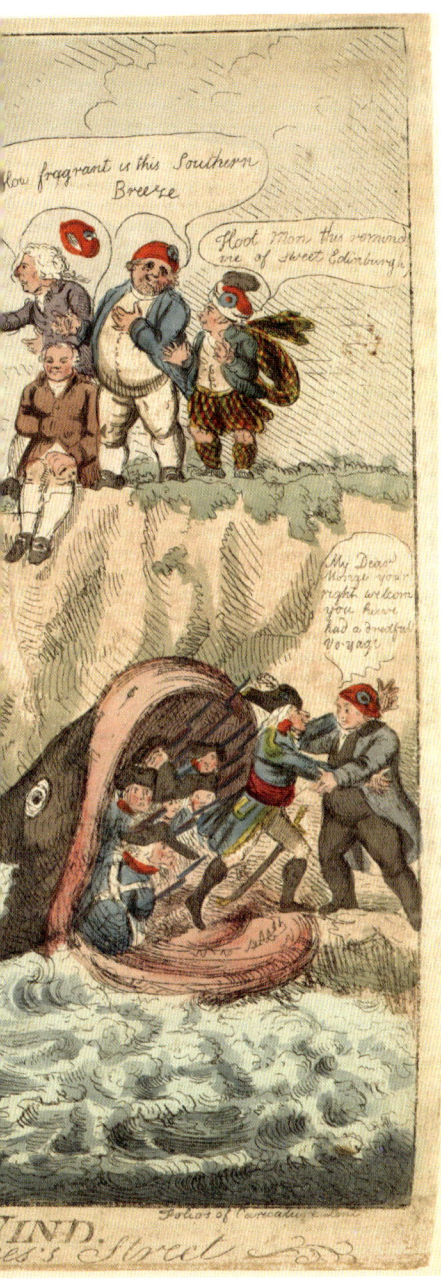

The Peace of Amiens — & Resumption of War

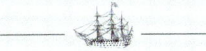

Populations on both sides hoped the treaty ratified in March 1802 would bring an end to wartime hardships. In Britain, peace was a condition of the change of leadership, following Pitt's resignation in 1801, when Henry Addington became Prime Minister. The most enthusiastic British cartoons hailed Napoleon as a bringer of peace – a seeming fulfilment of his revolutionary credentials. But in practice neither nation was prepared to make the territorial concessions agreed in the treaty. Britain resented resigning any colonies (this formed much of the burden of William Cobbett's objections in *Letters to the Rt. Hon. Henry Addington, on the Peace of Amiens, 1801*), and Napoleon needed conquests to cement his leadership. Under diplomatic wrangling, the Peace broke down. In 1803 William Pitt, still in retirement, organized a corps of volunteers at Walmer in Kent, to defend the Cinque Ports. War resumed in May 1803; Pitt returned to office a year later.

25

Roberts
John Bull's prayer to peace, or the flight of discord

Hand-coloured etching, 24.4 x 32.2 cm (subject)
Published [1801] by P. Roberts
Curzon b.12(59)
BMC 9737

In this unusual print the demon of discord is Pitt, who resigned in February 1801 over George III's refusal to countenance civil rights for Catholics after the Act of Union between Great Britain and Ireland. The new Government was led by Henry Addington, who immediately began negotiations with the French. The Peace of Amiens was perceived by Pitt's followers as too favourable to France, but opposition Whigs celebrated the success of Napoleon Bonaparte, whose military prowess was credited with bringing peace between Britain and France. John Bull prays for a restoration of liberties, a reference to the 'Two Acts'.

The journalist and publisher William Cobbett attached great importance to the appearance of images like this one.

At a print-seller's in St. James's-street, where a considerable crowd were assembled, a man approached the window, and pointing to a portrait of a Great Person…first made the motion of stabbing, and then of ripping up, grinding his teeth at the same time, and exclaiming, 'Ah! that I would! that I would!' – Then turning to a portrait of Mr. Pitt, 'Ah!' said he, 'and that long fellow too,' repeating, at the same time, the gesticulations expressive of his bloody wishes. After this he pointed to a portrait of Bonaparte, and, taking off his hat, gave three huzzas, in which he was joined by all those around him!!![33]

Cobbett called this behaviour 'infamously disloyal, not to say treasonable', and drew the controversial conclusion that popular support for the Peace was due not to war-weariness and the hope for lower food prices, but to pro-Bonapartist and republican feeling in England.

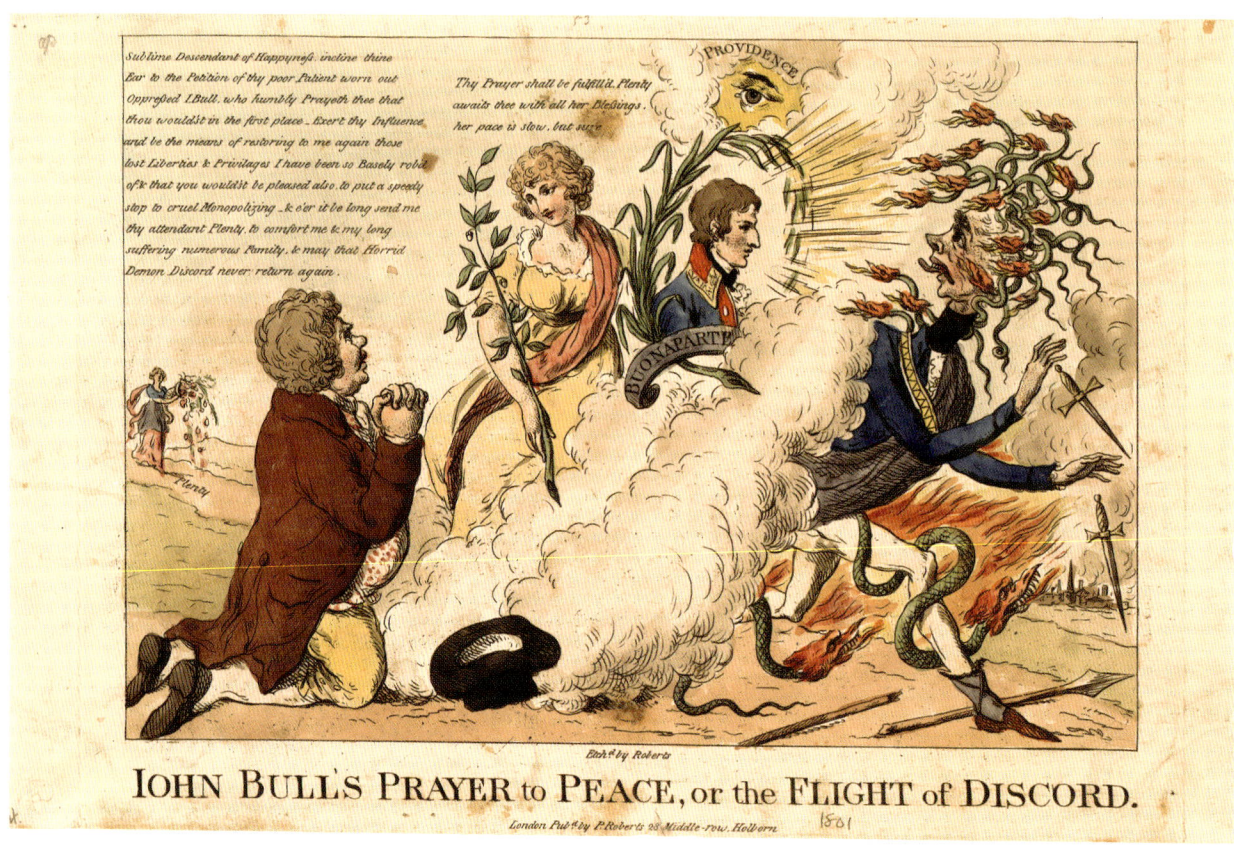

IOHN BULL'S PRAYER to PEACE, or the FLIGHT of DISCORD.

26

Commemorative medals of peace and war

The commemorative medals in this exhibition, loaned
by the Ashmolean Museum, Oxford, derive from a
number of sources. Some were clearly entrepreneurial
ventures, designed for a market which valued the
commemoration of the events of the day and
dependent for their profitability on capturing the
imagination and interest of the buyer. Others were
expressly commissioned, like the medals commemorating the Battle of the Nile, for which some £2,000
was paid to the silversmith Matthew Boulton.

Just as the cartoons in the exhibition use the portrayal
of individuals and events in such a way as to convey a
multiplicity of meanings, so too can the
commemorative medals be seen as an exercise in
miniature in the iconography of peace, victory, war and
leadership. In France as well as in England, medals
were produced to mark significant occasions and to
promote the names of military and political leaders,
especially Bonaparte.[34]

Some were designed for audiences across the Channel.
One medal celebrating the Peace of Amiens is inscribed
to Bonaparte by a Lancaster sympathizer, D. Eccleston,
whose pamphlet defending the first consul against the
'Black Legend' appears elsewhere in this exhibition (No.
77). Later, a French medal 'commemorating' the
invasion of England and inscribed 'Frappé à Londres'
was presumably intended not only to encourage the
French troops but to strike fear in British defenders.

Medals commemorating the Peace of Amiens, 1802

English Medals Trays 45 and 46
France Tray 25

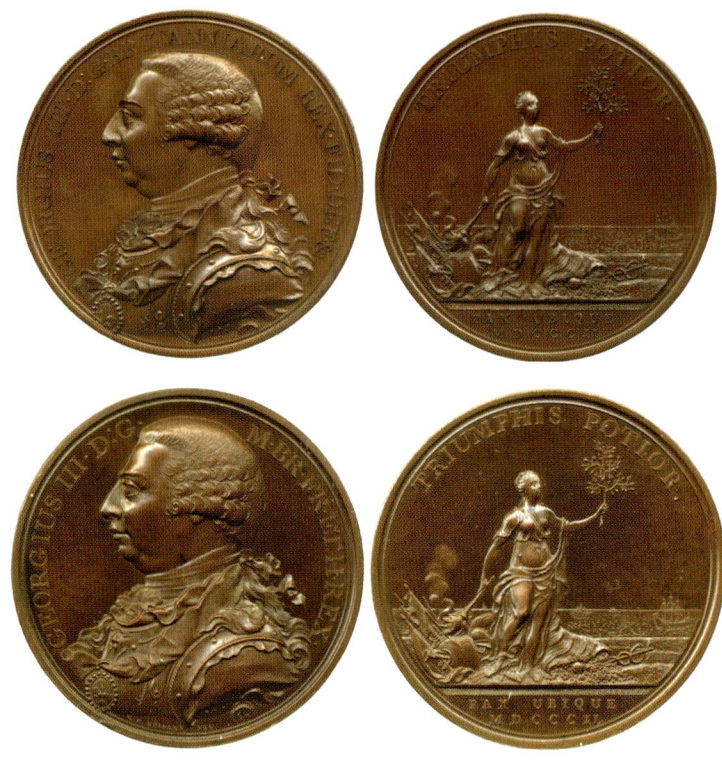

26a

C. H. Küchler

Obverse: Bust of George III, left profile: GEORGIUS III. D: G. M.BRITANIARUM REX FID.DEF.
Reverse: Peace setting fire to a pile of arms on the shore. TRIUMPHIS POTIOR
In exergue: PAX UBIQUE/MDCCCII
Bronze, 48 mm
Ashmolean Museum

26b

C. H. Küchler

Obverse: Bust of George III, left profile: GEORGIUS III. D: G. M.BR.FR.ET.H. REX.
Reverse: Peace setting fire to a pile of arms on the shore and holding an olive branch. TRIUMPHIS POTIOR
In exergue: PAX UBIQUE/MDCCCII
Bronze, 48 mm
Ashmolean Museum (Museum of the History of Science loan)

26c

H. Kettle

Obverse: British flag on an oval shield, mounted on crossed swords: PRELIMINARIES OF PEACE/ BETWEEN/GREAT BRITAIN AND FRANCE/ SIGNED/OCTOBER 1st 1801
Reverse: Peace standing on a quay holding an olive branch and emptying a cornucopia. Bales on the quay and ships at sea signify commerce. THEY SHALL PROSPER THAT LOVE THEE.
In exergue: ears of corn
White metal, 38mm
Ashmolean Museum

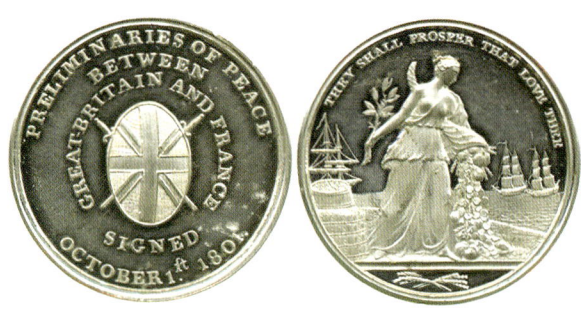

26d

J. G. Hancock

Obverse: Peace standing right holding scroll inscribed OCTO. 1801., raising kneeling female left. MY SOUL DOTH MAGNIFY THE LORD
In exergue: MARCH 27. 1802
Reverse: Religion holding cross and palm spray, right arm raised to heaven. St Paul's cathedral to left, medallion of King to right. WE PRAISE THEE O GOD
In exergue: THANKSGIVING JUNE. 1
Bronze, 38.5mm
Ashmolean Museum (M. H. Grant)

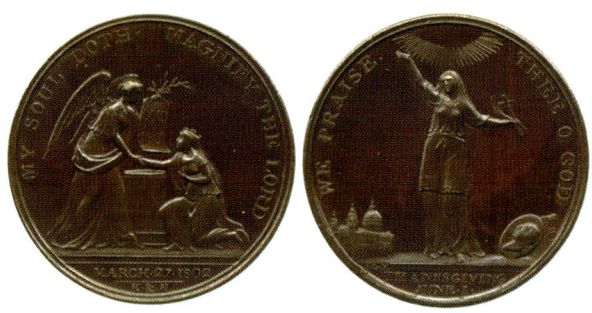

26e

L. Bramsen

Obverse: Head of Bonaparte, left profile, crowned with a laurel wreath: NAPOLEON BONAPARTE PREMIER CONSUL. Signed Dumarest F

Reverse: Peace holding an olive branch to Britannia: PAIX D'AMIENS

In exergue: LE VI GERMINAL AN X/ XXVII MARS/ M DCCCII

Bronze, 49.5 mm
Ashmolean Museum (Sir W. Calverley Trevelyan bequest)

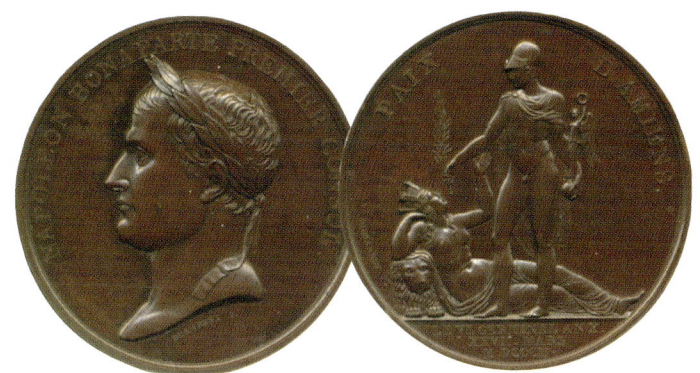

26f

J. G. Hancock

Obverse: Bonaparte, left profile: INSCRIBED TO NAPOLEON BONAPARTE BY D. ECCLESTON/ LANCASTER

Reverse: Globe: EUROPE/ASIA/AFRICA/EASTERN OCEAN: PEACE/HE GAVE TO FRANCE LIBERTY TO THE WORLD PEACE

In exergue: MDCCCII

Bronze with gilt, 57mm
Ashmolean Museum (M. H. Grant)

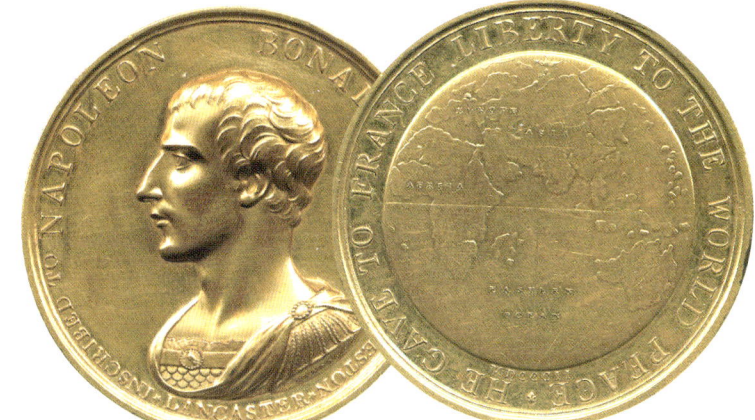

26g

F. Jeuffroy

Obverse: Three right profiles: CAMBACERES SECOND CONSUL. BONAPARTE PREMIER CONSUL. LEBRUN TROISIEME CONSUL. Signed Jeuffroy

Reverse: PAIX/ INTÉRIEURE,/PAIX/ ÉXTERIEURE encircled by: LE CORPS LÉGISLATIF AUX CONSULS DE LA RÉPUBLIQUE FRANÇAISE

In exergue: ARRÊTÉ DU 30 FLORÉAL AN X/ 20 MAI/ M D CCC II

Bronze, 68mm
Drilled top centre for hanging
Ashmolean Museum

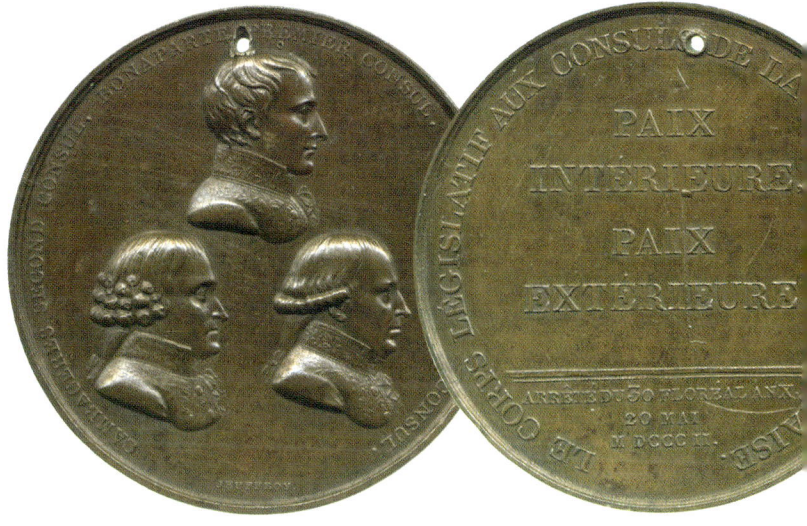

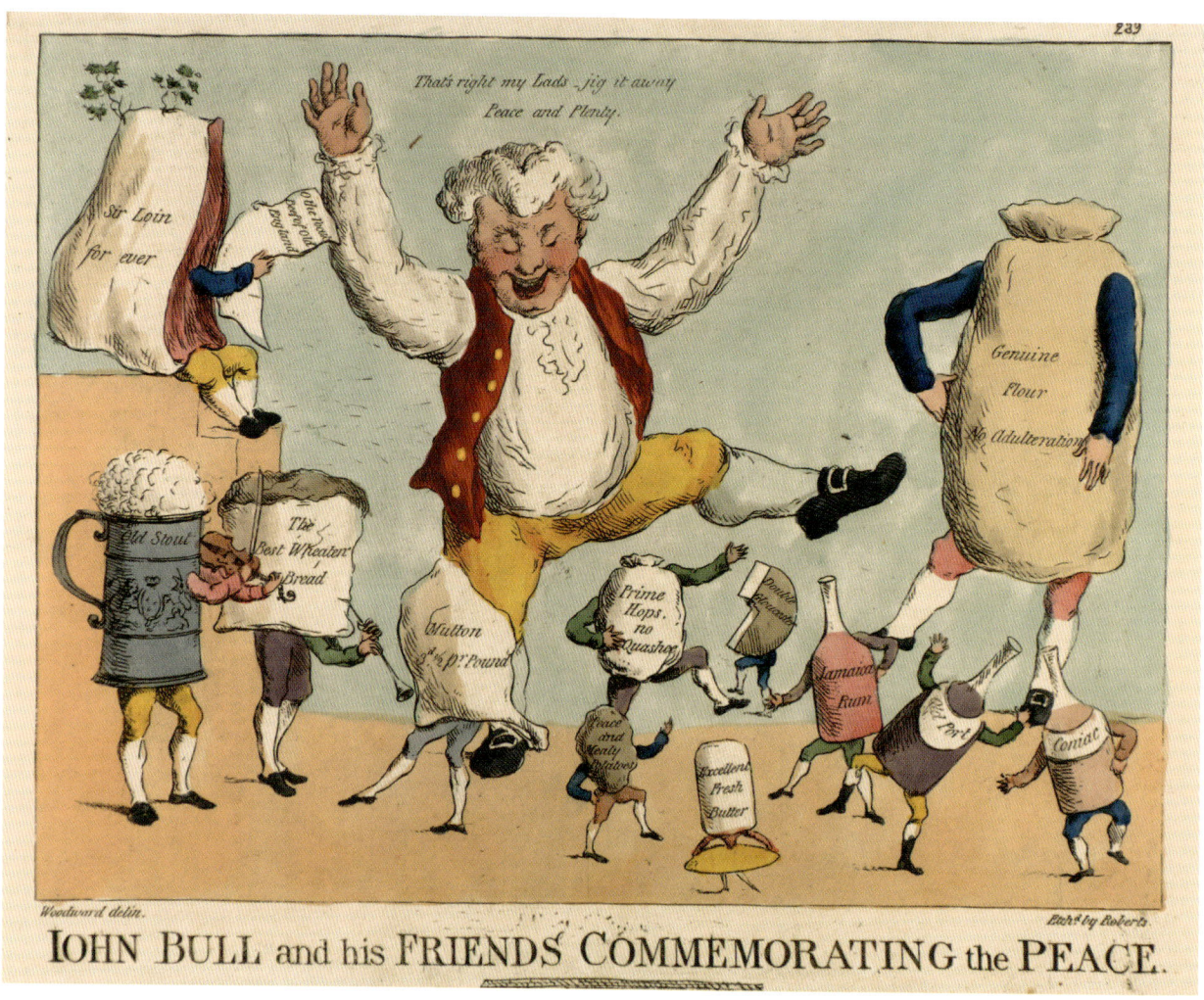

IOHN BULL and his FRIENDS COMMEMORATING the PEACE.

27

George M. Woodward (1760? –1809)

John Bull and his friends commemorating the peace

Hand-coloured etching 27.7 x 34.8 cm (platemark)
Etched by Roberts
Published [?March 1802] by P. Roberts
John Johnson Collection: Political Cartoons 1 (183)
BMC 9850

A happy John Bull dances with articles of food and
drink, now at cheaper prices, in anticipation of the
re-opening of trade with the Continent.

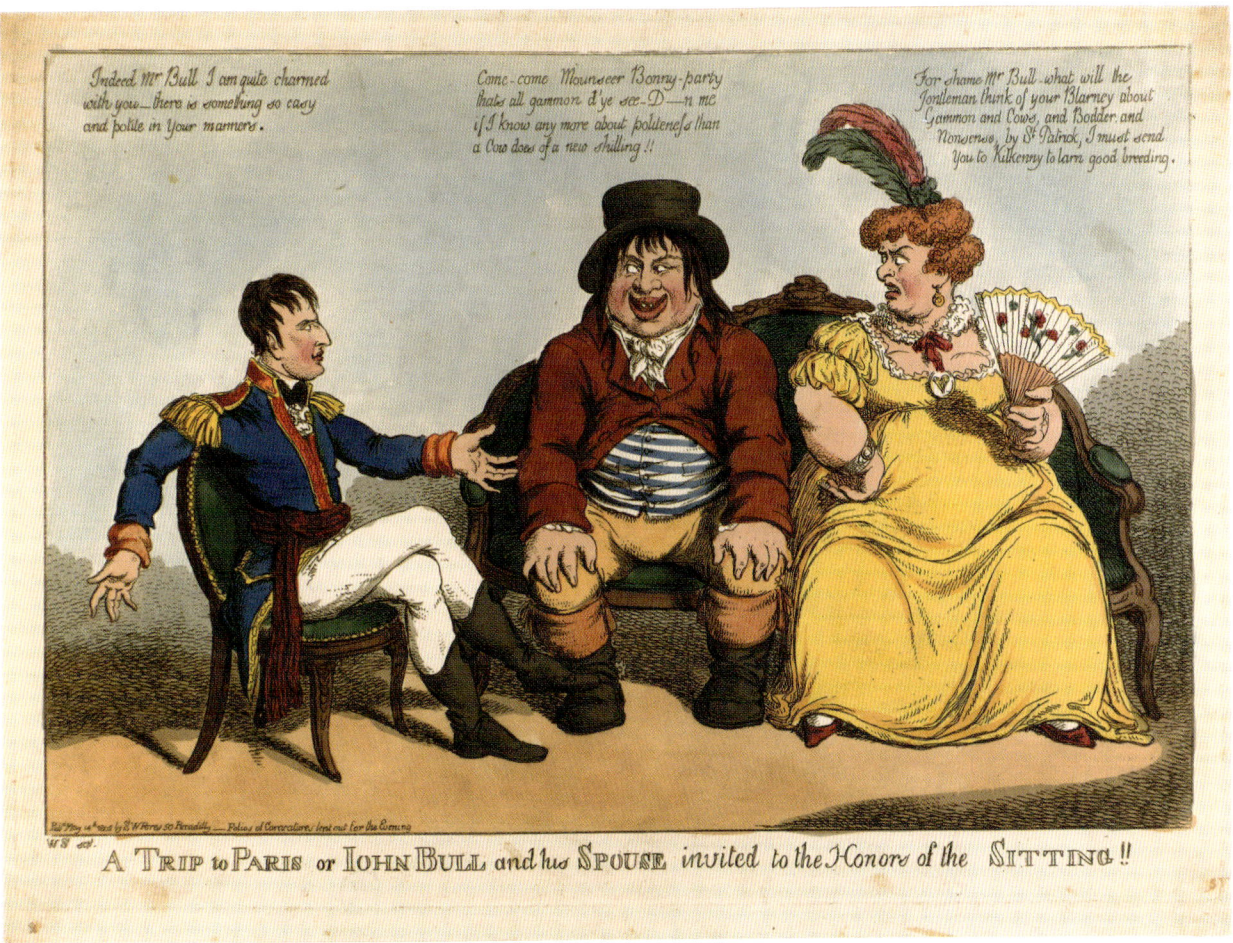

28

[C. Williams]

**A trip to Paris for John Bull and his Spouse
invited to the Honours of the Sitting!!**

Hand-coloured etching 25.2 x 36.8 cm (platemark)
Etched by W. S.
Published 14 May 1802 by S. W. Fores
John Johnson Collection: French Wars and Revolutions folder 6 (26)
BMC 9864

British visitors flocked to Paris during the brief period of peace in 1801–02. Many were able to see the First Consul in person at huge receptions in the Tuileries palace. Here John Bull and his wife Hibernia (Britain and Ireland after the Union of 1801) sit on a sofa, looking awkward beside their suave host. Napoleon is drawn in the now familiar profile, his expressive hands and carelessly crossed legs contrasting with the lumpish figures of John Bull and his wife. The face of Napoleon, so much reproduced in prints already, made a profound impression on some seeing him in person for the first time. Fanny Burney thought she saw, 'not only in the eye but in every feature…so penetrating a seriousness – or, rather, sadness, as powerfully to sink into an observer's mind.'[35] This interest in Napoleon's real face, as an expression of his character and destiny, accounts for the reluctance of cartoonists always to caricature him.

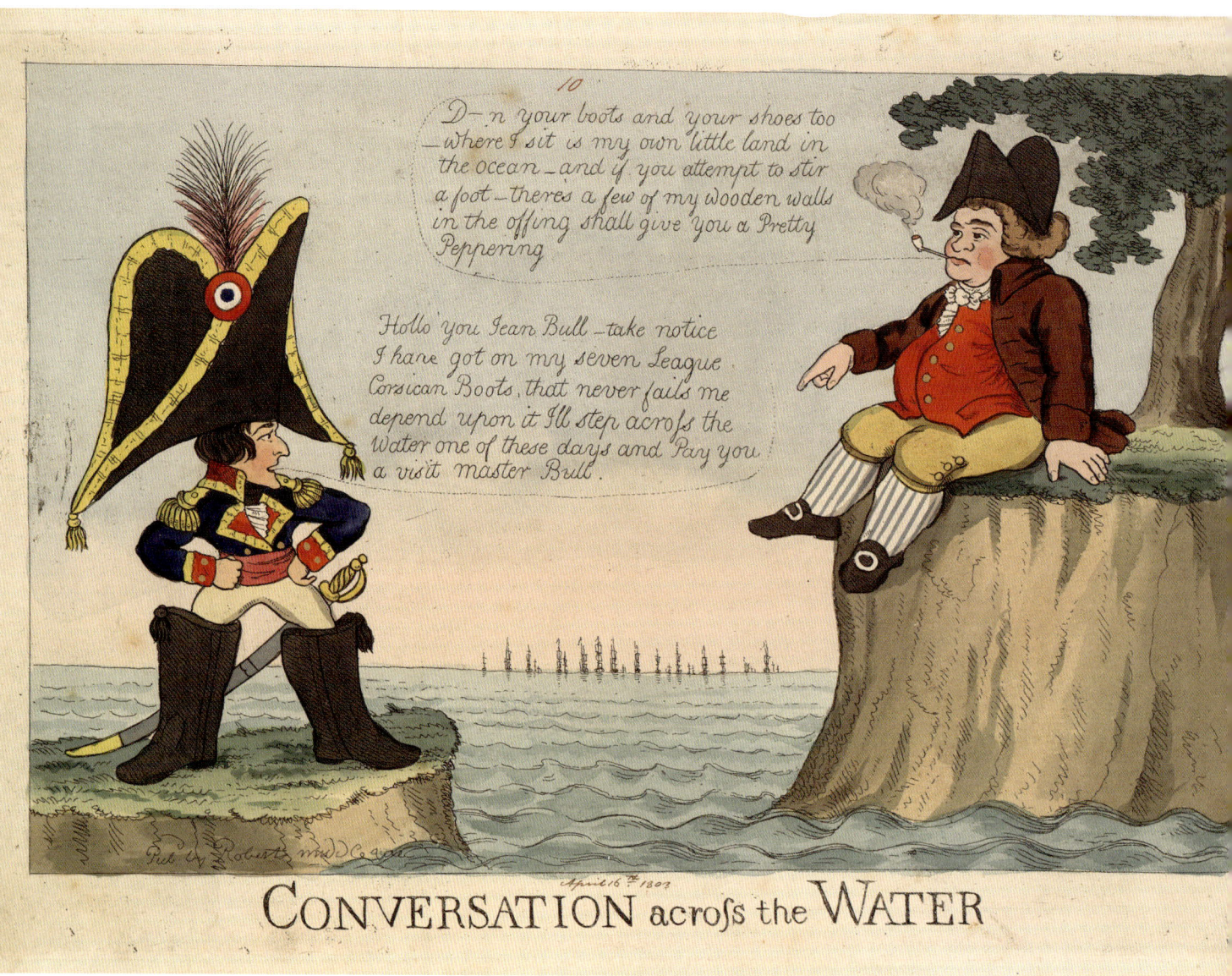

CONVERSATION across the WATER

29

Conversation across the water

Hand-coloured etching 25 x 35.3 cm (platemark)
Published [16 April 1803] by Roberts
Curzon b.12(7)
Broadley's collector's stamp
(Date in MS.)

Instead of confirming a Peace desired by populations
on both sides, the Treaty of Amiens proved to be only a
temporary truce. Neither side wanted to make the
territorial concessions agreed in the treaty and war
resumed on 18 May 1803.

30

[?George M. Woodward (1760?–1809)]

The three plagues of Europe

Hand-coloured etching 24.7 x 35.2 cm (platemark)
Published [August 1803] by McCleary, Dublin.
John Johnson Collection: French Wars and Revolutions folder 6 (23)
BMC 10084 [variant]

Napoleon as the peacemaker is replaced by 'General Fight-all'; Prime Minister Addington is 'Mr. Tax-all' and the Devil is the 'Revd. Mr. Take-all'. An old theme in popular imagery was known as the Four (or Five) Alls; the king who ruled for all, the priest who prayed for all, the soldier who fought for all and the peasant who paid for all. While acknowledging the role of each social order in preserving the kingdom, the design of the Four Alls also expressed the fatalism of ordinary subjects in the face of political turmoil and war, summed up in the motto, 'Whoever wins, I lose'. An earlier edition of this design was published on 1 June 1803 by William Holland.

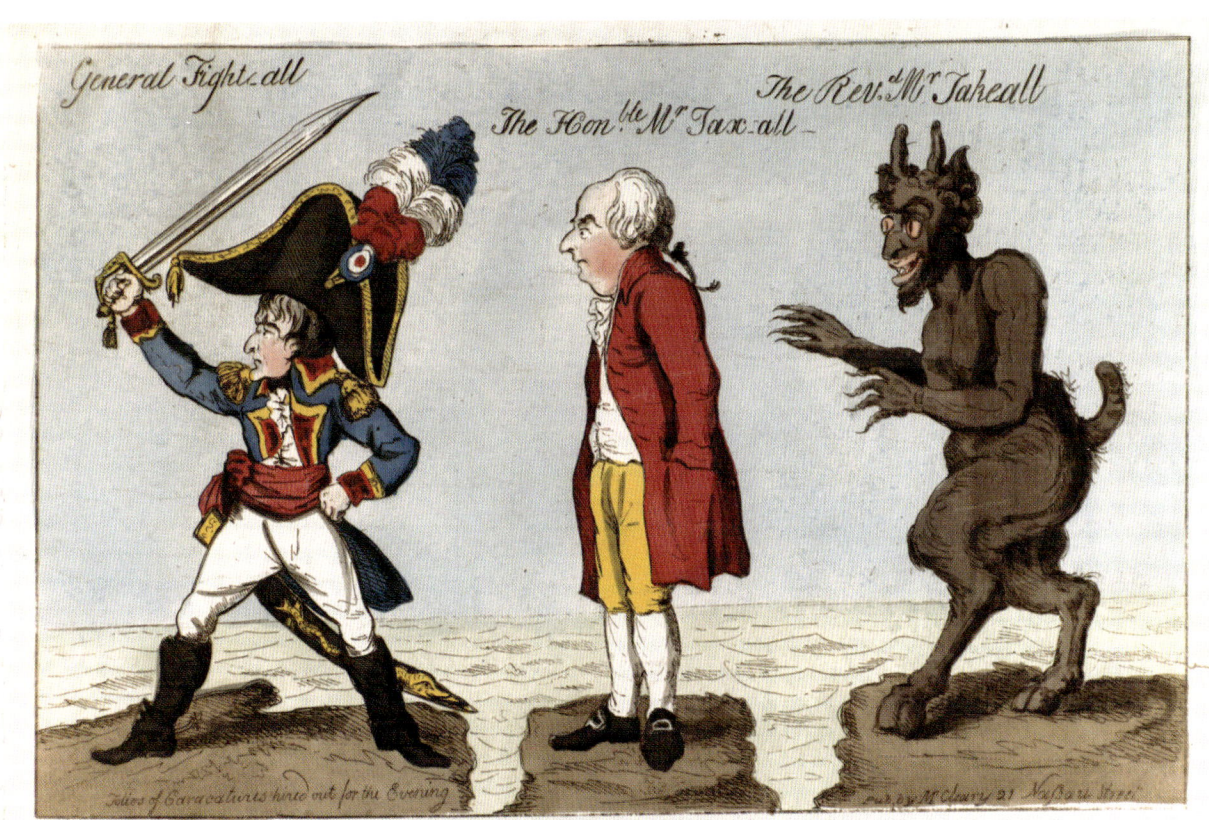

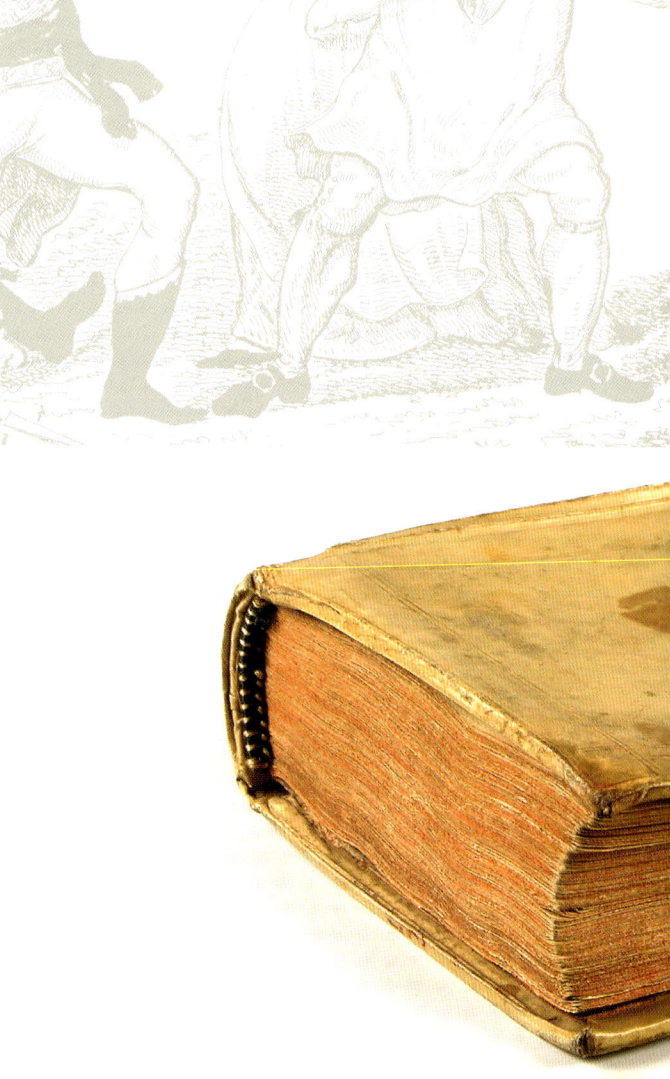

Preparing to Defend

Throughout the eighteenth century, Britain had built up her naval power. The 'wooden walls' were intended to keep out enemies and to transport soldiers, when needed, to colonial shores. Mobilizing the nation to defend British soil from an invasion was not only a new proposition but a potentially dangerous one, in the eyes of some military planners. Popular fervour in imitation of French revolutionary citizenship had never been encouraged by the Government. Now Parliament felt its own reliance on the numbers of British subjects volunteering for military service in defence of their localities. The vastness of the task could be measured also in the length of coastline to be defended. The orders to military commanders (No. 32) anticipate invaders advancing nearly to London before meeting strong resistance.

31

Charles-François du Périer Dumouriez (1739–1823)

[Memoirs on the defences of Great Britain and Ireland]

MS. Lyell empt. 48
Formerly in the collection of A. M. Broadley

Thoughts on invasion, December 1803

It is useful to consider the projected invasion at different times, when different means and methods may be used. Let us examine the principal points of attack which Bonaparte may make in December 1803. There are three great objectives he must fulfil.

First, to occupy London, in order to satisfy the army, to whom he was stupid enough to promise pillage, or to annihilate commerce and finance in this capital, as he has no chance of re-establishing the commercial and financial strength of France. Second, to destroy the ports and shipyards, so that they no longer support English dominance of the seas. Third, to profit from the rebellious spirit of the Irish nation (pp. 168–9).

By this time, Dumouriez shared the scepticism many felt about invasion and the view that the threats were made as much for the benefit of Napoleon's political power as in pursuit of military conquest. On the following page of the notebook (p. 170), he wrote: 'Bonaparte's grand plan has become a chimera, yet he is unable to abandon it – he persuades the French into new dangers, to reduce the danger to himself.'

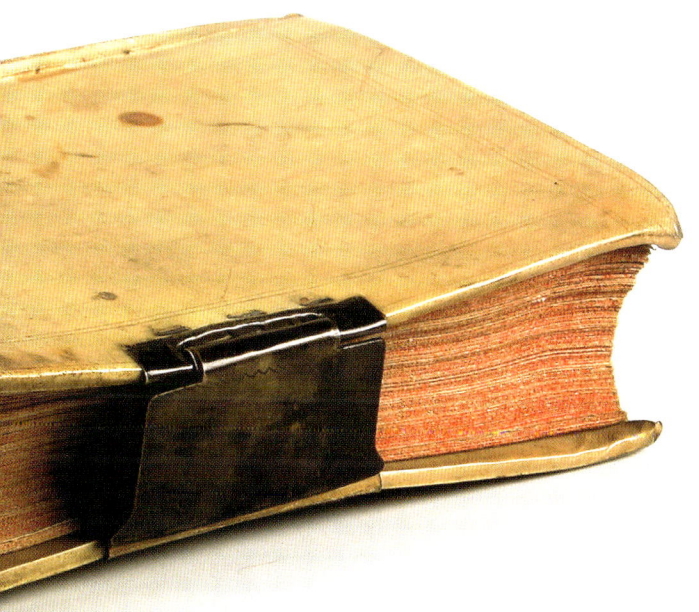

Dumouriez's *Memoirs on the defences of Great Britain and Ireland*
By Katrina Navickas

The memoirs were written by General Charles François Dumouriez (1739–1823) between November 1803 and May 1804, with further additions in 1805 and 1807. This manuscript contains his observations on the defence of every part of Great Britain and Ireland against the French fleets and the first attacks of their disembarking armies. It was designed as a detailed supplement to the British Commander in Chief's plans, from the point of view of a man who had designed an attack of England from France as Commandant of Cherbourg for Louis XVI over twenty years before. Dumouriez had been a military hero in the first years of the French Revolution for successes in Holland and against Austria, but in 1793 defected to the allied side and was determined to defeat Napoleon Bonaparte.

The direct influence of the memoir is ambiguous. Some suggestions were eventually implemented; for example, an increasing emphasis on mobile light artillery in response to the new tactics of the revolutionary armies and the military attack on Walcheren in 1809, which Dumouriez believed to be the key to solving the additional threat of Holland. The wider strategy he espoused, however, was too ambitious, far-reaching and expensive to be adopted as a whole by the British High Command. Furthermore, despite his connections with generals and politicians in London high society, he experienced anti-French prejudice, which he admitted prevented him from making the memoir as accurate as he would have liked.

Dumouriez's *Memoirs on the Defences of Great Britain* reflected his diverse experience as a military commander under both the Ancien Régime and the Revolution. He referred to his former abortive plans of 1779 for an invasion of Plymouth from Brest. His description of the defence of the Channel Islands was also taken from knowledge gained when he had organized an expedition to seize Jersey in 1777. Dumouriez had been Minister of the Interior and Commandant of Cherbourg under Louis XVI. He joined the Jacobins at the Revolution, and in 1792 he became Commander in Chief of the Army of the North, sharing the credit for the first great victory of the Republic, Valmy.[36] He then commanded the Army of Belgium and was honoured for winning the battle of Jemappes and conquering the country. He was defeated in an attempt to invade Holland. Disillusioned with the violent progress of the Revolution, he plotted with the Austrians. The Girondins denounced him as a traitor, his troops deserted him and he was forced to cross over into Allied lines. He spent the next seven years in exile, but eventually was offered a refuge and pension by Britain, temporarily in 1800, and permanently from 1803.[37] The manuscript was the product of his stay in Britain and, as it contains his own distinctive handwriting, was most likely his personal final draft for his own reference.

The memoir divided Britain into six military districts, as opposed to the ten or more arranged by the High Command. The defence of each county of Britain, including those of Scotland, is discussed in the plans. Although he did not perceive areas such as Cumberland and Wales as in great danger, Dumouriez was still diligent enough to compose provisional plans for their defence. His confidence in the staunch patriotic defence by the British people was counterbalanced by his concern for Ireland. He believed that it was almost impossible to defend the country's coasts because of the unreliability of the Irish militia and the certainty of civil war if the enemy were to invade. Mirroring the opinion of British military strategists such as Sir David Dundas, however, Dumouriez regarded the south east coast of England as the mostly likely landing spot for the invasion. The defence of Kent in particular is described in the greatest detail in the manuscript. Under the heading 'Project of Descent on Rye and Romney', Dumouriez wrote that he had studied the question in 1778: 'Its nature has altered only in so far that the English are better prepared to counter attack.' The extreme importance attached by Dumouriez to the defence of that part of Kent may have influenced the creation and positioning of the Hythe Military Canal.[38]

Dumouriez took pride in his knowledge of French military tactics and theory. He described himself as a 'defence advisor' to the War Office, although his role appears to have been unofficial. He refers to his work for the Government in the manuscript; for example, he claimed that he had been 'commissioned by the British Government' to undertake a scheme for the destruction of the enemy fleet in French waters, and thus a section of the memoir is dedicated to examining ports from which the French Navy would sail. He was alive to the threat from Holland and Flanders, but he underestimated the forces then mustering in and near Boulogne until 1805,[39] when he hastily composed another short memoir added to the manuscript regarding the new precautions to be taken on the Eastern English coasts. He also stated that he had written a single memoir, 'by order of the Commander in Chief', on the need of forming corps of light troops called *chasseurs* to harass the enemy from the flanks.[40]

A copy of the manuscript, not in Dumouriez's hand, exists in the War Office archives,[41] so it is clear that some notice was taken of the work, although perhaps too late to alter major plans already in place. Dumouriez knew of the general plan of defence drawn up by the Duke of York, submitted to the Minister at War on 25 August 1803, and he made continual references to it in the manuscript.[42] In his introduction, for example, he wrote:

I have nothing to add to the dispositions made by the Commander in Chief and his Staff in the matter of transport…as well as of signalling – the arrangements do honour to all concerned and they serve as models to any nation threatened with a naval invasion.

Broadley and Rose footnote this in their translation of the manuscript with the observation that the sentence 'proves' that the plan was designed to supplement that of the Duke of York.[43] The French general constantly praised the skills of the British Military High Command as well as the 'wonderful spirit of so energetic and powerful a nation'.[44] He also wished that the relevant parts of his plans would be communicated to each general commanding the Military Districts of the British Isles, although there is little indication that this was done directly.

Some suggestions within the manuscript were full of insight. Dumouriez recommended the use of light artillery and cavalry chasseurs as a response to the tactic developed by revolutionary France from 1792, 'the system of sharpshooter warfare which has disconcerted and vanquished all the armies of Europe'.[45] General Sir David Dundas adapted this policy for the organization of troops in southern England, especially regarding the militia and volunteer regiments. It is unclear whether Dumouriez's suggestions played a part in this, particularly as Dundas had his own strong views on methods of defence. Nevertheless, Dumouriez foretold the growing realization by British generals that the nature of warfare had changed, that the days of pitched battles had been superseded by a 'total war' involving the whole nation to be roused in defence.

The 'Military Principles' proposed by Dumouriez were on a large scale and thus were not implemented as a whole because of their ambition and their potentially ruinous cost. He envisaged a chessboard of defence, confined within twenty miles inland from the coast. This involved making traverse cuts all along the cliffs from Newhaven to Brighton, with lines of fortified camps garrisoned by heavy forces with mobile light divisions acting in support, so as to sweep that coast with fire at all points.[46] Dumouriez assumed that no extensive coast defence was impregnable, that preparation should be made to outflank an enemy who had landed.[47] This formed an alternative to the Government's new plan of building Martello towers, a policy with which Dumouriez disagreed. Another element of British strategy which Dumouriez believed was impracticable was the 'driving' of the country of its inhabitants, cattle and horses on the approach of the invader, contained in the 1798 Defence Act. Eventually, however, in 1804, under the pressure of the lords lieutenant on the southern coasts, the policy was scaled down.[48]

The French general admitted that he did not consult with any military authorities and had to rely on out-dated maps and his own theory to devise the scheme of defence. Under a section entitled 'The Army', he wrote that the nature of troops to be used in defence was 'a very delicate matter to treat of, particularly for a foreigner, whom national jealousy, rightly or wrongly understood, has denied access to communications that are essential on this head'.

Dumouriez's position as a former Revolutionary general clearly still aroused some suspicions against him at this time of state-sponsored Francophobia. He thus apologized for the errors in the work, particularly the topographical mistakes: 'due to the varying correctness of the small-scale maps that have been vouchsafed to me as my only help. I have been refused even the permission to verify them on the spot.'[49] He was still offering his services to William Pitt when he had finished his memoir on defence in May 1804, mentioning the plans as proof of his capability as a military adviser.[50] Six weeks later, he wrote to Pitt asking him to read the memoir, which he had already sent to the former Prime Minister Addington the previous December. He requested to be employed in the 'service of a *patrie* which I now regard as my country and for its own glory'.[51]

Dumouriez resided at the respectable location of Gunnersbury Lodge in Acton and received a pension from the British Government. It may have been through Admiral Nelson's influence that he was able to find this comfortable exile in England. He corresponded regularly with Nelson and met him in Hamburg in October 1800. Nelson was complimentary about the French general and forwarded his letters to Addington in 1801.[52] Dumouriez's military prestige was recognized in October 1803, when he was invited to be present at the grand review of volunteer corps by the King in London, just before he began to compile his plan of defence contained in the manuscript.[53] He counted Nelson, George Canning and Lord Auckland amongst his friends. His position was secured by his frank detestation of Napoleon Bonaparte, a motif of the manuscript and all his writings. He could thus allay the criticisms against his own 'treason' against the French Republic with his belief that Bonaparte had betrayed France by his 'tyrannical' conduct and ambition for power.

Dumouriez also used the manuscript to sketch out wider strategy beyond internal defence. He astutely calculated that an attack on Walcheren was the key to eliminating the additional threat of Holland,[54] an idea that was (unsuccessfully) put into practice by the Duke of York in 1809. The scheme of defence in the memoir also includes notes on Portugal and Ireland composed in 1807. He had predicted that the Continent would be the main focus for military engagements, and in November 1805 he undertook a secret mission to the Continent under obscure motives and with minimal success. He fell into debt on the trip, but the Government refunded him.[55] As the threat of invasion receded, however, Dumouriez found himself increasingly redundant and he resorted to inundating military celebrities, notably Lord Wellington, with his views on every strategic and tactical issue that came to prominence.[56] With the final defeat of Napoleon in 1815, he found himself relegated to relative insignificance. He died at Henley-on-Thames in 1823.[57] This marked a poignant end to a great French military strategist who had adopted Britain as his home and had hoped to awaken more rapidly the response of British generals towards the new kind of warfare waged by the revolutionary armies on the Continent.

34

To

Major General Finch.

1st
2d
3d   The same as to Major General Hope
4th
5th

The particular situation of the Brigade under your command will render the instructions that are necessary for your particular guidance with respect to your first movements very short.

The object of your Brigade in the first instance is the speedy support of that under the command of Major General Bellworth I as that officer is instructed as to the case in which he is to call upon you, you will please to follow such directions with respect to movement as you may at any time receive from him.—

In no other case that I am aware of except within the limits of the part of the coast with the care of which Major Genl Bellworth is charged can you receive accounts of the landing of an Enemy or of his appearance in force through any channel by which they will reach you with more expedition than those which it shall be my care to send to you and as these shall be accompanied with directions for your proceeding no other Instructions appear to be necessary on that head.

32

Copy Book of Military Orders, Eastern Military District, 1803–04

Given by S. A. Warner, 1940
MS. Eng. hist. c.263 f.1–2

This manuscript is a copy book of the orders given by Lieutenant General Sir James Henry Craig (1748–1812), General Officer Commander of the Eastern Military District, to the generals under his command, from about May 1803 to August 1804. To protect the huge expanse of coastline from Essex to Suffolk, Craig ordered the generals to position regiments of dragoons and militia at strategic points close to the most vulnerable areas. If the French landed successfully, volunteer corps were to be given the role of harassing the enemy, shooting at the French from 'behind every tree and stone', before the Army arrived to launch a full counter-attack. Even ordinary inhabitants might serve as guides with local knowledge, especially in 'driving' the land, that is carrying out the 'scorched earth' policy of removing all useful livestock and equipment to prevent the invaders from gaining supplies.

Lieut. General Sir James Henry Craig's orders to commanders in the Eastern Military District, 1803–04
by Katrina Navickas

Great Britain was divided into ten Military Districts for defence. The Eastern District, which Lieutenant General Craig commanded, covered Essex, Norfolk, Suffolk, Hampshire and Cambridgeshire. It was considered to be at the second greatest risk from the invading fleet after the Southern District (the Kent coast). The south coast of Essex was especially vulnerable as it formed the top of the mouth of the Thames, providing a quick route towards London. Lieutenant General Sir James Craig had command over ten major generals, whose regiments were quartered at Ipswich, Chelmsford, Colchester, Norwich and Great Yarmouth. The regular forces amounted to over 1,800 cavalry, 4,500 infantry and 8,600 militia.[58] It was an impressive force, led by prominent and experienced generals such as Lord Charles Fitzroy, who commanded the garrison at Ipswich, and Major General Edward Finch MP, who had served in the Netherlands and Egypt before taking the command of the first brigade of guards, stationed at Chelmsford. Lieutenant General Sir James Henry Craig himself had fought in America during the War of Independence, and in the 1790s served in the Netherlands as Major General under the Duke of York. The order book indicates the much larger scale and complexity of the duty now bestowed on him.

The first series of orders in the book exhibit an acute sense of anxiety about the impending invasion, in particular the uneasy feeling that Bonaparte could land anywhere at any time. Craig wrote to Major General Sir Eyre Coote, who was stationed at Ipswich:

This constant state of preparation is the more expedient on the present occasion, from the impossibility of foreseeing the movements of the Enemy...his arrival on our Coast may be look'd for at a moment when on every ordinary principle that directs movements of the nature of that which he has to undertake he ought to be the least expected.

Hence his orders were very detailed and attempted to prepare for every eventuality. The chief strategic concern was to prevent the enemy from advancing beyond the shoreline and acquiring a base area within the country; if this failed, then the aim was to attack the invader,

continually to impose delay and keep his troops confined to the smallest area possible.[59] Control of the routes from the sea inland was a key consideration. In his order to Major General Stoke, he advised: 'The knowledge of the roads and communications must not be confined to the country in your front or between you and the sea – it is equally essential that those in your rear leading towards Harwich and the Stow and towards this place should be known.'

General Craig's orders were formulated partly in response to the new modes of warfare the British Army had experienced on the Continent during the 1790s, when the old-style pitched battles had given way to attempting to fight huge revolutionary armies who relied on tactics of surprise, light infantry and ravaging the surrounding countryside for supplies. The Military High Command realized that an approach was necessary which mirrored the elements of rapidity, the use of almost guerrilla-like sharp shooters and light artillery and the mobilization of the mass population in defence. It was conjectured that the likely places of a French landing in the Eastern District included Lynn, Cromer and Great Yarmouth in Norfolk, Hollesley Bay in Suffolk and the Blackwater and Crouch estuaries in Essex.[60] The corresponding points of assembly and advanced posts for the troops were laid out and they were generally followed by Craig in his orders of 1803. For example, both identified that a landing at Hollesley Bay or near Landguard Fort would mean that Bonaparte was intending to head as quickly as possible to London, and that General Manners' brigade should immediately march from Bradfield to back up the rear of the brigade defending the fort, and roads leading towards Colchester and London should be blocked.

In June 1803, General Craig sent a memorandum of his orders to the Commander in Chief, the Duke of York. He explained that it was 'utterly impossible to guard every spot of so extensive a coast', and thus the best means of defence was to place troops 'in central positions to be able to march at the shortest notice'.[61] Craig was most anxious about various points on the coasts of Suffolk and Essex. Two entrenched camps, one near Colchester between the rivers Colne and Stour, the other on the high ground above Chelmsford, were brought back into use. Additional works were prepared between Sudbury and Gun Hill to cover an enemy's line of approach from the direction of Harwich.[62]

The defence of Harwich harbour and Colchester in particular was the constant preoccupation of the military authorities, as they were perceived to be vulnerable and easy routes towards London. The general command was thus based at Colchester, with infantry brigades being positioned at the surrounding small towns. Craig feared that if the French were to succeed in getting through Harwich harbour, they could be in possession of Colchester within a few hours. The garrison at Colchester hosted among others, the 42nd (Black Watch) and 92nd (Gordon) Highlanders, the former having been welcomed by the inhabitants with ringing of bells in honour of their service in Egypt.[63] Landguard Fort, which protected Harwich Harbour on the approach to Colchester, was however, in a bad state of repair in 1803. Craig believed that the Navy would help to ward off invading French or Dutch troops in the area, but if they did reach the shore, the fort's batteries were extremely deficient, with only a couple of hundred 'invalids' to operate them. He thus urgently called for the fort's reconstruction, but this was to take shape only very slowly.[64] Another point of danger was Norman Cross in Cambridgeshire, where General Este commanded a garrison which held over 6,000 French Prisoners of War. Craig advised General Este that if Bonaparte was to land at Lynn, he should immediately remove the prisoners from Norman Cross and with the help of the volunteer corps, destroy all the bridges and roads leading towards the prison.

The order book, among his other correspondence, illustrates General Craig's ardour in forwarding defence measures. He was not only an excellent strategist regarding the placing of troops, but he also pioneered the experimental firing of a line of beacons as a means of communication, in order to make response to invasion as rapid as possible. Beacons were placed at various points along the coasts of Essex, Suffolk and Norfolk. He also instituted a system of semaphore, which was intended to convey messages towards London; one was placed on the steeple of the parish church of Colchester. The General continued to improve these systems of communication until after the invasion scares had passed.[65]

The inclusion of the volunteer forces into the military's plans is a crucial indication of how the nature of war had changed. The two spheres of defence, military and civil, generals and lords lieutenant, co-operated successfully to integrate their plans. General Craig attended the meeting of the Essex Lieutenancy on 24 June 1803, which decided how ordinary civilians were to be used in defending the county, in particular as volunteer corps, 'pioneers' and 'drivers' of the countryside.[66] The Duke of York had instructed the generals commanding military districts that volunteers were to 'harass, alarm and fatigue the enemy'. This policy was exemplified by the orders given by Craig to the generals under his command. Although he reported that definite plans involving their detachment could not yet be drawn up as the volunteer system was not yet complete, he nevertheless envisaged their utility 'as light and regular troops in constantly harassing the Enemy, outposts and columns of march'. He placed vivid significance on mobilizing the general population through volunteer corps: 'these must be used as irregulars – they must be in almost continual action, firing from behind every tree and every stone.'

For the first time, the generals trusted the masses to be armed and to fight as auxiliaries to the Army. It reflected a shift within the generals' plans of defence, one which had been germinating gradually during the revolutionary wars: a recognition of the usefulness of the patriotic efforts of the civilian population, through training them to arms, or in other means such as providing food for the Army or as wagonners to transport troops or their supplies. In some respects, this new policy was enforced on the British Army and Government through lack of manpower, when many of Britain's troops were serving on the Continent rather than on the immensely long periphery which made up the British coastline. The Napoleonic period, especially during the invasion scares, marked the point when the military forces realized they could not rely on the Navy alone.

33

Orderly-book of the Desborough Troop of Armed Yeomanry commanded by Capt. Sir John Dashwood King, Bart.

[c. 1795]
MS. DD Dashwood c.14 F2/3/2
Reproduced by kind permission of Sir Edward Dashwood

34

Orderly book

[c. 1795–8]
MS. DD Dashwood c.14 F2/3/3
Reproduced by kind permission of Sir Edward Dashwood

F2/3/2

Orderly - Book

27ᵗʰ April 1799.

Common Exercise

1. By fours to the Right wh...
2. D°
3. By D° — to the right about wheel
4. By fours to the left wheel
5. D°
6. By D° to left about wheel
7. By half ranks to the Right wheel
8. By D°
   By half ranks to the right about wheel
   By half ranks to the left wheel
   By D°
   By half ranks to the left about wheel
   The whole to the right wheel
   D° —
   The whole to the right about wheel
   The whole to the left wheel
   D°

35

Accounts of the Desborough troop of Armed Yeomanry

[c. 1795–8]
MS. DD Dashwood c.14 F/2/2/7
Reproduced by kind permission of Sir Edward Dashwood

36

Volunteers of the United Kingdom, 1803

(House of Commons Papers, 9 and 13 December 1803)
PP Eng. 1803/I

Volunteer regiments had been organized on a large scale in 1798 to meet the first invasion threat. Nothing better expresses the sense of danger in 1803 than the 463,134 men in Great Britain and Ireland who volunteered during the summer. The 'Terms of Service' specified here show the localism of many corps. Large cities like London organized several volunteer regiments under different commanders. The uniforms and terms of service of some of these were commemorated in No. 68, *Loyal Volunteers of London and Environs*.

John Eastwood King Bar.[ ] on Account of the Provincial Cavalry for
to the shop &c Commands.

Contra — Cr

By first Dr.[ ] received from Mr. Box — 350:—:—
2.[ ] D.[ ] from D.[ ] — 170:—:—

£ 520:—:—

John Bull Guarding the Toy Shop

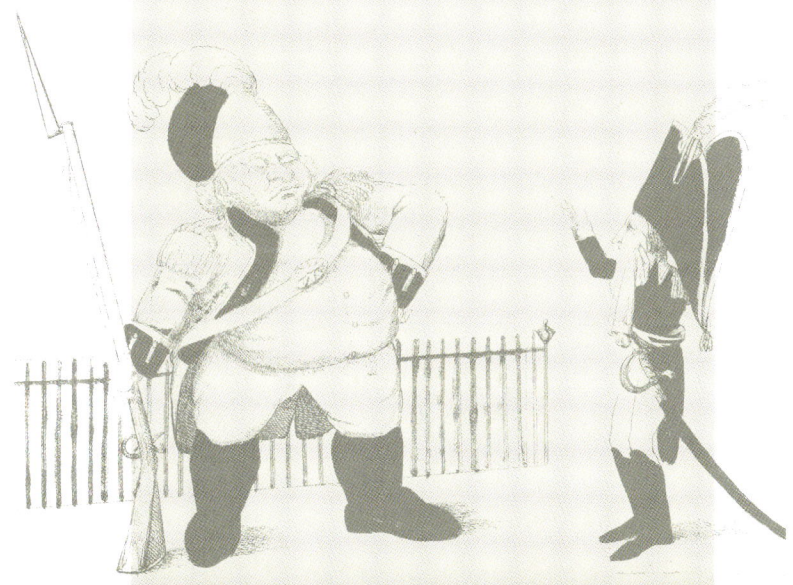

From the 1780s, John Bull appeared in cartoons as an Englishman defending his rightful liberties, usually while enjoying the material comforts of a prosperous commercial nation – a pipe of tobacco and a tankard of ale. In 1803, cartoons and broadsides reinvented John Bull from a stolid civilian to a citizen in arms, one of the hundreds of thousands who were called upon to volunteer for military service to defend Britain against Napoleon.

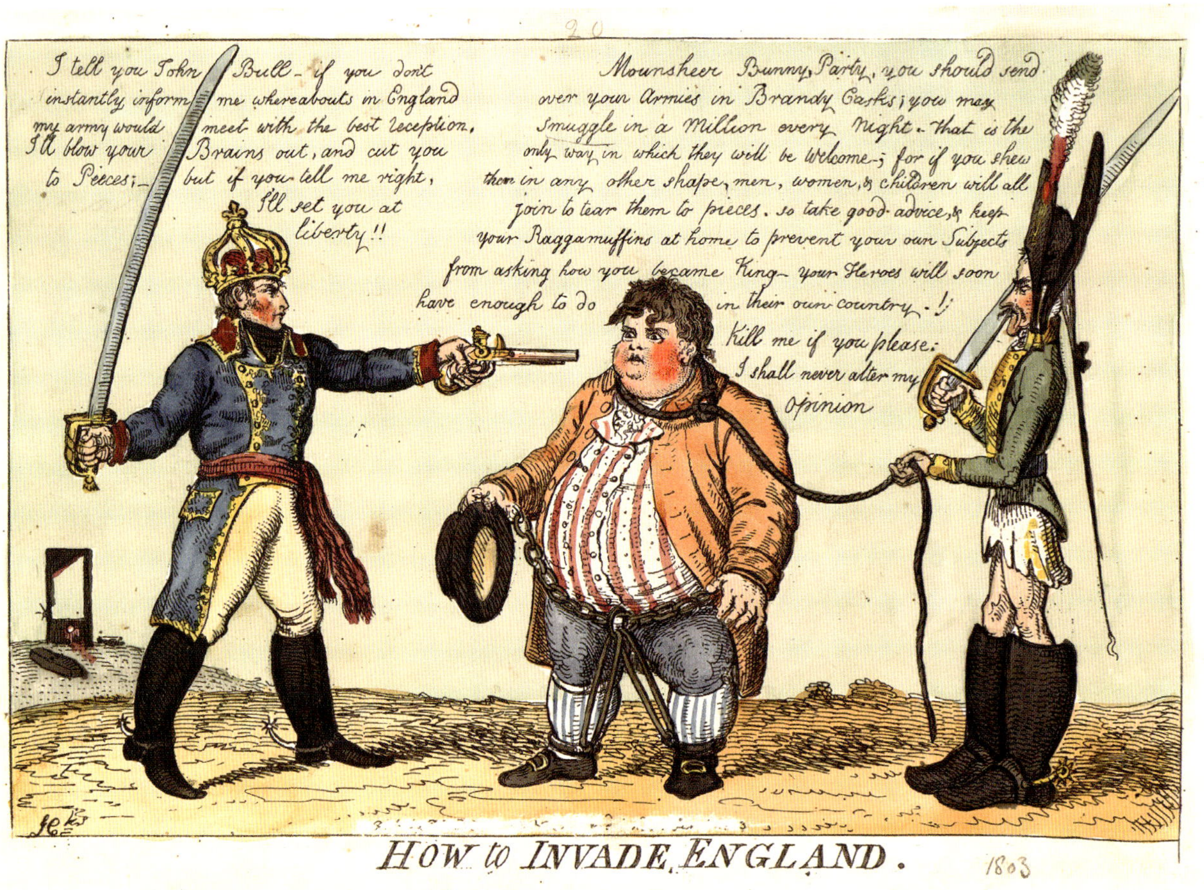

I tell you John Bull - if you dont instantly inform me whereabouts in England my army would meet with the best reception, I'll blow your Brains out, and cut you to Peeces; but if you tell me right, I'll set you at liberty!!

Mounsheer Bunny Party, you should send over your Armies in Brandy Casks; you may smuggle in a Million every Night. that is the only way in which they will be Welcome; for if you shew them in any other shape, men, women, & children will all join to tear them to pieces. so take good advice, & keep your Raggamuffins at home to prevent your own Subjects from asking how you became King - your Heroes will soon have enough to do in their own country. -!

Kill me if you please: I shall never alter my Opinion

HOW to INVADE ENGLAND.   1803

37

Isaac Cruikshank (1764 – 1811?)

How to invade England

Hand-coloured etching, 21.8 x 33 cm (subject)

[Published 6 June 1803 by Williamson]

Curzon b.11(99)

[Imprint obliterated]

38

Isaac Cruikshank (1764–1811?)

How to stop an invader

Hand-coloured etching, 18.6 x 25.3 cm (subject)

Published 28 July 1803 by Williamson

Curzon b.11(43)

BMC 10042

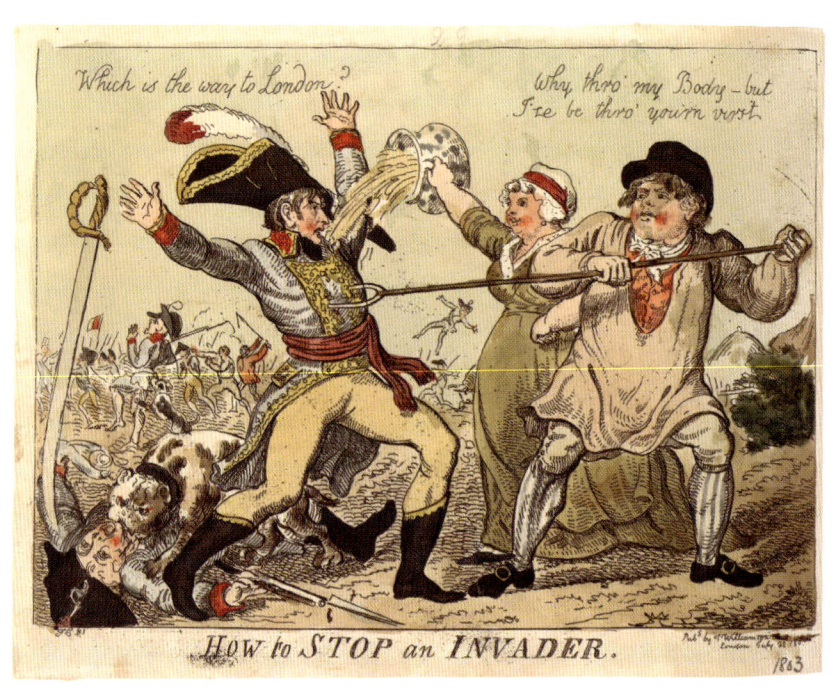

39

J.B.

John Bull guarding the toy-shop, – or Boney crying for some more play things

Hand-coloured etching, 23.1 x 32.3 cm (subject)
Published 29 October 1803 by S. W. Fores
Curzon b.3(1)
BMC 10118

The publisher slyly advertises his own wares. The
window panes of London print shops were usually
filled with prints for sale; the 'toys' depicted in this shop
are London buildings representing the royal and
financial establishment of England. Napoleon demands
the Bank, to the indignation of John Bull.
Establishments such as the Bank of England and the
East India Company raised their own regiments of
volunteers for defence in case of invasion or
insurrection, as can be seen in the parliamentary
returns of volunteers (No. 36).

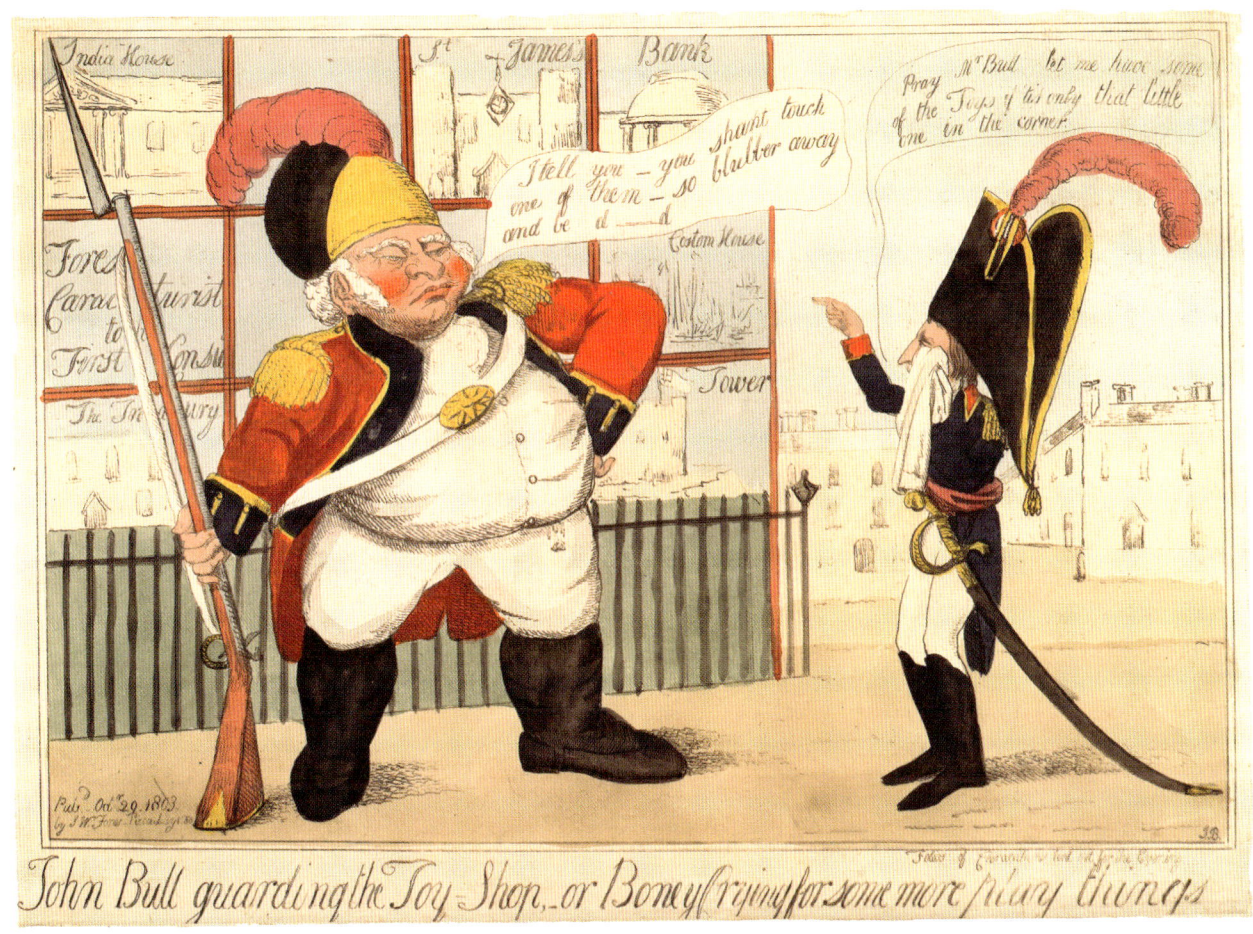

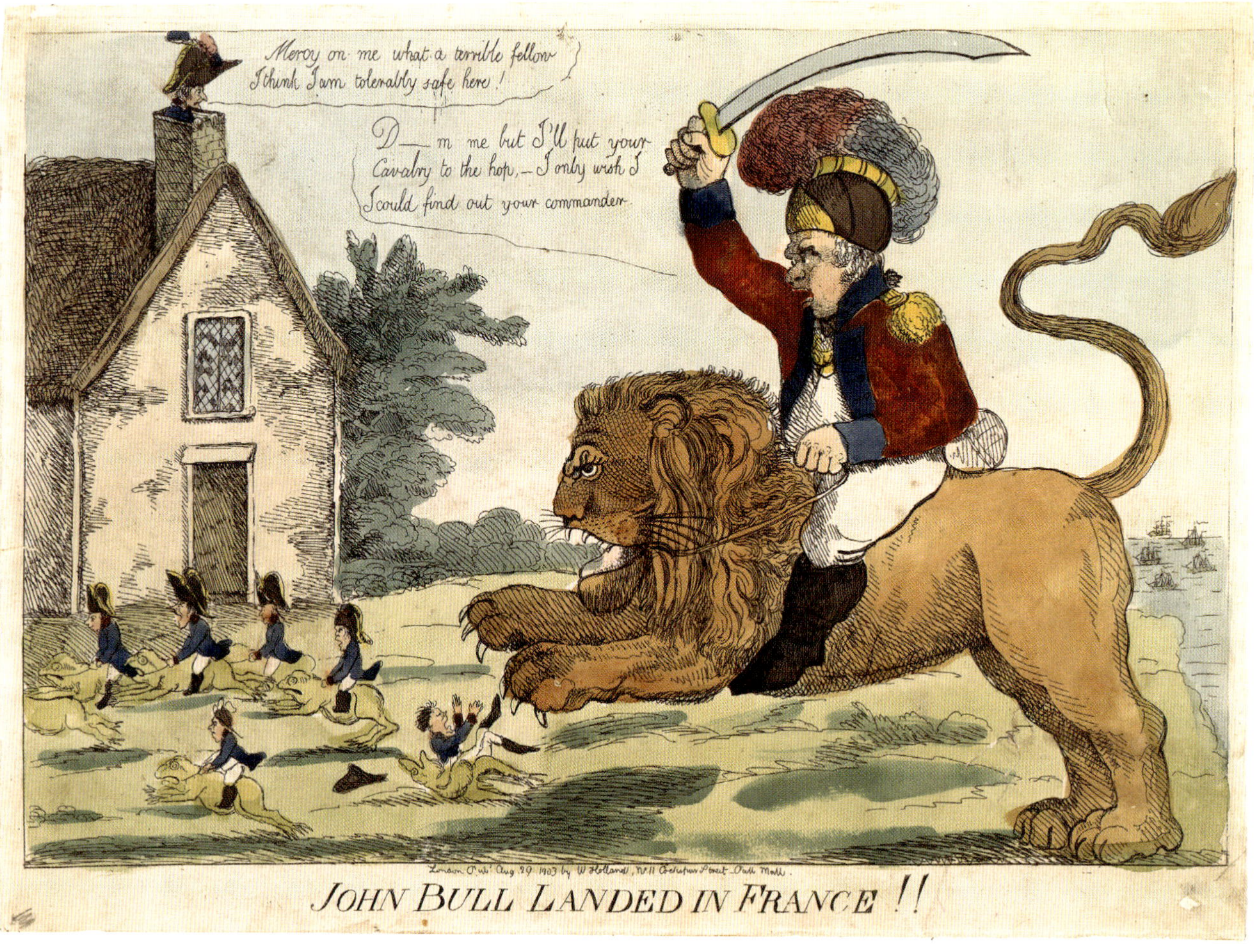

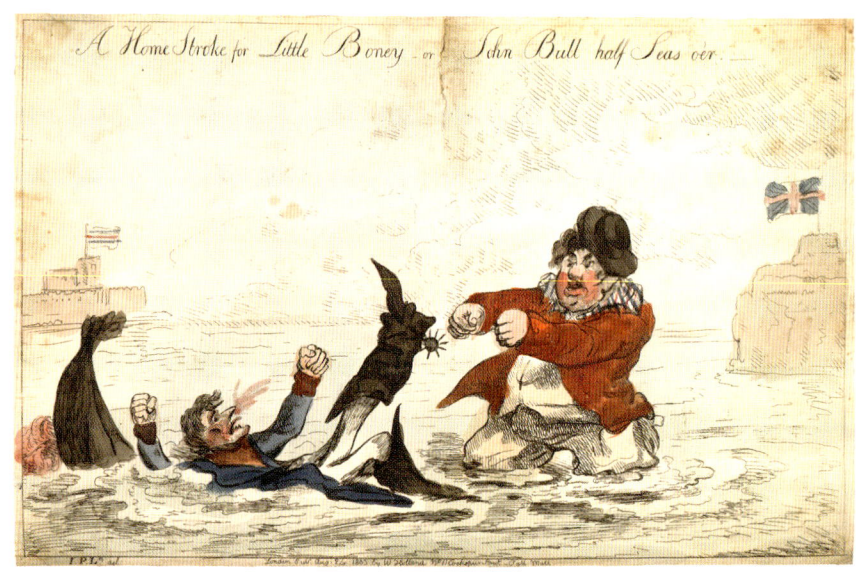

40

John Bull landed in France!!

Hand-coloured etching, 22.7 x 33.7 cm
(subject)
Published 29 August 1803 by W. Holland
Curzon b.4(55)
BMC 10078

41

A home stroke for little Boney, or John Bull half seas o'er

Designed by I.P.Ln.

Hand-coloured etching, 26 x 41 cm
(subject)
Published 24 August 1803 by William
Holland
Curzon b.11(2)

42

John Bull clipping the Corsican's wings!!

Hand-coloured etching, 33.9 x 23.6 cm (subject)
Published September 1803 by William Holland
Curzon b.11(47)

43

John Bull bringing Bonaparte to London!!

Hand-coloured etching, 22.3 x 33.9 cm
Published 8 August 1803 by William Holland
Curzon b.4(34)

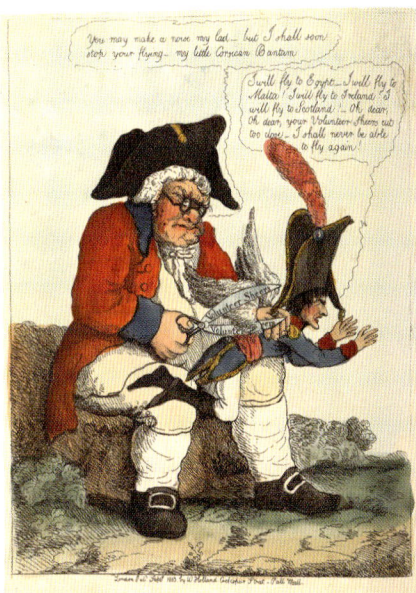

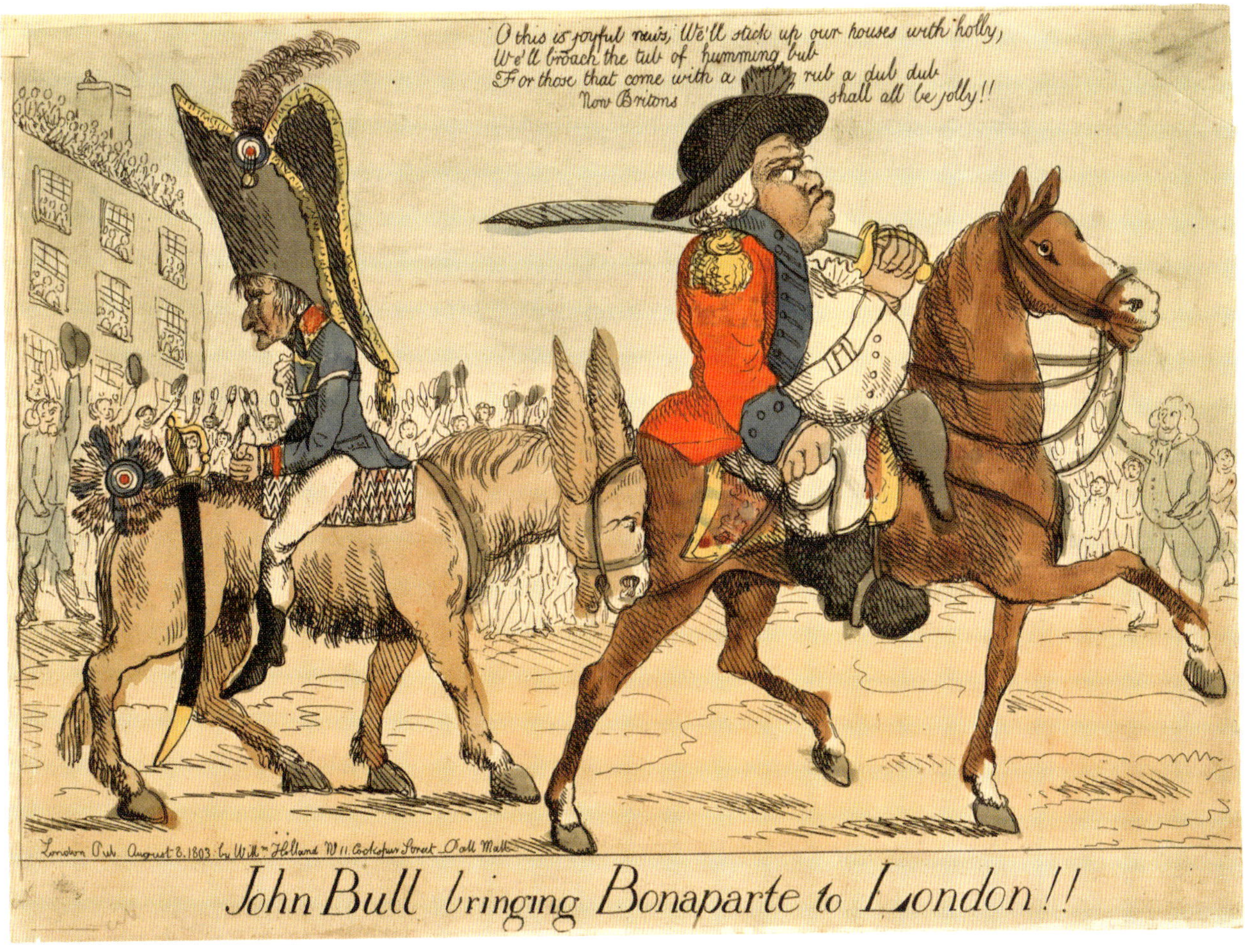

JOHN BULL clipping the CORSICAN'S WINGS!!

The Invasion Threat,
1803

The war resumed in May 1803. There
was now constant speculation about
the troops being massed by Napoleon
at Boulogne for a possible invasion
of England.

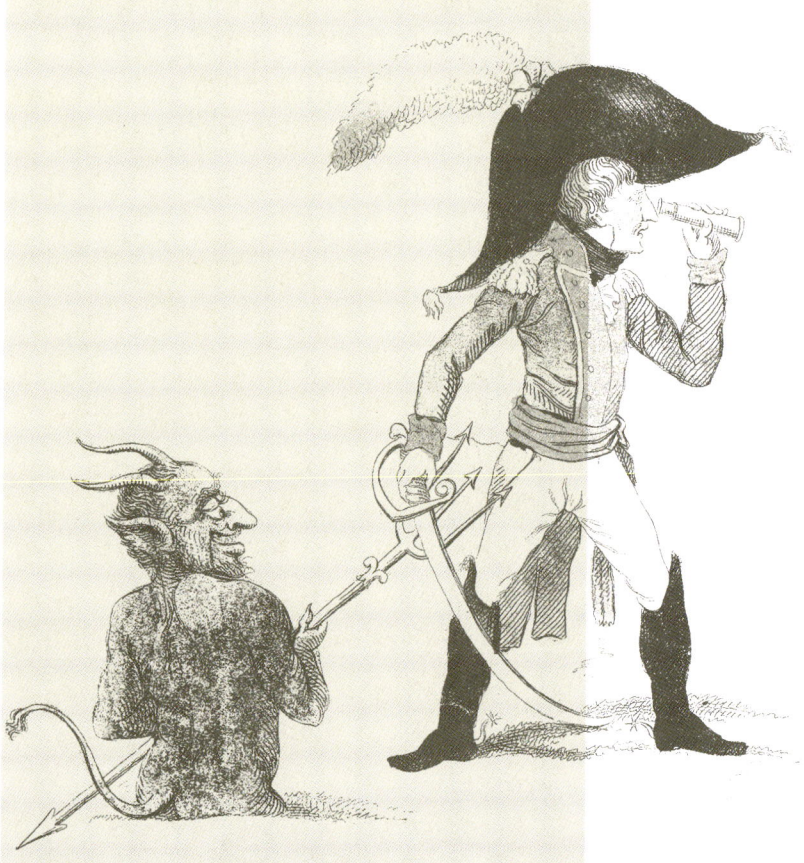

44

[James Gillray (1756–1815)]
John Bull and the alarmist
Hand-coloured etching, 31.8 x 35.6 cm (sheet)
Published 1 September 1803 by Hannah Humphrey
John Johnson Collection: French Wars and Revolutions folder 6 (3)
BMC 10088

In a sign of the change in attitudes since 1798, the Whig politician and playwright Richard Brinsley Sheridan spoke on the Volunteers Bill, 10 August 1803, appealing for a suspension of political animosities in the face of 'the greatest danger with which we were ever threatened'. Here Gillray satirized the fevered tones of loyalist papers, including the patriotic speech from Sheridan's play Pizarro, which was reprinted in 1803 as a handbill titled 'Sheridan's Address to the People'. It included the lines, 'We serve a monarch whom we love – a God whom we adore…The throne we honour is the People's Choice.'

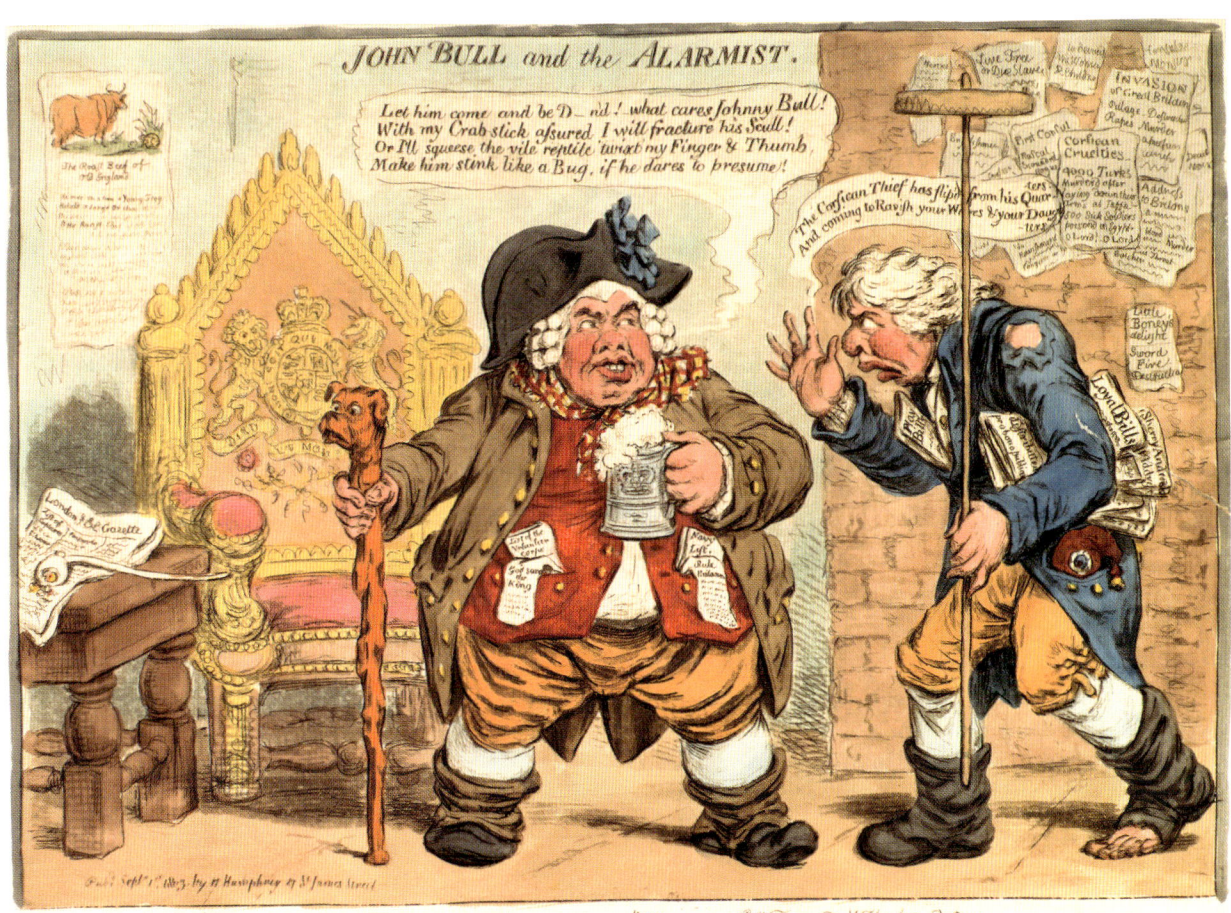

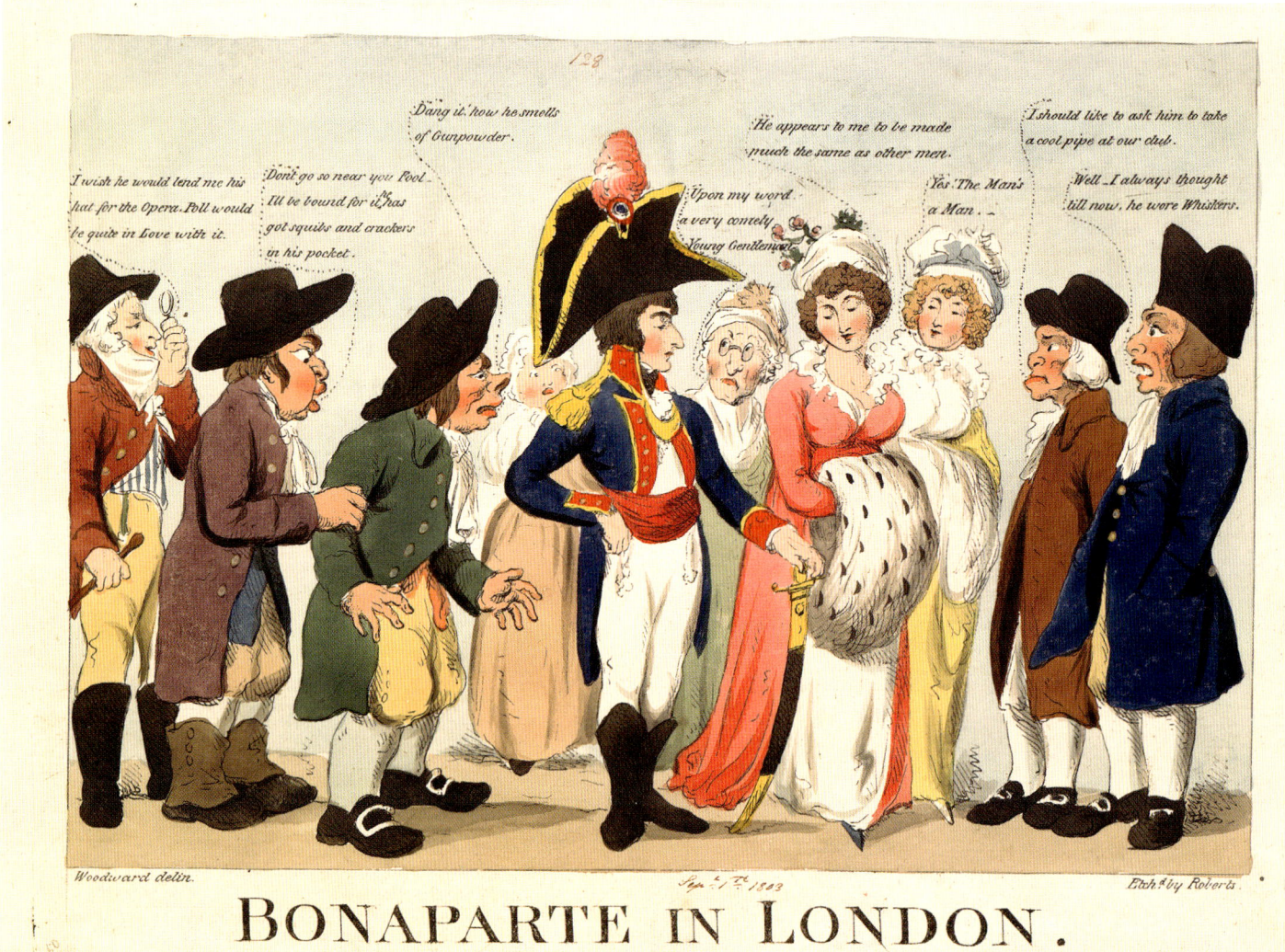

45

George M. Woodward (1760?–1809)
Bonaparte in London
Hand-coloured etching, 22.3 x 32.8 cm (subject)
Etched by Roberts
Published [1 September 1803] by P. Roberts
Curzon b.12(57)

In this cartoon Napoleon is not caricatured, but shown as a dashing officer. The English ladies comment favourably on his manly and military appearance.

46

[C. Williams]
The consequence of invasion – the hero's reward
Hand-coloured etching, 26 x 39.1 cm (sheet), 22.7 x 34 cm (subject)
Published 1 August 1803 by S. W. Fores
John Johnson Collection: French Wars and Revolutions folder 5 (Db10)
BMC 10047

A British volunteer holds a grisly prize: the severed heads of French invaders, topped by the head of Napoleon himself. Here the ladies of London desert their foppish mates to shower kisses on the stout defender.

47

After the invasion – the levée en masse – or Britons strike home

[C. Williams]

Hand-coloured etching, 23 x 34.3 cm (subject)
Published 6 August 1803 by S. W. Fores
John Johnson Collection: French Wars and Revolutions folder 5 (Db1)
BMC 10052

The Levy en masse Act, for the compulsory military training of men between the ages of 17 and 55, was passed on 27 July 1803. It was quickly superseded by the numbers volunteering. The language of these three recruits emphasizes the pragmatic and local concerns which were put forward in patriotic writings of 1803: property, family and village society. This cartoon imitates the Gillray print, 'Buonaparte 48 hours after landing!'. In both of these prints Napoleon's profile is handsome and fine, in contrast to the country bumpkin faces of England's defenders. This characterization appeared in other descriptions of the French leader. In a poem imagining a successful invasion, J. Amphlett described Napoleon as 'thoughtful', 'musing', 'languid', 'pensive' and 'sad'.[67]

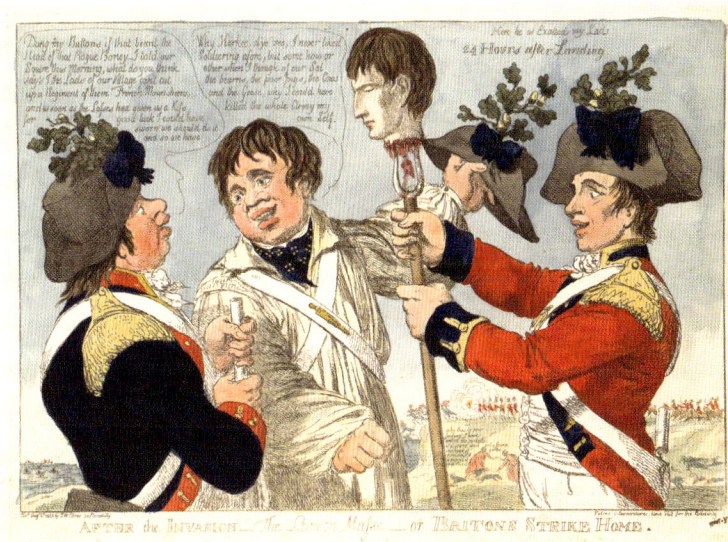

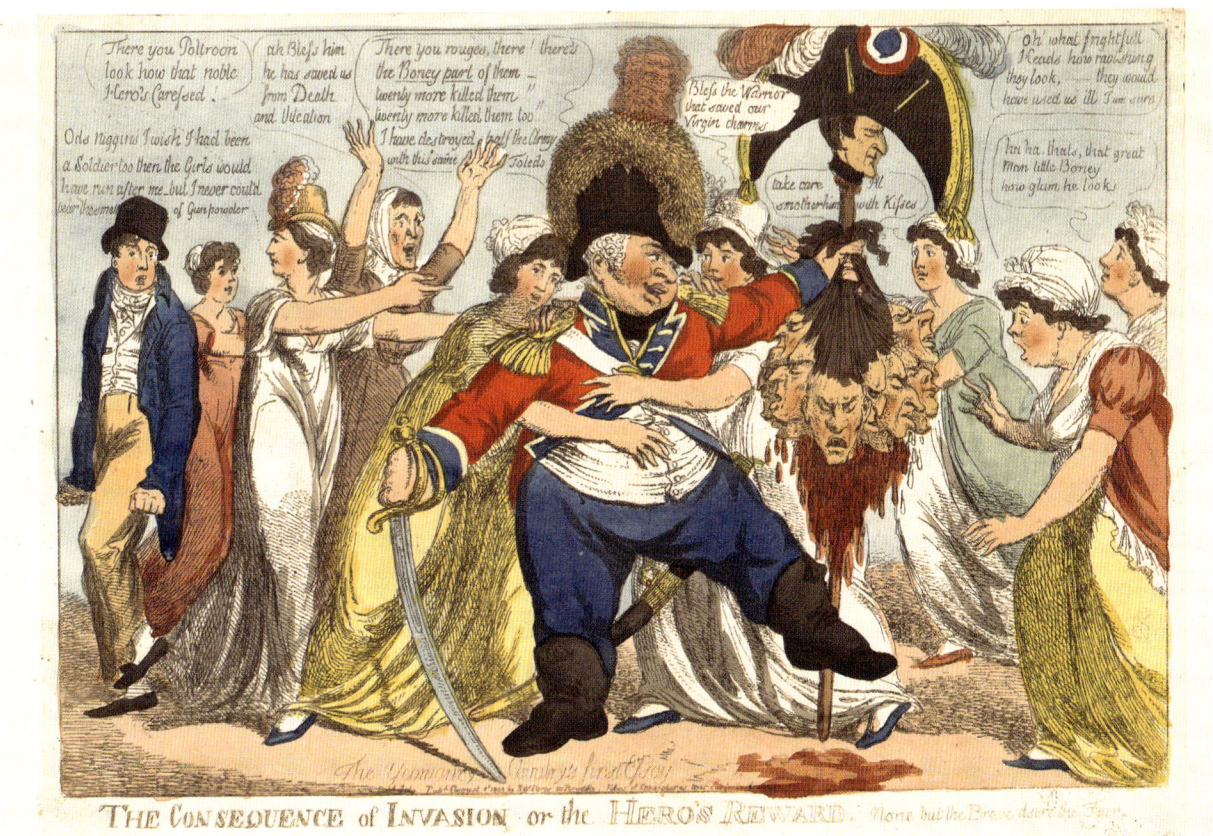

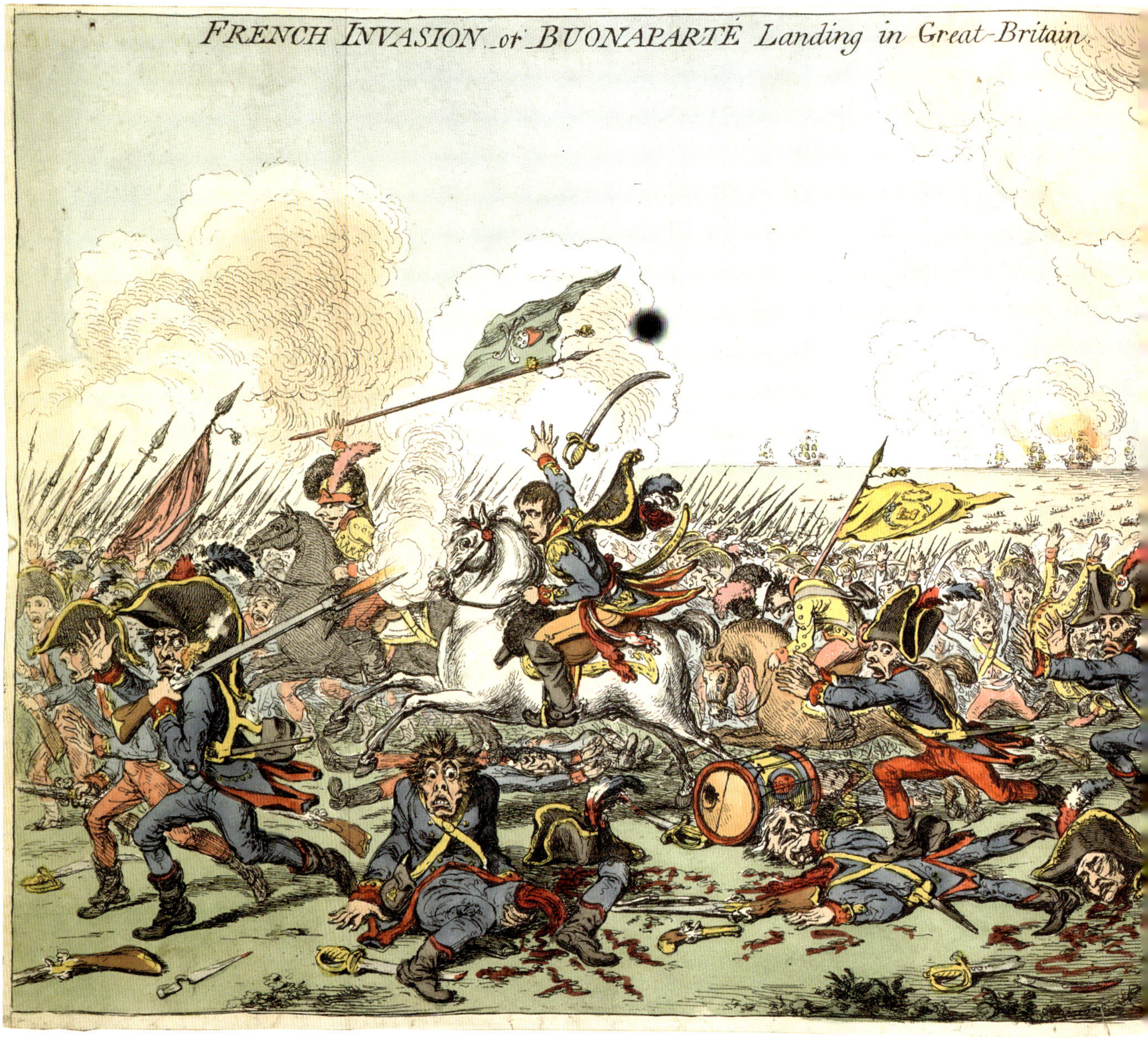

FRENCH INVASION _or_ BUONAPARTÉ Landing in Great-Britain.

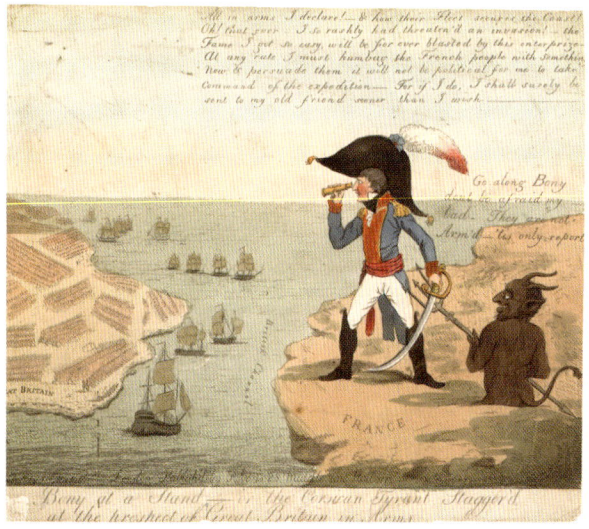

48

J. T. Mitchell

Bony at a stand – or the Corsican tyrant stagger'd at the prospect of Great Britain in arms

Hand-coloured etching, 24.6 x 29.2 cm (sheet)
Published [1803] by Roberts
Curzon b.23(242)

Political cartoons pretended to report the inner thoughts of leaders, suggesting human motivations behind diplomacy and war. Here, Bonaparte's first concern is for his personal reputation and safety. The volunteers assembling on the English shore are reduced to a mass of single strokes.

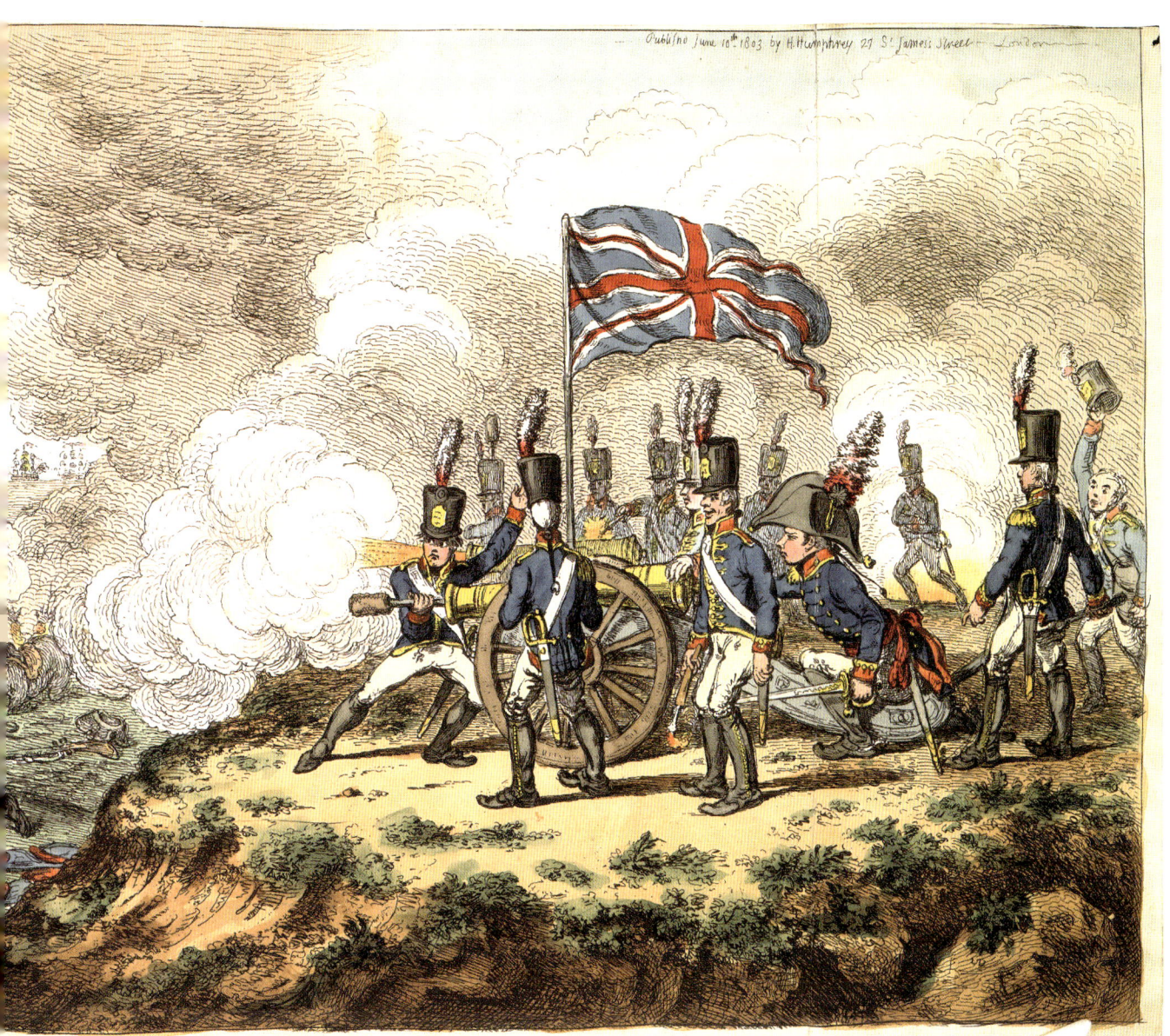

Publish'd June 10th 1803 by H. Humphrey 27 St. James's Street — London

49

James Gillray (1756–1815)

**French invasion or Buonaparte landing in
Great-Britain**

Hand-coloured etching, 28.5 x 67.6 cm (sheet)
Published 10 June 1803 by Hannah Humphrey
Curzon b.22(62)
BMC 10008

Gillray imagines the invasion force, including Napoleon himself on a white horse, put to flight as soon as it lands on the English shore. In fact, English preparations provided for only a small force at any of the possible landing points and by 1803 only a few places along Britain's coasts were sufficiently fortified to hold off an invasion for any length of time. It was assumed that the main stand would be made in or near London itself.

Defenders of Britain

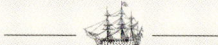

At the beginning of the wars against Revolutionary France in 1793, Britain's defence strategy rested on the performance of an elite officer corps with a conscripted army and militia. In 1803, the Government turned to national popular mobilization as a means not only of raising the strength of the home defence, but also of generating patriotism. Many of these cartoons represent the nation's defenders as John Bull in the uniform of a volunteer, or as Jack Tar, the archetypal British sailor. The portrayal of George III as an active defender of the nation further enhanced his status, though as in the Gillray cartoon 'St George and the Dragon' (1805) (Fig. 2, *illus. p. 21*), this image could be ridiculed.

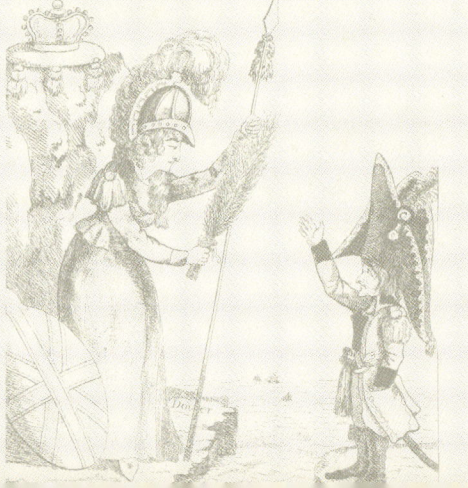

50

Bicester Independent Company of Volunteer Infantry – Muster Roll, 1803–08

MS. Top. Oxon.c. 223

This muster roll records the names and occupations of 120 inhabitants of Bicester, Oxfordshire, who signed up to form a local Volunteer Corps of Infantry in response to the threat of invasion in August 1803. They provided 'a proper military uniform' with scarlet jackets at their own expense and agreed to serve on permanent duty for a total of twenty days per year, anywhere in the county, or in case of invasion, anywhere in Great Britain. The names are ranked in order of seniority; the main officers were: Henry Walford, Captain-Commandant of the Corps, Lieutenant William Wharton and Ensign William Shillingford. Henry Walford was a local attorney, and the mainly artisanal membership of the corps is reflective of its parochial nature, when compared to the more socially prominent leadership of the nearby Oxford Loyal Volunteers and the Oxford University Volunteer Corps. The popularity of the Bicester Volunteers is indicated by the continual addition of names to the roll from its inception until the Corps's dissolution around 1809.

The Bicester Volunteers
By Katrina Navickas

The offer of the Bicester Volunteers to serve was accepted by the Government on 17 August 1803.[68] The population of the market town of Bicester in 1801 was only just under 2,000,[69] so the raising of 120 men was a significant patriotic achievement in 1803, twice the number of men enlisted in response to the earlier invasion scare of 1798.[70] The varied artisanal occupations of the members, most of whom could write their own name, perhaps represent a section of Bicester society who had enough time and resources to spare to join the Corps in a patriotic endeavour. Half of Bicester's population were employed in agriculture and some farmers are evident amongst the names. However it is such myriad and skilled trades such as silversmith, watchmaker, shoemaker, cabinet maker and cottage textile industries including 'breeches maker', 'laceman' and 'flax dresser', which reflect the composition of Bicester's economy, not dominated by any one industry, as was typical of many small market towns in the south of England. The local nature of the Bicester Volunteer Corps is indicated by the fact that its commandant, Henry Walford, was not a gentleman of leisure, but an attorney and deputy steward for the nearby manors of Islip and Launton. Neither was he a prominent landowner in Bicester and he probably could not provide uniforms for all the men he commanded.[71] The rest of the inhabitants of Bicester therefore raised a subscription fund to pay the expenses of the Corps.[72] The patriotism of the Bicester Volunteers was parochial, amateur but sincere. They requested arms and ammunition from Government, and also the services of a drill sergeant 'to instruct the corps in the use of arms',[73] as for most of these men, this would be the first time they had ever held a musket or pike. Mass military mobilization of the civilian population through volunteering thus reached even the smallest towns and villages, even if their only activity was to learn drill exercises for a couple of hours a week. The Bicester Volunteers travelled out of the town once to serve their obligatory twenty days; in July 1804, they were kept on permanent duty at Chipping Norton, about twenty miles away, for which the rank and file received a shilling a day.[74]

The Bicester Volunteers swore their oath of allegiance (loyalty to the King for defence of the country) before John Coker, Esq. Coker was the lieutenant appointed to oversee the military division which covered Oxford and a large area stretching eastwards from the city. He was lord of the manor, built a large mansion and owned much land in Bicester.[75] His social prominence explains why he led a more important regiment, the University of Oxford Volunteer Corps, while the Bicester Volunteer Corps was raised by a more local and less dominant figure in society. Coker did, however, donate the large sum of £100 to the subscription fund, and other notables living nearby also felt obliged to donate money, as they did not take part in the Corps. Bicester was renowned as a centre for horse racing and hunting,[76] and thus aristocracy and gentry must have passed through the town when the season arose, but the inhabitants of the town itself were left to get on by themselves, and this is illustrated by the humble muster list. It is notable that the only 'gentleman' mentioned in the muster list, George Howlett, was only a private, which suggests that social boundaries were crossed in bringing the community together through this expression of military patriotism. The Corps's membership expressed a quiet but confident local patriotism, that the inhabit-ants of Bicester were able to defend themselves and their King and constitution, without the need for show or ostentation that obsessed other volunteer corps whose officers were members of the higher social classes.

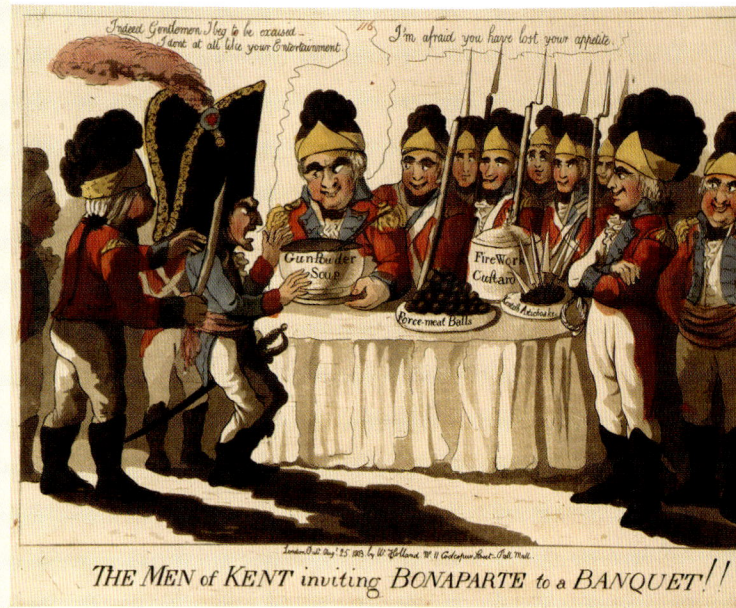

THE MEN of KENT inviting BONAPARTE to a BANQUET!!

51

The Men of Kent inviting Bonaparte to a banquet!!

Hand-coloured etching, 24.9 x 35.2 cm (platemark)
Published 25 August 1803 by William Holland
Curzon b.12(4)
BMC 10074

52

The lion and the frog!!

Hand-coloured etching, 24.9 x 35.3 cm (platemark)
Published 30 July 1803 by William Holland
Curzon b.12(54)

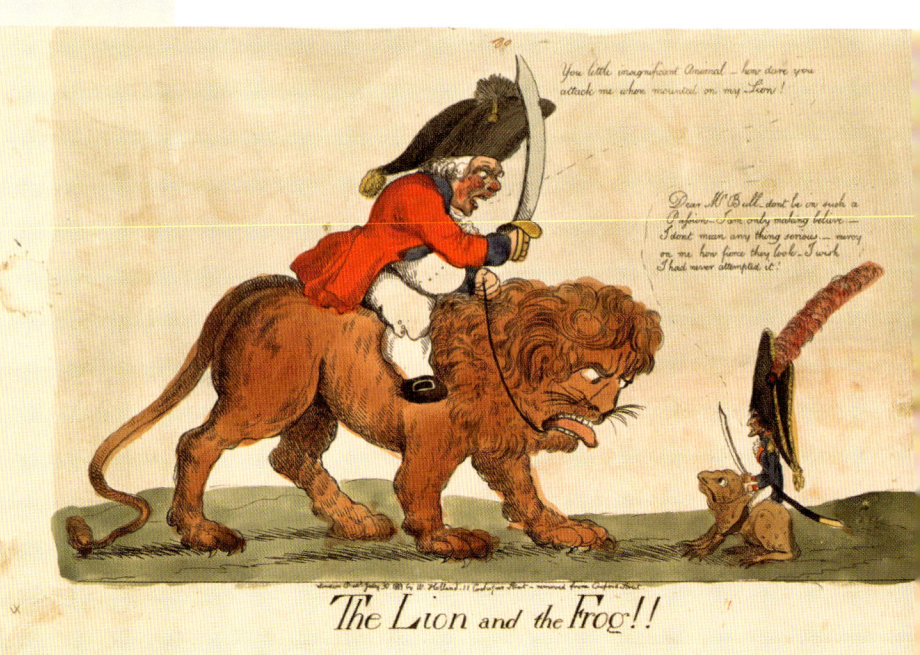

The Lion and the Frog!!

53

[Designed by] A. M.

Boney attacking the English hives or the Corsican caught at last in the island

Hand-coloured etching, 23.8 x. 18.4 cm (sheet)
Published August 1803 by S. W. Fores
Curzon b.11(11)
BMC 10079

George III is here identified with the nation as a whole, and protection of England equated with loyalty to the King, as he shelters behind the beehives representing coastal counties mobilized to resist invasion. The 'Royal London Hive' may refer to the loyal 'Declaration of the Merchants, Bankers, Traders, and other Inhabitants of London', in June 1803. The businessmen subscribed money to a Patriotic Fund for the defence of the kingdom. Napoleon's comment, 'I did not think this Nation of Shopkeepers could have stung so sharp', highlights the message that Britain's strength lay in her prosperity as well as the size of her army.

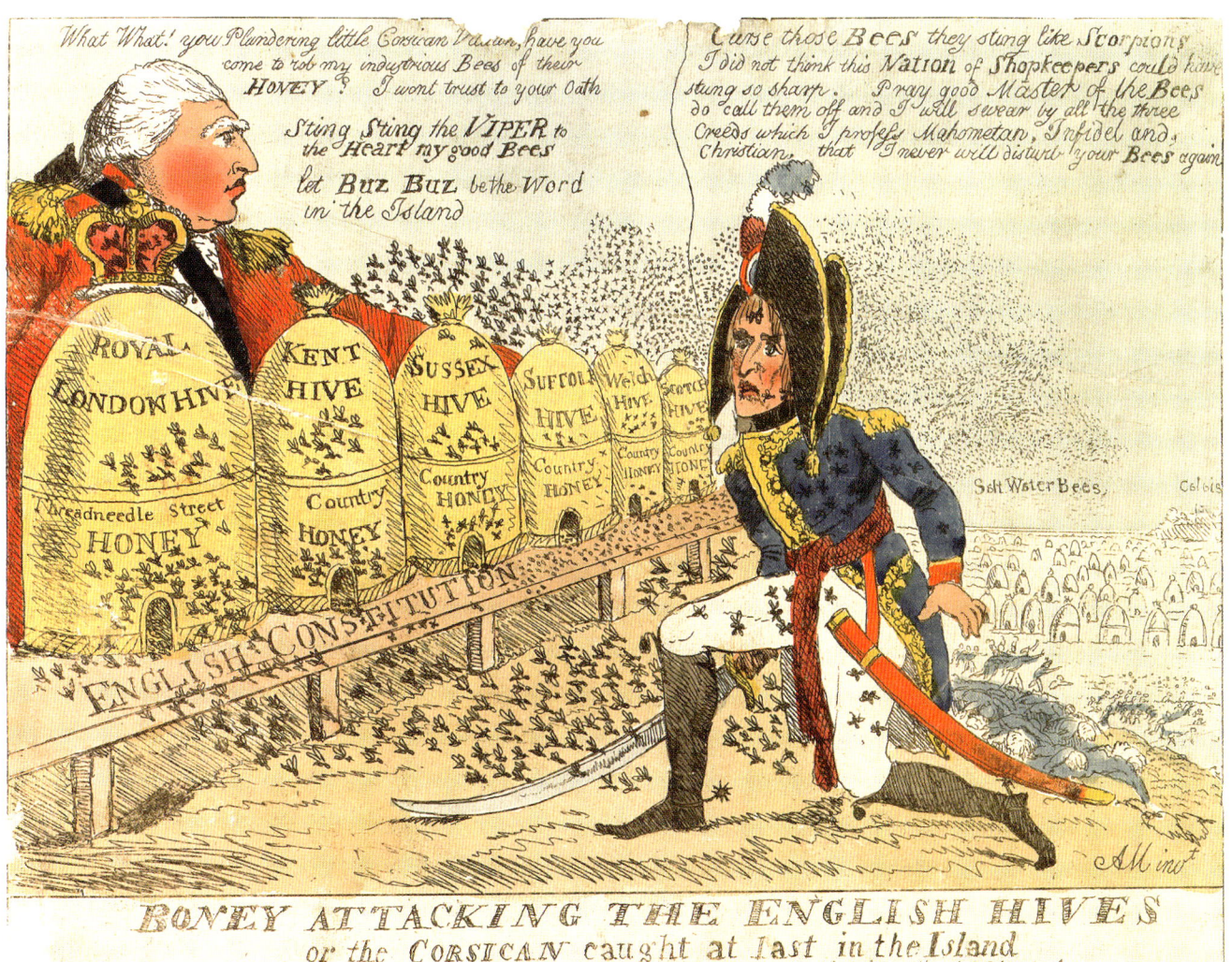

BONEY ATTACKING THE ENGLISH HIVES
or the CORSICAN caught at last in the Island

54

The British mower and the Lilliputians!

Hand-coloured etching, 35.1 x 24.8 cm (platemark)
Published 20 July 1803 by William Holland
Curzon b.12(51)

George III – 'Farmer George' – is the giant mower
cutting down the French Army with a scythe.

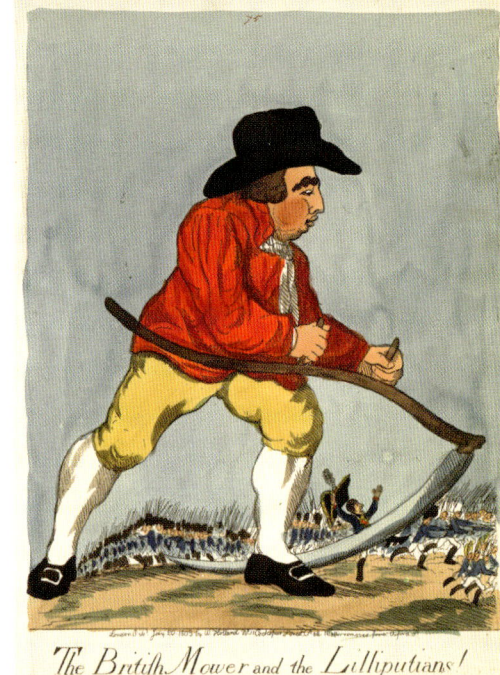

The British Mower and the Lilliputians!

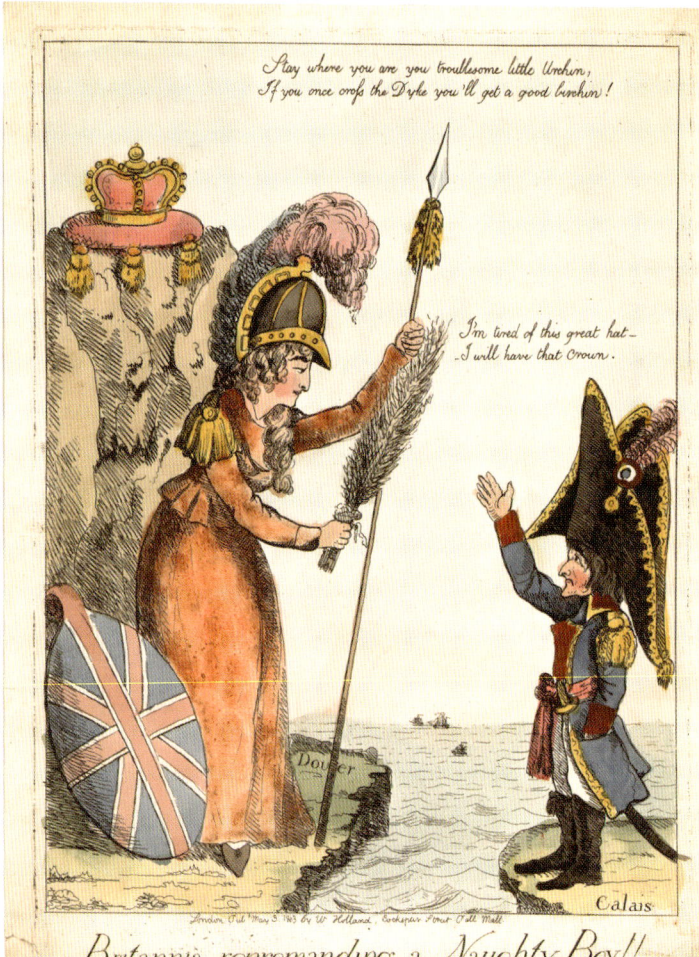

Britannia repremanding a Naughty Boy!!

55

Britannia repremanding a naughty boy!!

Hand-coloured etching, 31.6 x 23.8 cm (subject)
Published 3 May 1803 by William Holland
John Johnson Collection: French Wars and Revolutions
folder 5 (Db7)
BMC 9987

Britannia appeared less frequently in the
cartoons of 1803 than her counterpart John
Bull. Likewise the song *Rule Britannia* was
replaced by *God save the King* as the national
anthem during this period, emphasizing an
increasingly royalist tone to official patriotism,
temporarily displacing commercial strength
and naval power as expressions of British
superiority. Still, she was the primary figure in
appeals to the patriotism of sailors. This
important group formed the basis of much
popular patriotic symbolism. Recognition of
their distinctive dress, songs and spirit, were
acknowledged in printed ballads and in the
musical theatre, especially in the very popular
productions by Charles Dibdin (1745–1814).
From the 1780s Dibdin was mainly known for
his sea songs. His 1803 production was
entitled *Britons strike home!*, and in that year he
received a pension from the Government after
a long career as a composer and performer.

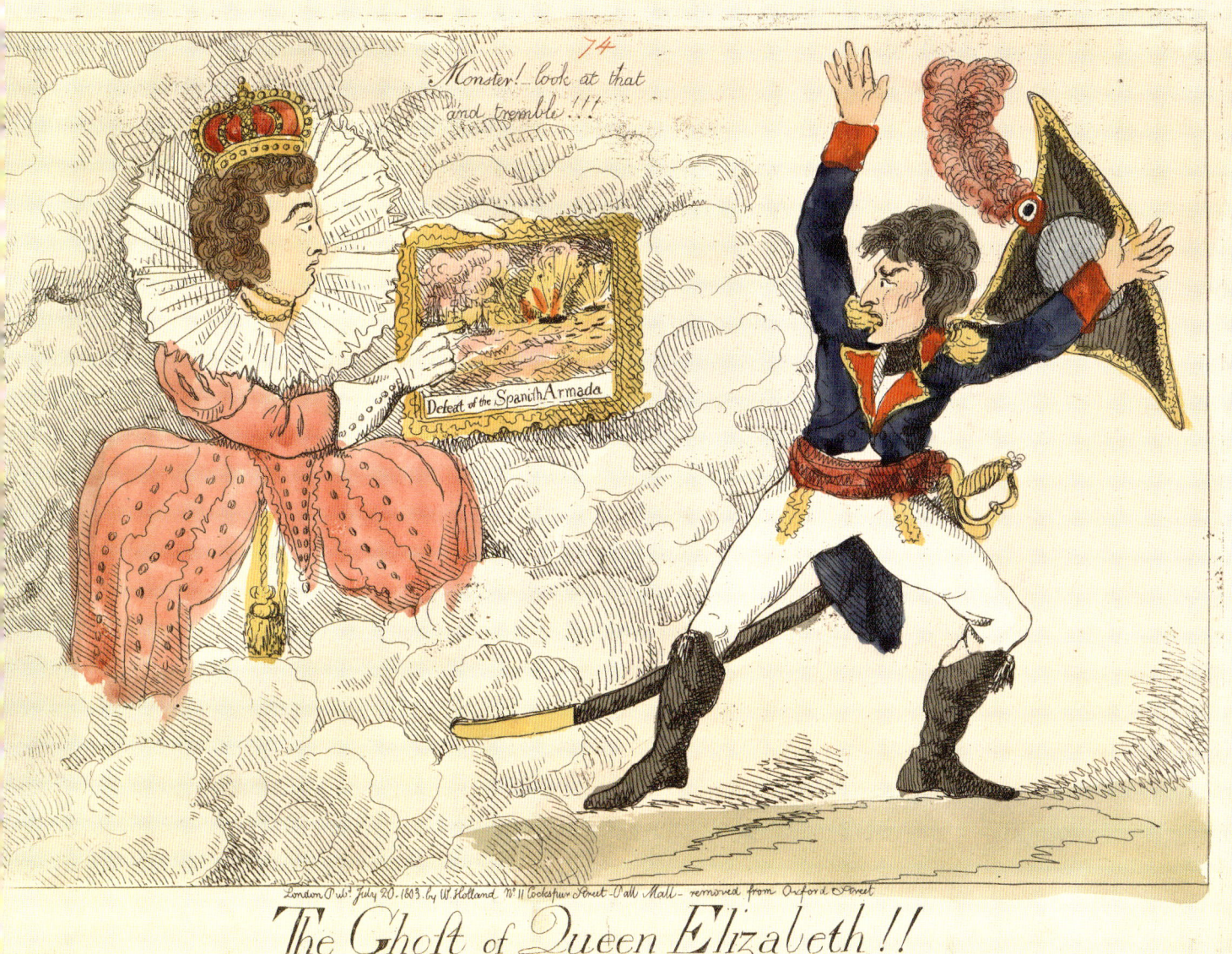

The Ghost of Queen Elizabeth!!

56

The Ghost of Queen Elizabeth!!

Hand-coloured etching, 25.1 x 35.2 cm (platemark)
Published 20 July 1803 by William Holland
Curzon b.12(8)

The rousing speech of Elizabeth to her troops at Tilbury in 1588, as they awaited the powerful Spanish Armada, was reprinted as a broadside in 1803, *Queen Elizabeth's speech to her people when threatened by the Spanish Armada*. The sixteenth-century precedent offered not only the example of a failed invasion attempt, but the memory of 'Good Queen Bess', credited with uniting a turbulent nation and setting England on a career of colonial conquest. Elizabeth was viewed through rose-tinted glasses, and some compared her favourably with the current monarch,

George III. At the height of the invasion scare in August, the radical MP Francis Horner wrote:

I have been lately fortifying myself by some favourite historical precedents – the invasion of Greece by Persia, Holland by Louis XIV, and England by Philip [the Armada in 1588]. What a mortifying contrast the behaviour of Elizabeth forces us to make with some characters of the present age; so much spirit, caution, and generous confidence, contrasted with bigotry, mean jealousy, and a selfish stupid coldness towards the people.' Horner referred specifically to the King's rejection of civil rights for Catholics in England and Ireland.[77]

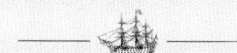

Gulliver

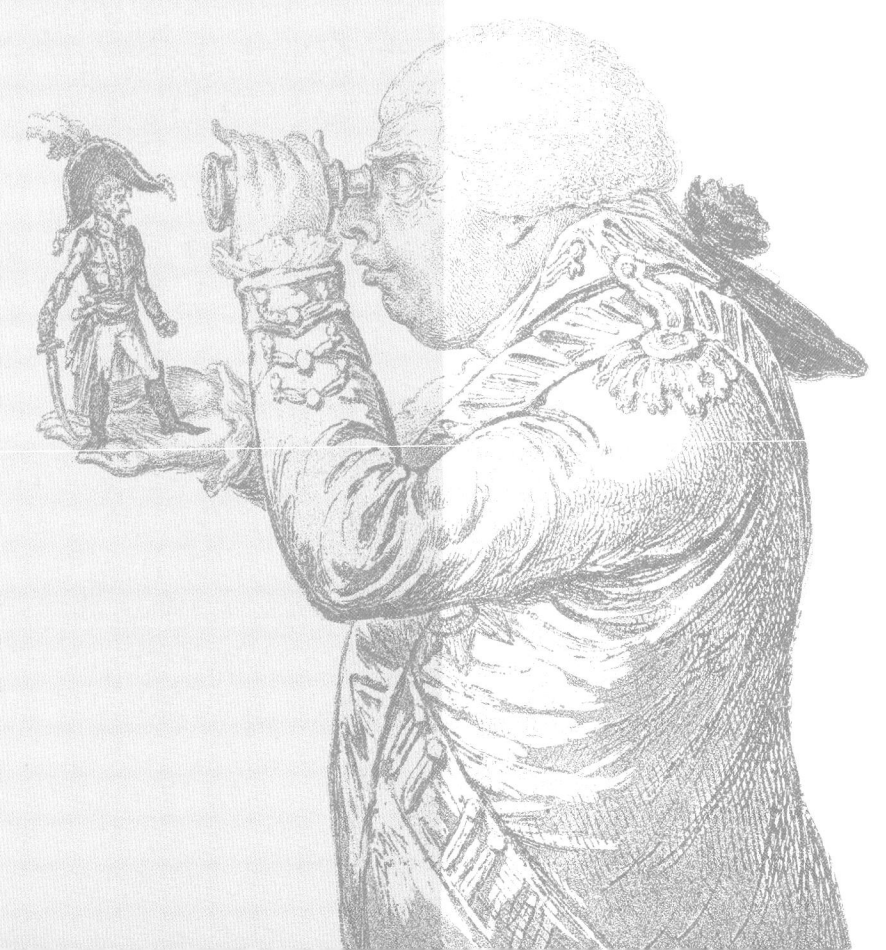

James Gillray invented the caricature of
Napoleon as 'Little Boney' in a cartoon
of 1 January 1803. The artist's etching
of Napoleon as Gulliver and George III
as the King of Brobdingnag is one of
the best-known of these images.

57

[?West]

Amusement after dinner, or The Corsican fairy displaying his prowess!

Hand-coloured etching, 25.1 x 35.2 cm (platemark)
Published July 1803 by W. Holland
Curzon b.12(70)
BMC 10034

58

[? Designed by George M. Woodward (1760?–1809)]

A peep at the Corsican fairy

Hand-coloured etching, 24.8 x 34.6 cm (subject)
Published [?July 1803] by Roberts
Curzon b.3(164)
BMC 10032

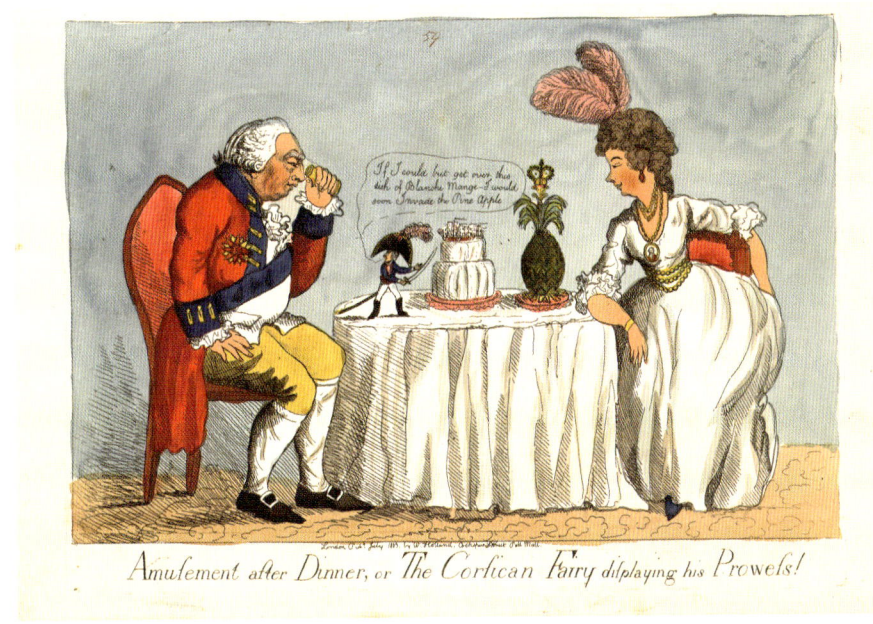

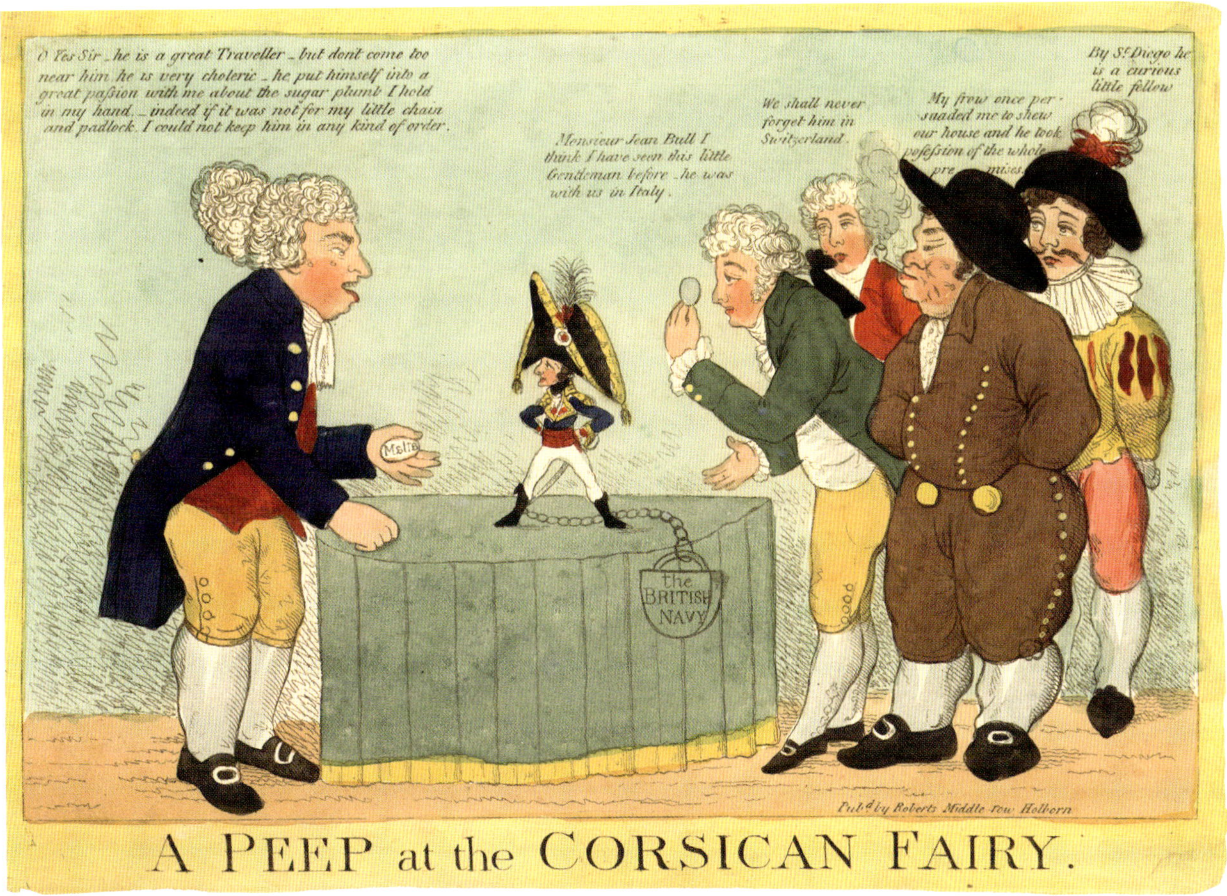

Amusement after Dinner, or The Corsican Fairy displaying his Prowels!

A PEEP at the CORSICAN FAIRY.

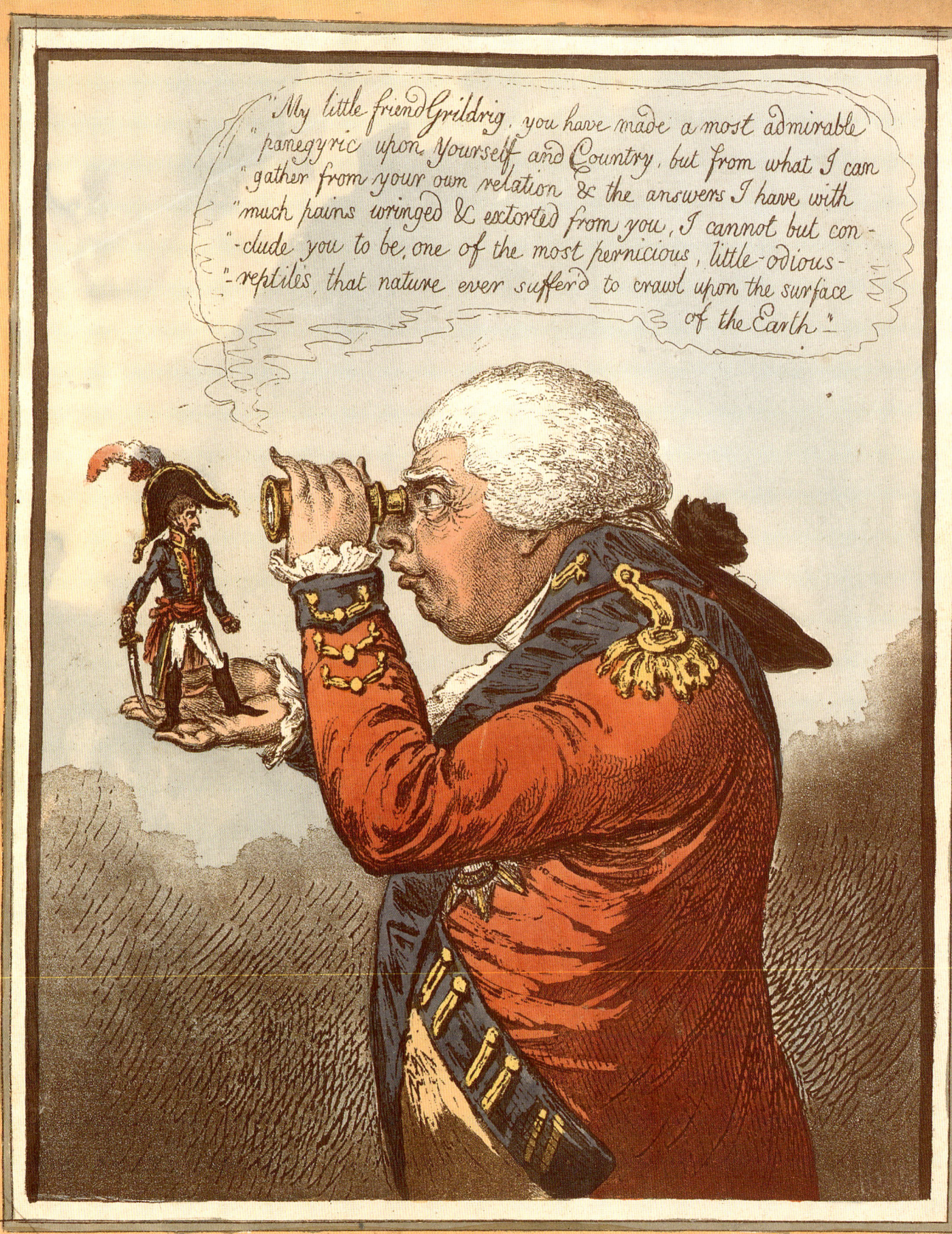

The KING of BROBDINGNAG, and GULLIVER.

_ Vide. Swift's Gulliver: Voyage to Brobdingnag

59

Designed by Lt. Col. Thomas Braddyll (1776–1862); etched by James Gillray (1756–1815)

The King of Brobdingnag and Gulliver

Hand-coloured etching, 30.3 x 24.3 cm (subject)
Published 26 June 1803 by Hannah Humphrey
Curzon b.4(22)
BMC 10019

60

William Charles (d. 1820)

Gulliver and his guide, or a check string to the Corsican

Hand-coloured etching, 21.5 x 33.7 cm (subject)
Published August 1803
Curzon b.4(41)
BMC 10051

The pose of the King is copied from Gillray's print, 'The King of Brobdingnag and Gulliver' (No. 59). Napoleon's guide is Jack Tar, the typical English sailor. He speaks in naval slang and recites a bit of Thomas Dibdin's song, *The tight little island*, from *The British Raft*, a musical play produced during the first invasion scare of 1797–8.

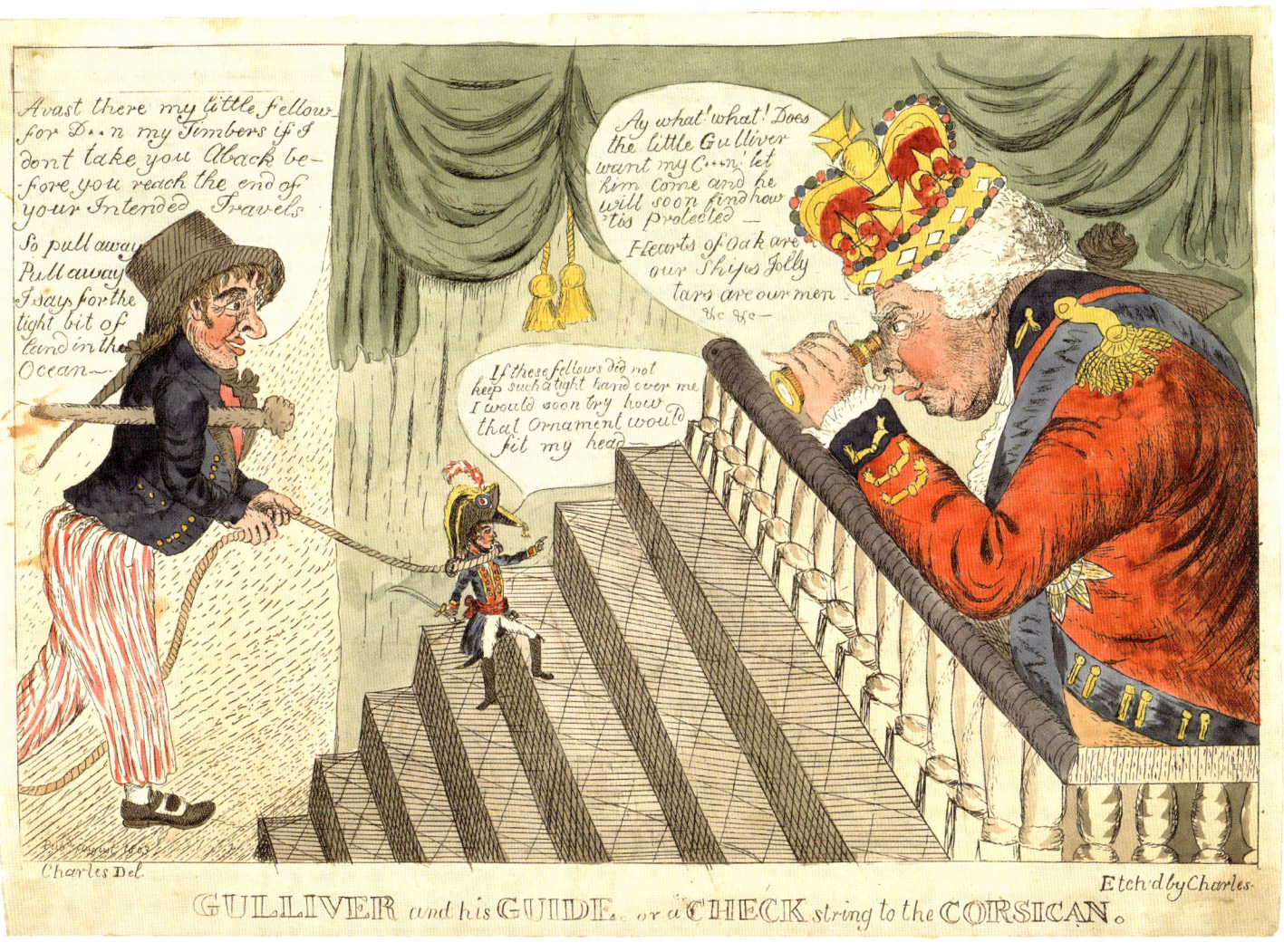

61

The Corsican Cesar presented to Mr. and Mrs. Bull!!

Hand-coloured etching, 22.4 x 33.4 cm (subject)
Published December 1803 by W. Holland
Curzon b.4(64)

62

The coffin expedition or Boney's invincible armada half seas over

Hand-coloured etching, 22.5 x 33.6 cm (subject)
Published 6 January 1804 by S. W. Fores
John Johnson Collection: French Wars and
Revolutions folder 5 (Db9)

Any French invasion required at least
temporary control of the Channel, as
Napoleon acknowledged. As winter
deepened, the prospects looked worse
for a French attempt.

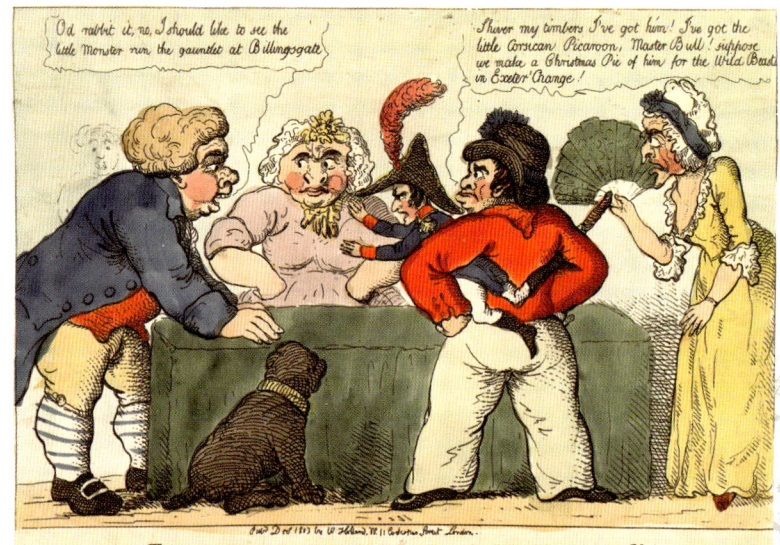

THE CORSICAN CESAR presented to Mr & Mrs BULL!!

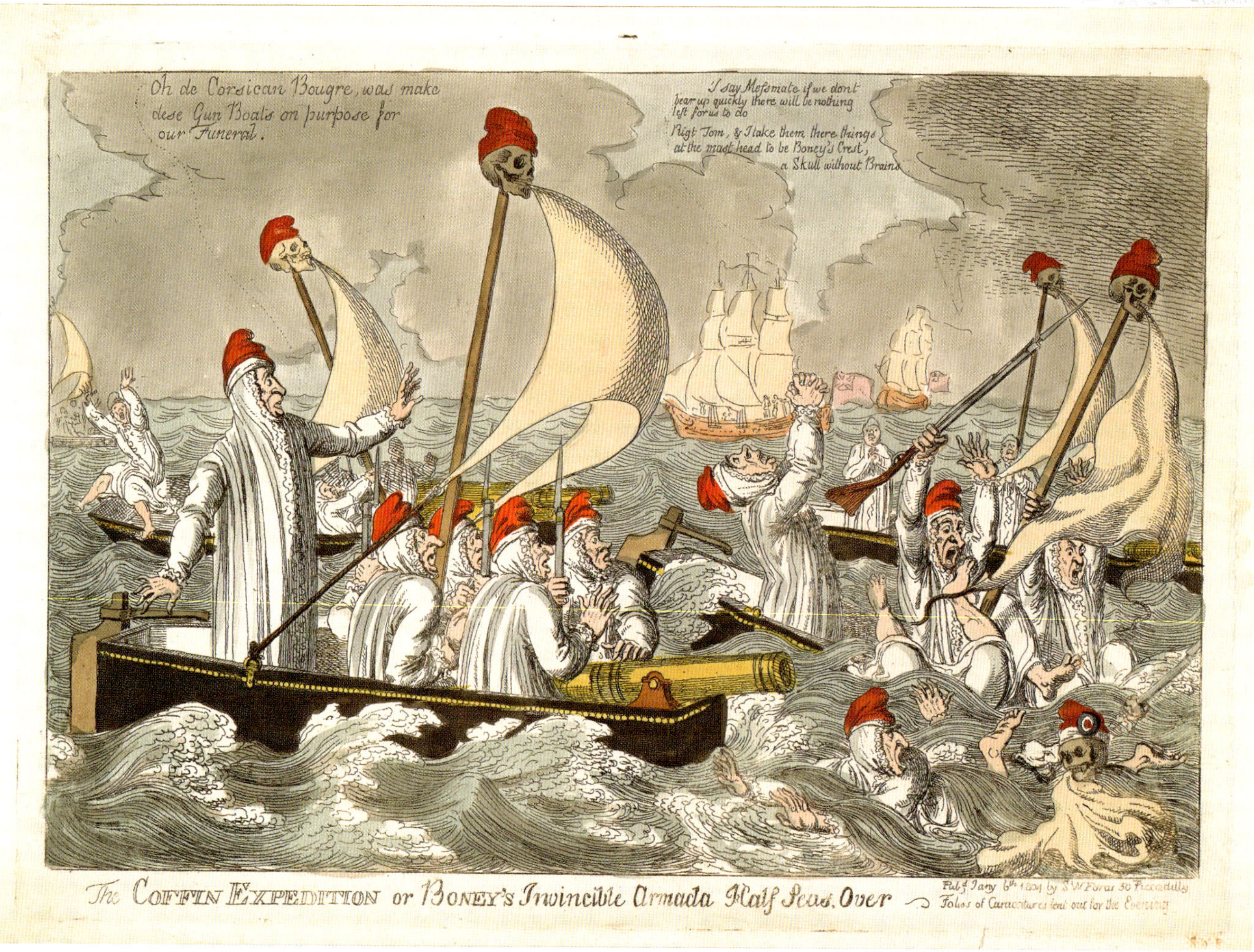

The COFFIN EXPEDITION or BONEY's Invincible Armada Half Seas Over

Imagining 'La Descente en Angleterre'

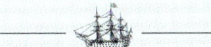

Radical agitation was a real concern in 1803, when events seemed to prove the continued underground existence of republican societies. The previous November, Government spies had uncovered a conspiracy to seize the Tower of London and the Bank of England, and to assassinate the King. The leader, Edward Despard, was linked to English and Irish republican groups. In 1803 a desperate rebellion in Ireland, led by Robert Emmet, was crushed. Emmet and Despard and their followers were executed for treason. The reformist politician Francis Burdett was caricatured as a sympathizer of these movements in another print, 'The Crown and Anchor Despar(d)ado' (8 August 1803, BMC 10054), after a speech denying the patriotic duty of Britons to serve in a war on behalf of the ministry he opposed.

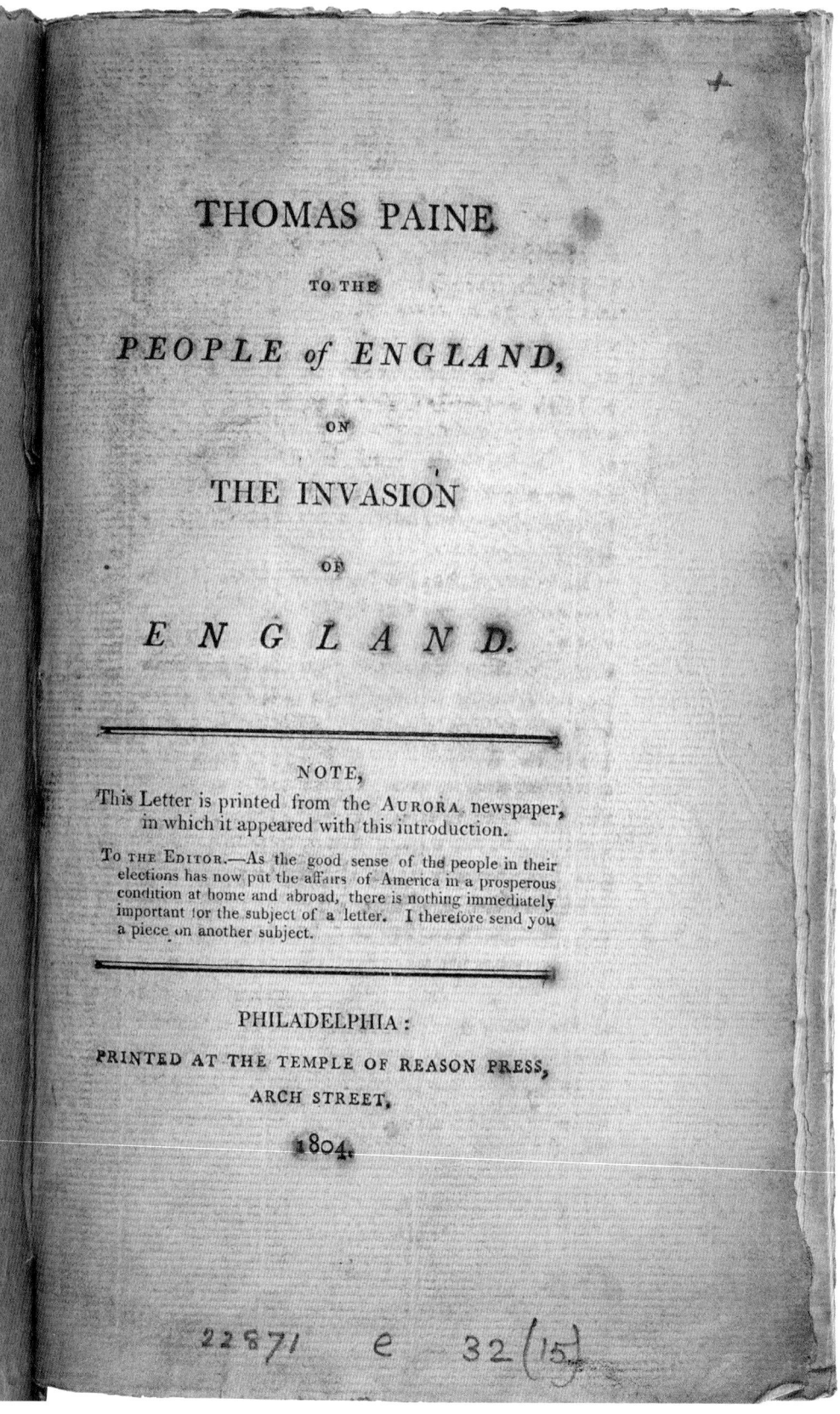

THOMAS PAINE

TO THE

PEOPLE of ENGLAND,

ON

THE INVASION

OF

ENGLAND.

NOTE,

This Letter is printed from the AURORA newspaper, in which it appeared with this introduction.

TO THE EDITOR.—As the good sense of the people in their elections has now put the affairs of America in a prosperous condition at home and abroad, there is nothing immediately important for the subject of a letter. I therefore send you a piece on another subject.

PHILADELPHIA:

PRINTED AT THE TEMPLE OF REASON PRESS,

ARCH STREET,

1804.

22871 e 32 (15)

63

Thomas Paine, **To the people of England, on the invasion of England**
Philadelphia, Temple of Reason Press, 1804
22871 e.32(15)

Paine remarked bitterly that the Government had not trusted Britons to read his book, *The Rights of Man*, without turning to treason in 1792, yet in 1803 relied on patriotic fervour to preserve the King and constitution.

By the experiment of raising the country in mass the government have put arms into the hands of men whom they would have sent to Botany Bay but a few months before, had they found a pike in their possession (p. 15).

The imprint 'Temple of Reason Press' may shield a printer hesitant to put his own name on a pamphlet by Paine, who was by 1804 a controversial figure, even in America, for his radicalism and atheism.

64

Medals of the *'Descente en Angleterre'*

Medals 'commemorating' the intended invasion were intended to infuse his own army with vigour and frighten the English. Their novelty value made them collectors' items in England after the war. These medals were inspired in their use of miniaturization. Perhaps the most extreme example is that depicting the Camp at Boulogne, in which the geometric dimensions of the Camp are displayed, numbered and carefully footnoted – no small achievement in a coin of 41mm diameter!

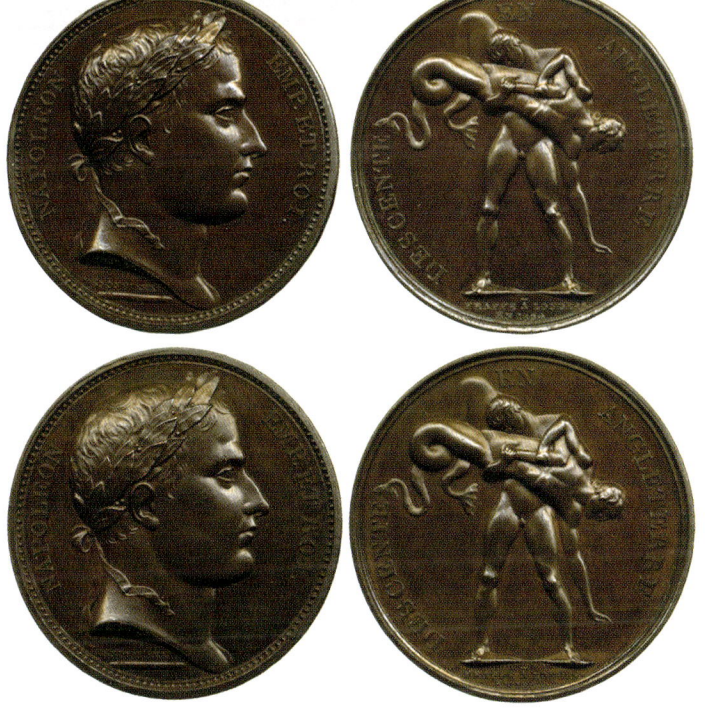

64a

Mudie; copy made in England of a French medal by J. P. Droz
Obverse: Head of Napoleon in right profile, crowned with a laurel wreath: NAPOLEON EMP.ET ROI
Reverse: Hercules crushing the giant Antaeus by lifting him in the air: DESCENTE EN ANGLETERRE
In exergue: FRAPPÉ A LONDRES 1804

The original cast was made in Paris under Napoleon's instructions and designed by Droz. Few medals were struck and few survived. Copies of the medals, such as these, became prized collectors' items after the conclusion of the war.
Bronze, 41 mm
Ashmolean Museum (Douce Collection)

64b

L. Bramsen: copy made in England of a French medal by J.P. Droz.
Bronze, 41 mm
Ashmolean Museum (M. H. Grant)

64c

L. Bramsen, F. Jeuffroy and Denon

Obverse: Above, plan of Boulogne Camp in semi-circular layout, with reference numbers. Below, SERMENT DE L'ARMEE. D'ANGLETERRE/ A L'EMPEREUR NAPOLEON

No 1. CAVALLERIE 2. INFANTERIE/ 3. GÉNÉRAUX. 4. DRAPEAUX. 5 LÉ/GIONNAIRRE. 6 GARDE DE L'EMPER^EUR. 7 MUSICI^ENS ET T^ROUPS 8.ET M^OR D^SC^S 9. R^TM^ORC^AL. 10 LE TRONE

Reverse: Emperor Napoleon awarding medals to four soldiers: HONNEUR LEGIONAIRE AUX BRAVES DE L'ARMÉE

In exergue: A BOULOGNE LE XXVIII THERM. AN XII. XVI AOUT MDCCCI. Signed Denon D. Jeuffroy F.

Bronze, 41 mm

Ashmolean Museum (Sir W. Calverley Trevelyan bequest)

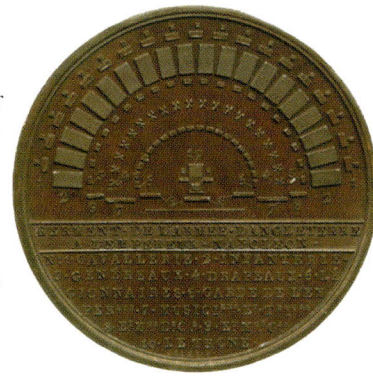 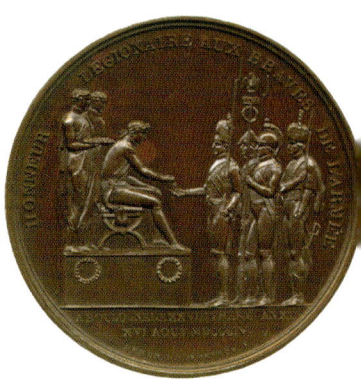

64d

L. Bramsen, Andrieu et Brenet

Obverse: Head of Napoleon identical to 64a

Reverse: Eagle robed, with tokens of war: L'EMPEREUR COMMANDE LA GRANDE ARMÉE

In exergue: LEVEE DU CAMP DU BOULOGNE LE XXIV AOUT MDCCCV/ PASSAGE DU RHIN LE XXV SEP^BER MDCCCV

Bronze, 40mm

Ashmolean Museum (R. Finch bequest)

This medal commemmorates the disbandment of the Boulougne camp as Napoleon's attention turned to war in the east, with the crossing of the Rhine in September 1805.

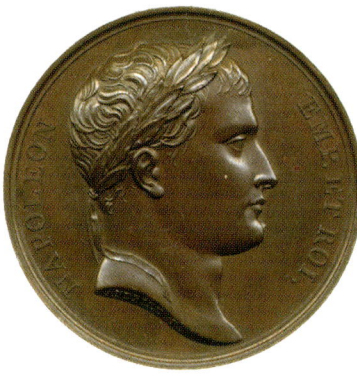 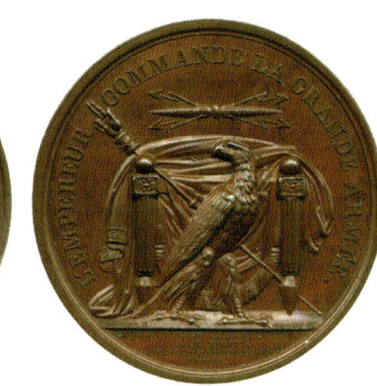

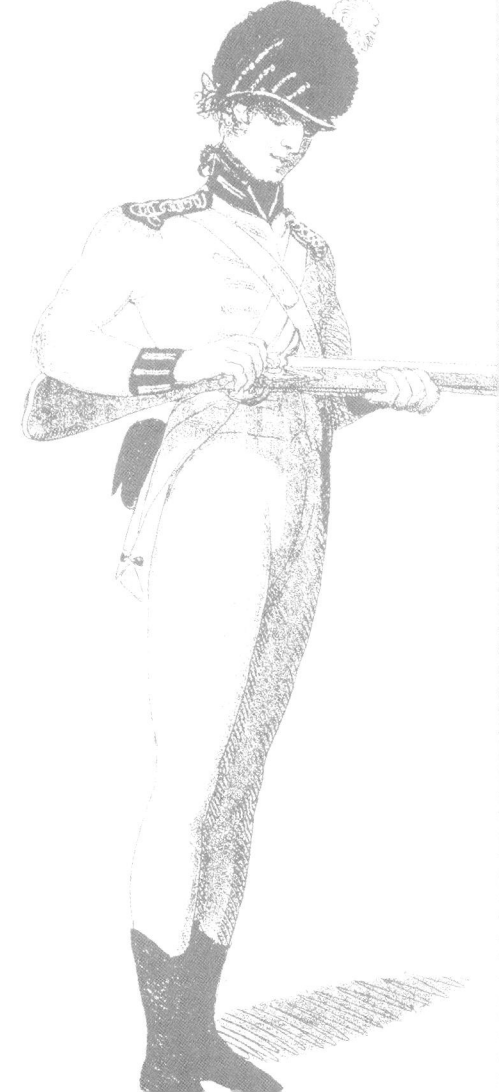

Loyalism in Print

The variety of items represented here invited various expressions of patriotism from different audiences. Humorous cartoons and picture puzzles were intended to appeal to a popular audience, and the 'Loyalists alphabet' makes patriotism as simple as A,B,C – while flattering the viewer who can 'solve' the riddles of what each letter represents.

The book of plates by Thomas Rowlandson, meanwhile, was a lavish production intended, its publisher wrote, as a monument 'to the credit of those Volunteer Corps, who, in the moments of alarm and of imminent dangers, so readily and honourably stood forward, at their own expense, to assist the Civil Magistrates, and to preserve the tranquillity of this Great and Commercial Emporium; and to defend the Property of their less qualified neighbours from the ruffian hands of interested depredators, and from the malicious schemes of disloyalty.' The emphasis here was on civic duty – and display.

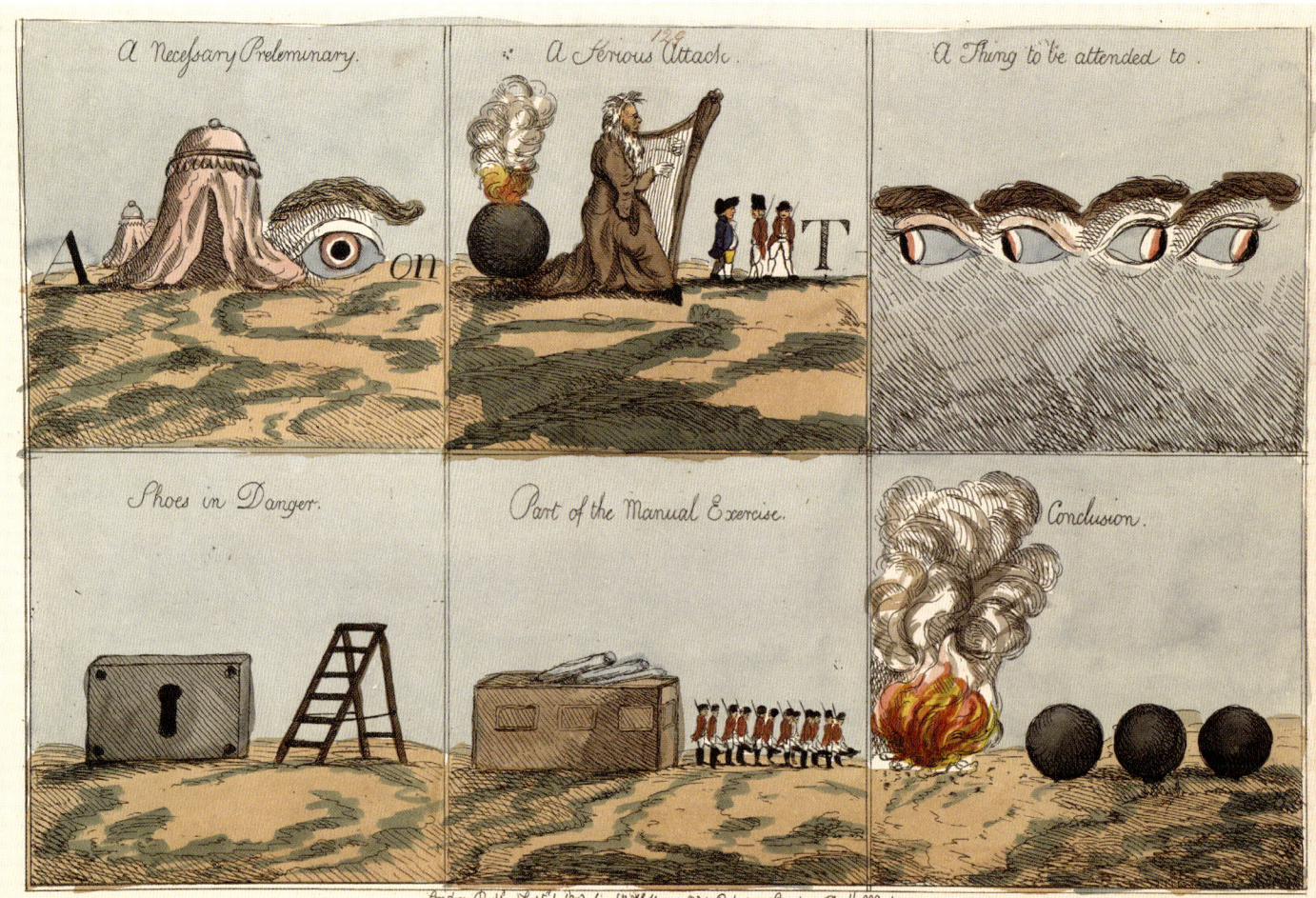

65

Puzzles for volunteers!!

Hand-coloured etching, 22 x 33.4 cm (platemark)
Published 1 September 1803 by William Holland
Curzon b.12(2)

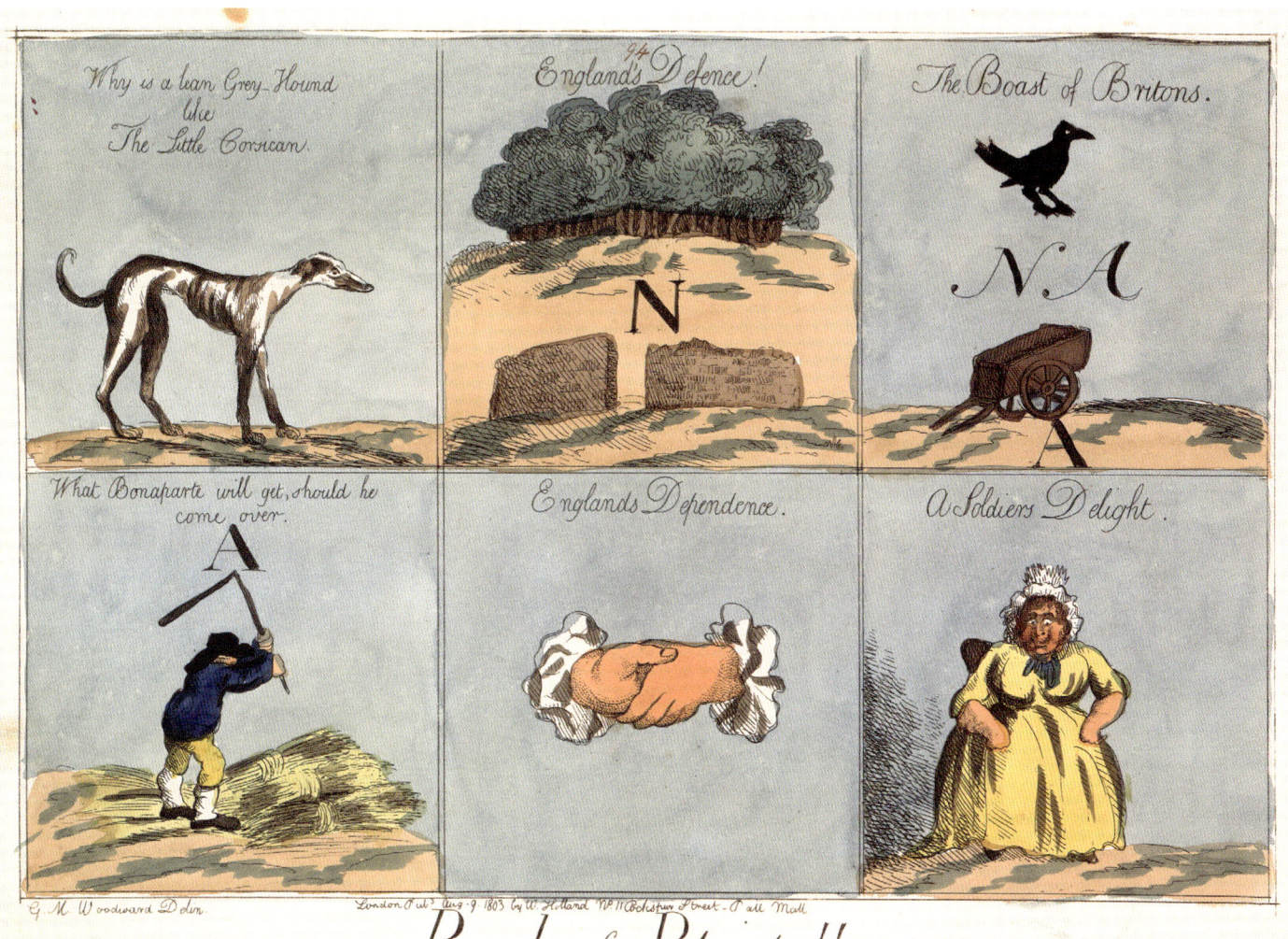

66

George M. Woodward (1760?–1809)
Puzzles for patriots!!
Hand-coloured etching 25 x 35 cm (platemark)
Published 9 August 1803 by William Holland
Curzon b.12(53)

67

James Bisset
The loyalists alphabet
Hand-coloured etching 34.9 x 23.4 cm (sheet)
Published 3 September 1804 by Laurie & Whittle
John Johnson Collection: French Wars and Revolutions folder 6 (10)
BMC 10276

'I' is for invasion – a fear now consigned to the past,
according to this print, although the continued threat
inspired the construction of Martello towers on British
and Irish coasts after 1804. 'J' may refer to the French
general, Junot, a staunch supporter of Napoleon. 'L'
and 'M' emphasize the antiquity of British
constitutional liberties and their link to the Church and
Crown, in contrast to French republicanism.

James Bisset (1762?–1832) was, like Gillray and
Cruikshank, a Scottish migrant to England, in his case
to Birmingham where he worked as a portraitist and
composed topical verses, as well as keeping a 'museum'
and shop selling commemorative medals of his own
designs. In 1803 he published *The Patriotic Clarion, or
Britain's Call to Glory, original Songs written on the
threatened Invasion.*

68

Thomas Rowlandson (1756–1827) (illus.)
**Loyal volunteers of London & environs,
infantry & cavalry, in their respective uniforms.
Representing the whole of the manual,
platoon, & funeral exercise, in 87 plates.
Designed & etch'd by T. Rowlandson**
London, R. Ackermann, 1799

Plate No. LII
Langbourne Ward Volunteers
Reproduced by kind permission of the governing body of Trinity
College, Oxford

The Langbourne Ward Volunteer Corps was formed in
May 1798, Sir John Eamer, Knight and Alderman, in
the Chair, when they resolved to furnish themselves
with Arms and Clothing at their own expence; and that
is be understood the persons forming this Association
are not to be considered as enlisted Soldiers, but as
Citizens, learning the use of Arms for the sole purpose
to protecting their own Property, and of supporting the
Chief and other Magistrates, in case of Invasion,
Rebellion, Insurrection, Riot, &c.

A similarly forthright statement of the inspiration
behind volunteering came from the Union Volunteers,
covering part of Tower Hamlets, who vowed to 'protect
our Liberties and Properties, but also to defend our
invaluable Constitution (consisting of King, Lords, and
Commons) under which we live, from all the attacks of
its avowed and secret enemies'. The plates by
Rowlandson show volunteers in uniforms of the
different corps performing moves from the drill.

The printed list of subscribers to this book included
George III and his sons, and the directors of the East
India Company, as well as foreign monarchs. The
publisher Rudolph Ackermann (1764–1834) was born
in Saxony and worked as an artist and printseller before
establishing a business on the Strand in London. The
firm became well known for producing fine art prints
and illustrated books. Rowlandson also contributed
plates to Ackermann's popular serial publication, the
Repository of Arts, Literature, Fashions, Manufactures, &c.

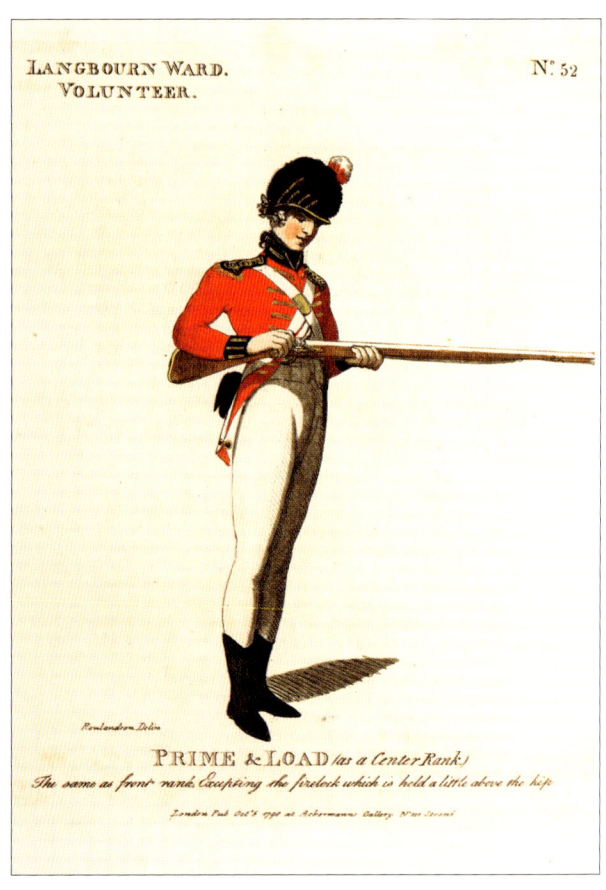

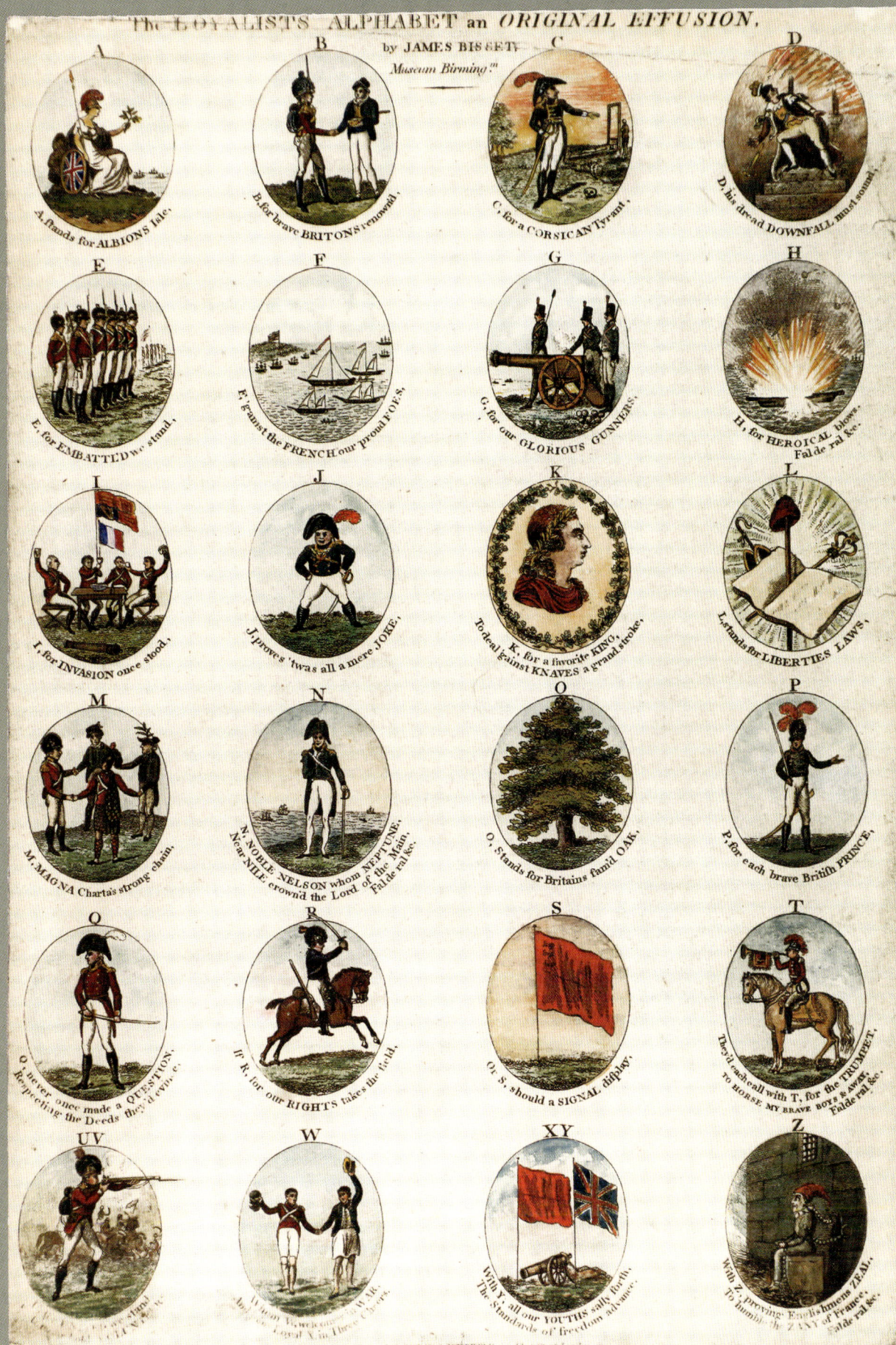

The LOYALIST'S ALPHABET an ORIGINAL EFFUSION.
by JAMES BISSET.
Museum Birming.m

A, stands for ALBIONS Isle.

B, for brave BRITONS renown'd.

C, for a CORSICAN Tyrant.

D, his dread DOWNFALL must sound.

E, for EMBATTED we stand.

F, 'gainst the FRENCH our proud FOES.

G, for our GLORIOUS GUNNERS.

H, for HEROICAL blows.
Falde ral &c.

I, for INVASION once stood.

J, proves 'twas all a mere JOKE.

K, for a favorite KING,
To deal 'gainst KNAVES a grand stroke.

L, stands for LIBERTIES LAWS.

M, MAGNA Charta's strong chain.

N, NOBLE NELSON whom NEPTUNE,
Near NILE crown'd the Lord, of the Main.
Falde ral&c.

O, Stands for Britains fam'd OAK.

P, for each brave British PRINCE.

Q never once made a QUESTION,
Respecting the Deeds they'd evince.

R, for our RIGHTS takes the field.

Or, S, should a SIGNAL display.

They'd each call with T, for the TRUMPET,
TO HORSE MY BRAVE BOYS & AWAY.
Falde ral &c.

U V

W, Whom Volunteers in W.W.
And Loyal N. in Three Cheers.

X Y, all our YOUTHS sally forth,
The Standards of freedom advance.

With Z, proving Englishmens ZEAL,
To humble the ZANY of France.
Falde ral &c.

69

Jack Junk's new jester, or Bony taken in tow in a new way (?1807)

London, J. Ker, [1807]
Harding E 242(2)

The jokes and anecdotes in this chapbook were ostensibly directed at sailors. One concerns a dream of 'Jack Junk' who imagined Bonaparte cornered by a bulldog while attempting an invasion of England.

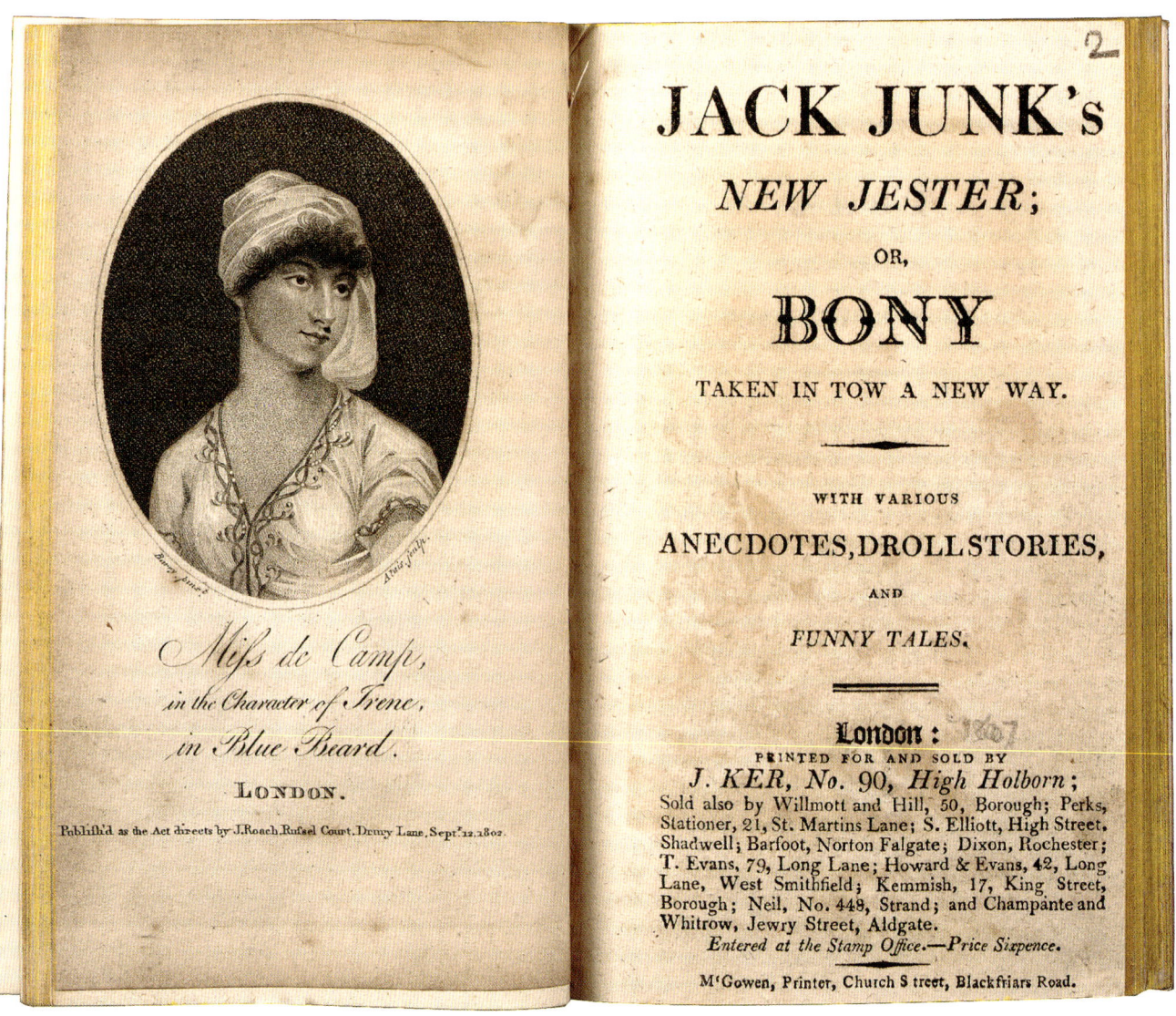

Miss de Camp, in the Character of Irene, in Blue Beard. LONDON.

Publish'd as the Act directs by J. Roach, Russel Court, Drury Lane, Sept.r 12. 1802.

JACK JUNK's
NEW JESTER;
OR,
BONY
TAKEN IN TOW A NEW WAY.

WITH VARIOUS
ANECDOTES, DROLL STORIES,
AND
FUNNY TALES.

London :
PRINTED FOR AND SOLD BY
J. KER, No. 90, High Holborn;
Sold also by Willmott and Hill, 50, Borough; Perks, Stationer, 21, St. Martins Lane; S. Elliott, High Street, Shadwell; Barfoot, Norton Falgate; Dixon, Rochester; T. Evans, 79, Long Lane; Howard & Evans, 42, Long Lane, West Smithfield; Kemmish, 17, King Street, Borough; Neil, No. 448, Strand; and Champante and Whitrow, Jewry Street, Aldgate.
Entered at the Stamp Office.—Price Sixpence.

M'Gowen, Printer, Church Street, Blackfriars Road.

Napoleon's Career 1

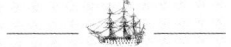

1798: Ambition

Napoleon led an expedition to Egypt
in 1798, designed to extend France's
colonial power and to demonstrate the
intellectual advances made possible by
the French Revolution. Admiral
Nelson's victory at the battle of the
Nile in August 1798 cut off the
French Army and resulted in
Napoleon's withdrawal from Egypt.

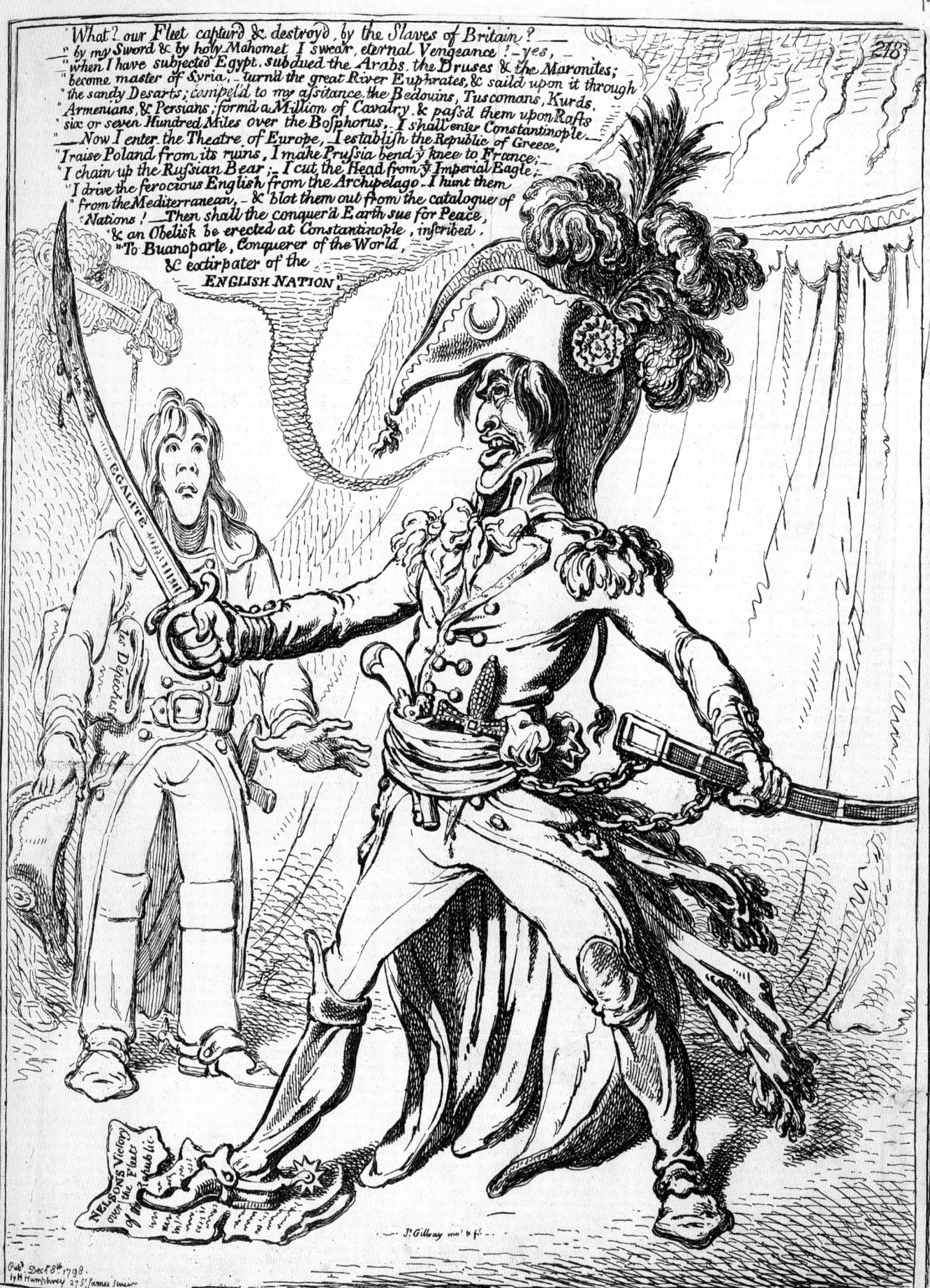

BUONAPARTE, hearing of Nelson's Victory, swears by his Sword, to Extirpate the English from off the Earth.
See Buonaparte's Speech to the French Army at Cairo; published by authority of the Directory, in Volney's Letters.

70

James Gillray (1756–1815)
Buonaparte hearing of Nelson's victory
Etching, 33.4 x 25.2 cm (subject)
Published 8 December 1798 by Hannah Humphrey
Curzon b.20(179r)
BMC 9278

Napoleon's speech is paraphrased from an article by one of his supporters, predicting French success in Egypt and promising that Napoleon would follow this with an entry onto the 'Theatre of Europe'.

71

Plan of the Battle of the Nile on the 1st of Augt. 1798 by the late R. W. Miller, Esqr. Captain of H.M.S. Theseus
25 x 20 cm (sheet)
Curzon b.18(34)

This plan shows Nelson's tactic of 'turning the line', by attacking the French squadron at right angles rather than broadside to broadside.

72

Medals of the French Egyptian expedition and the Battle of the Nile

(1798)

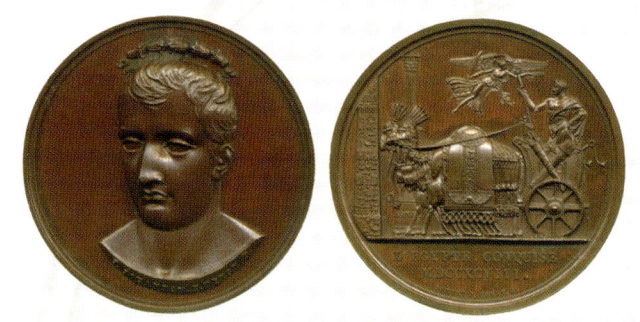

72a

J. Jouannin (obv.) and Brenet (rev.)
Obverse: Head of Napoleon wreathed in laurel
Reverse: Manned chariot pulled by camels; obelisk and column in left background; Nike above centre: L'EGYPT CONQUISE/MDCCXCVIII [sign. Brenet. F. Denon D.]
Bronze, 40.5 mm
Ashmolean Museum (Douce collection)

72b

[Another copy]
Ashmolean Museum (R. Finch bequest)

72c

T. Wyon Sr.
Obverse: Bust of Napoleon: NAPILONE BUONAPARTE, GENERAL OF THE FRENCH ARMY IN EGYPT
Reverse: Tokens of war in front of pyramids
In exergue: LANDED AT ALEXANDRIA/ JULY 2 1798/ MDCCXCIX
Bronze, 38.5mm
Ashmolean Museum (M.H. Grant)

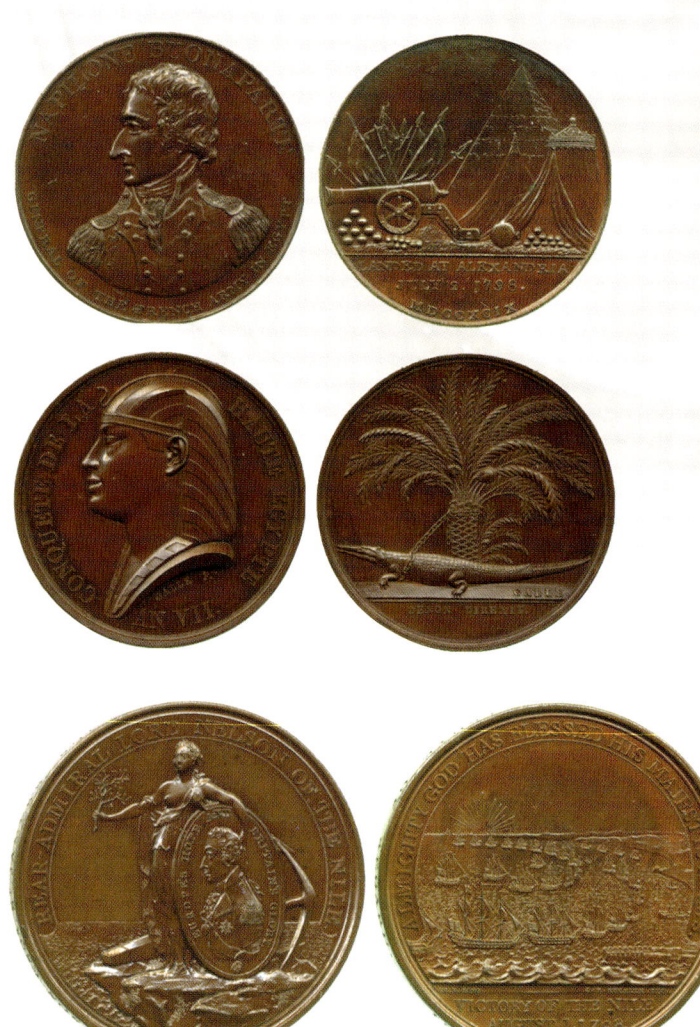

72d

Jouannin, Brenet and Denon
Obverse: Egyptian head. Signed Galle. Inscription below, CONQUETE DE LA HAUTE EGYPTE AN VII
Reverse: Crocodile chained to palm tree, signed Galle
In exergue: DENON DIREXIT
Bronze, 37mm
Ashmolean Museum (Sir W. Calverley Trevelyan bequest)

72e

C.H. Kuchler, struck by M. Boulton
Obverse: Peace holding an olive branch and leaning on a shield bearing a profile bust of Nelson and the inscription EUROPE'S HOPE AND BRITAIN'S GLORY. REAR-ADMIRAL LORD NELSON OF THE NILE. [Signed CHK on rock]

Reverse: Scene of naval battle of Aboukir Bay, the French at anchor, the English fleet going into action: ALMIGHTY GOD HAS BLESSED HIS MAJESTY'S ARMS

In exergue: VICTORY OF THE NILE/AUGUST 1. 1798. Signed M.B. Soho C. H. Küchler, Fec.
Edge inscribed: FROM ALEX^R DAVISON, ESQ^R St JAMES SQUARE – A TRIBUTE OF REGARD

Bronze, 48mm
Ashmolean Museum (M. H. Grant)

72f

[Another copy, in gilt]
(Reverse)
Ashmolean Museum (M. H. Grant)

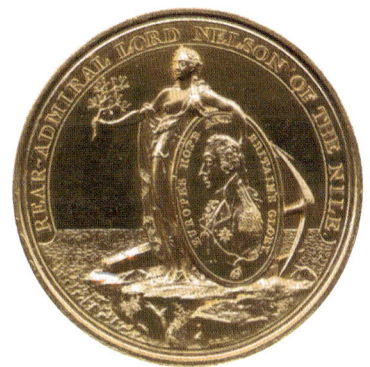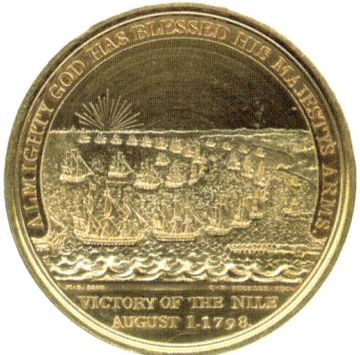

Alexander Davison was appointed by Nelson as the sole prize agent for the ships captured at Aboukir Bay. He had these medals struck from the profits and distributed them to members of the ships' companies; copies in precious metals were for the senior officers.

72g

T. Wyon

Obverse: Bust of Horatio Nelson in three-quarter profile portrait: ADMIRAL LORD NELSON OF THE NILE. Below: BRITAIN'S GLORY & DEFENCE

Reverse: Three ships engaged in battle ALMIGHTY GOD HAS BLESSED HIS MAJESTY'S ARMS

In exergue: FRENCH FLEET DEFEATED/ AUGUST 1. 1798

Bronze, 38mm
Ashmolean Museum (Muirhead transf.)

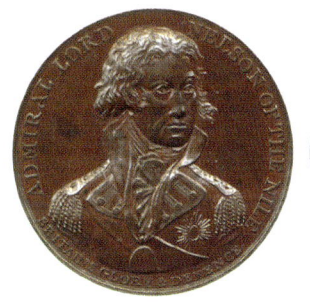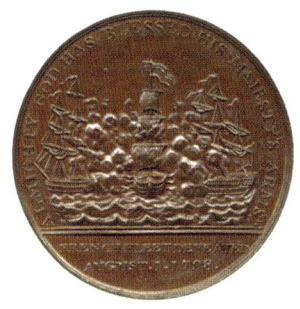

72h

T. Wyon Sr

Obverse: Victory seated holding a plaque with the bust of Lord Nelson, a lion, palm tree and harp, before a pyramid: VIRTUTE NIHIL OBSTAT & ARMIS (nothing withstands valour and arms)

In exergue: VICTORY OF THE NILE/ AUG^T 1 1798

Reverse: A shield and foul anchor on which: NOV 29 LAUS DEO 1798. Above: SUB HOC SIGNO VINCES (under this sign thou shalt conquer)

Bronze, 38mm
Ashmolean Museum (Keble College loan)

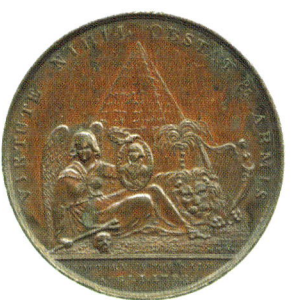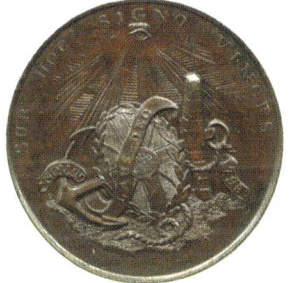

73

Representation of the defeat of a squadron of French ships under the command of Admiral Brueys, by a squadron of English ships under the command of Admiral Nelson of [sic] Bay Aboukir on the 1 August 1798

Hand-coloured aquatint and etching, 43.1 x 57.4 cm (sheet)
Engraved by Frederick Weber
Published [1798] by S. Tessari &
Fr. Weber
Curzon b.18(17)

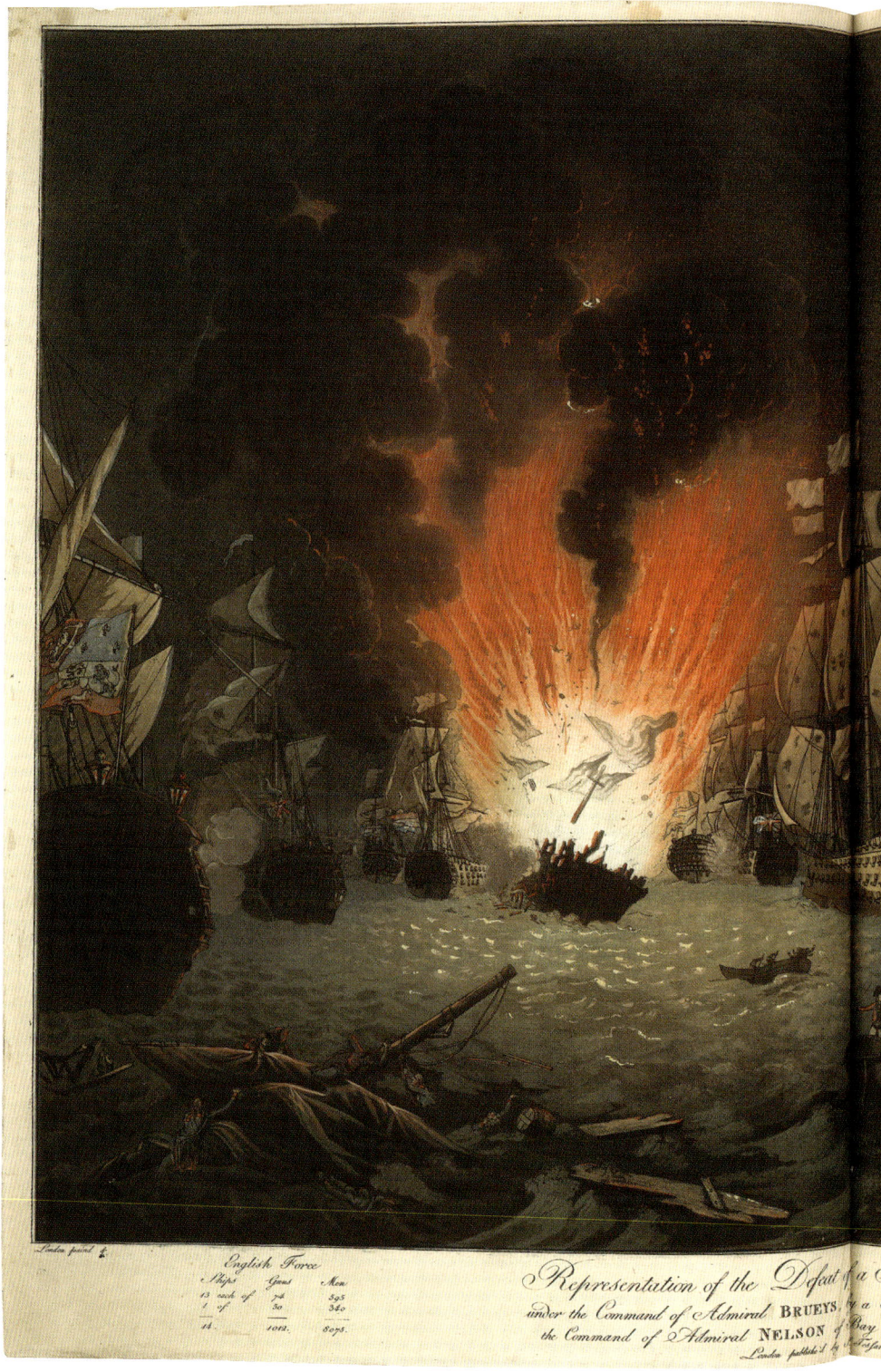

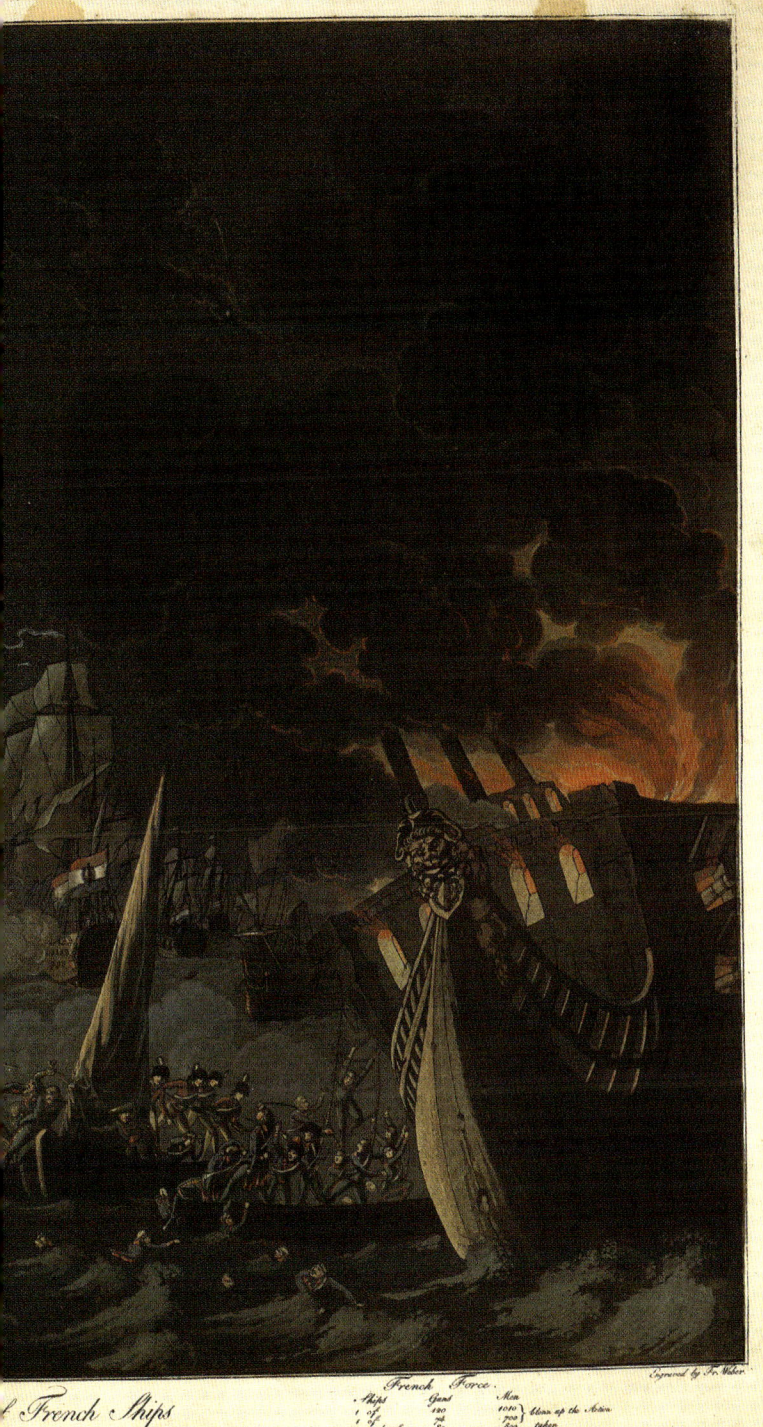

French Ships

...nglish Ships under

...e 1 August 1798.

Engraved by Fr. Weber

French Force.

Ships	Guns	Men	
1 of	120	1010	blown up the Action
1 of	74	700	taken
4 each of	80	800	taken
7 of	74	700	
1 each of	44	300	escaped
3 each of	36	250	blown up the Action
17	1186	10810	

1803: Reputation

Despite his retreat from Egypt, Napoleon had sufficient support in Paris to carry off the coup on Eighteenth Brumaire Year VII (10 November 1799) by which he became First Consul. His detractors, both the British themselves and French emigrés in Britain, continued to circulate the stories which comprised the 'Black Legend', of atrocities during the Egyptian campaign.

A SECOND DIALOGUE

BETWEEN

BUONAPARTE

AND

JOHN BULL

SCENE.---CALAIS.

Buonaparte. HOW do you do, Monfieur *Anglois?*

John. What's that to you?

Buon. Nay, John, don't be angry.

John. Angry! I am angry, and I will be angry.

Buon. But ftill, John, a little Civility to your Betters------

John. Betters! And pray who are my Betters!---Not fuch a Vil-----

Buon. There! there! Now you are going to be rude again. I hate Rudenefs. You look like a fenfible Man; cannot you and I difcufs this Matter coolly?

John. I have nothing to difcufs with you :---Keep out of my Reach, I advife you.

Buon. One Moment, my dear Friend. You feem hurt at the Word BETTERS. For myfelf, indeed, I have no Vanity of any Kind; and yet, when you confider my Atchievements----------

John. Name them!

Buon. The Battle of Lodi----------

John. What! Where, with equal Ignorance and Barbarity, you facrificed Six Thoufand of your beft Troops in forcing a Pafs, which you might have taken, by croffing a few Furlongs above, without the Lofs of a Man!

Buon. The Storming of Alexandria, then-------

John. There, indeed, the Sacrifice was lefs*. But is it not a pitiful Vanity in you to boaft of ftorming a Place without a Garrifon, and open on every Side? And why do you fupprefs all Mention of the Maffacre which took Place there, when your brutal Soldiery, BY YOUR ORDERS, entered the Mofques, which were filled with defencelefs Citizens, and " FOR THE SPACE OF FOUR HOURS," in the Words of one of your own Officers, " *indifcriminately put to the Sword,* MEN, WOMEN, AND CHILDREN AT THE BREAST!"

Buon. You are always fo warm. If you would but take Time for Reflection, you would perceive that this MASSACRE, (as you perverfely call it,) was an Act of Mercy.

John. MERCY!

Buon. Yes, John, Mercy. It was calculated to ftrike Terror into the Enemy, and prevent the Neceffity of recurring to fuch Meafures in future.

John. But when the Example had operated, and FOUR THOUSAND Turks furrendered, you ftill had Recourfe to the fame Act of " MERCY," and SAVAGELY BUTCHERED THEM ALL, IN COLD BLOOD. Where was the " NECESSITY" of this?

Buon. I wifh you would come a little nearer: I really do not hear you.

John. I believe you:---but I will fpeak louder. It was MERCY, then, that induced you to POISON your own Soldiers!

Buon. Yes, it was; and fo you will allow, when I have explained the Matter to you. But why POISON? Was it not ENDING THEIR DAYS BY A SOPORIFIC? I hate that unmannerly Way you Englifhmen have of calling every Thing by its vulgar Name.

* " We loft 150 Men, all of whom we might have faved, by only fummoning the Town." General Boyer's Difpatch.

John. And I abhor ftill worfe that deceitful Method you have of gloffing over the greateft Enormities with fpecious Titles.----But come, let me have your Explanation.

Buon. What could I do? I had 580 Men in the Hofpital. Of thefe, fome had loft an Arm, or a Leg, and were totally unferviceable; others had been badly wounded, and would have required MORE TIME THAN I COULD SPARE to cure; and not a few were labouring under temporary Blindnefs. In this Situation, a Burden and a Difgrace to their Country, I ordered them to be judicioufly dofed with Opium; and all but eleven went off as quietly as Lambs.--------

John. Stop, Sir! Do you term thofe who fuffer in fighting the Battles of their Country a Burden and a Difgrace to it? You have never been in England, and you never will come there, except as a Fugitive and a Prifoner; but if you could fee our Hofpitals of Chelfea and Greenwich you would find that we think very differently on the Subject. A Soldier or a Sailor, who has fhed his Blood in the Service of his Country, and is requited with a comfortable Refidence for Life, in the moft magnificent Palaces in England, or perhaps in Europe, is to us an Object of heart-felt Pride and Pleafure.

Buon. I know nothing of this. You will grant, however, that MY METHOD OF PROVIDING FOR MY INVALIDS, is not fo bad as you imagined.

John. It is, perhaps, not altogether fo cruel as BURYING THEM ALIVE†; which was your conftant Practice in Italy!---but fufficiently fo, to ftigmatize you for the moft barbarous and bloody Villain that ever difgraced Humanity.

Buon. Since you are determined to keep no Meafures, Sir, I can be as plain as you. I fhall be in England foon, and if I once get upon you---

John. You will ride us to the Devil;---that I believe. I would not advife you, however, to make the Attempt: we are apt to kick and fling, and he muft be a much better Horfeman than you that could keep his Seat for a fingle Moment. You fay, I am PLAIN, and I have given you a Proof of it. For the reft, I defy the Devil and all his Works. I HAVE A KING THAT I LOVE!---God blefs him! I HAVE A COUNTRY THAT IS FREE!---God blefs that, too! and I HAVE A WILL OF MY OWN, that will make me as ftrong as Forty *French* Slaves. To conclude, Citizen, you will never get to England.

Buon. I will try, however.

John. Do, and the fooner the better.

Buon. Yes, and I will try, too, to teach YOU good Manners.

John. And I will try to teach YOU the Difference between an Englifhman and a Frenchman, of which you know nothing. You may ride THEM, if you pleafe; they are Slaves by Nature, and will carry well :--- but if you touch an Englifhman, nay, if you do but look at an Englifhman, and he does not like your Looks, he'll knock you down. You teach!----teach a Pudding's End! But I am talking when I fhould be in Action. Adieu! I am not much given to prophecy, but for once I'll venture :---Your Reign will be fhort; you will not die in your Bed; and the Devil, whom you faithfully ferve, will have you as foon as the Breath is out of your Body. Once more, Citizen Conful, adieu! We fhall never meet again in this World, nor---in the next.

Buon. Morblieu!---I fear it.   *Exeunt, different Ways.*

† Buonaparte was formally charged with throwing his wounded Soldiers into the Ditches, without Examination ! ! !—The Writer of this has feen the horrible Details which were brought forward, not long before the Firft Conful failed for Egypt, and fuppreffed for that Time by the Director Barras.

PRINTED FOR J. HATCHARD, No. 190, PICCADILLY.

Price Sixpence per Dozen.   THALES, PRINTER, OLD BOSWELL COURT.

74

A Second dialogue between Buonaparte and John Bull

John Johnson Collection: French Wars and Revolutions folder 5 (191)
Published [1803] by J. Hatchard
Hales, Printer, Old Boswell Court

In this imagined meeting, an irritable John Bull bridles at the suggestion that Napoleon is his superior:

Buonaparte: How do you do, Monsieur Anglais?
John Bull: What's that to you?
Buon. Nay, John, don't be angry.
John. Angry! I am angry, and I will be angry.
Buon. But still, John, a little civility to your Betters –
John. Betters! And pray who are my Betters! Not such a Vil –

The broadside ends with John Bull's staunch assertion of his patriotism:

John. 'I HAVE A KING THAT I LOVE! – I HAVE A COUNTRY THAT IS FREE! – and I HAVE A WILL OF MY OWN!'

75

The trial of John Peltier, Esq.

London, Cox, Son, and Baylis, 1803
80 Z 601 Jur.

Following the Treaty of Amiens, Napoleon took action against the French émigré Jean Peltier's pamphlet, *L'Ambigu*, which criticized his despotic rule as First Consul. The woodcut frontispiece was one of the offending items mentioned in the case; it shows Napoleon as a sphinx (referring to his Egyptian campaign), on a plinth inscribed SPQR, correctly prophesying Napoleon's coronation as emperor in 1804.

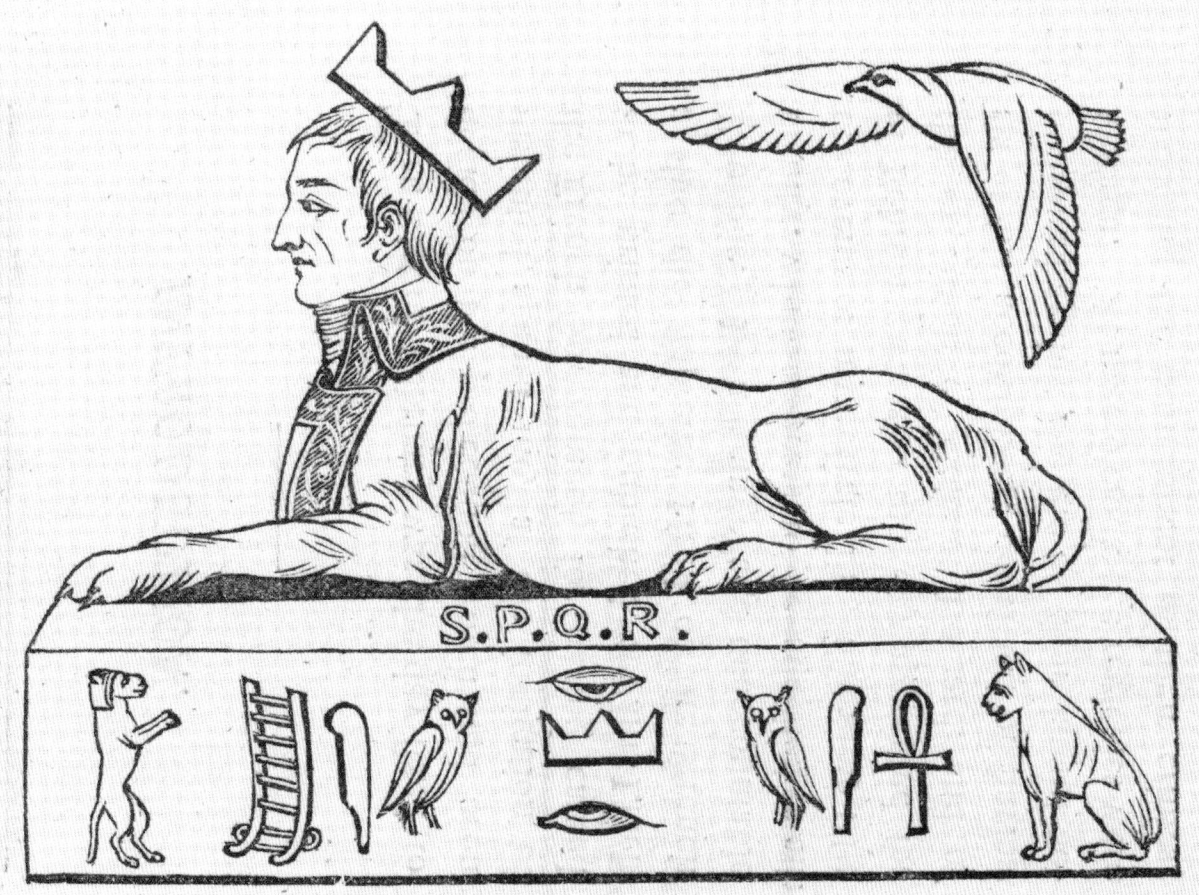

Trouvé dans les Tombeaux des Rois de Thebes,
Et réimprimé par Cox, Fils, et Baylis, Great Queen Street, Paroisse de Saint-Giles, à Londres.

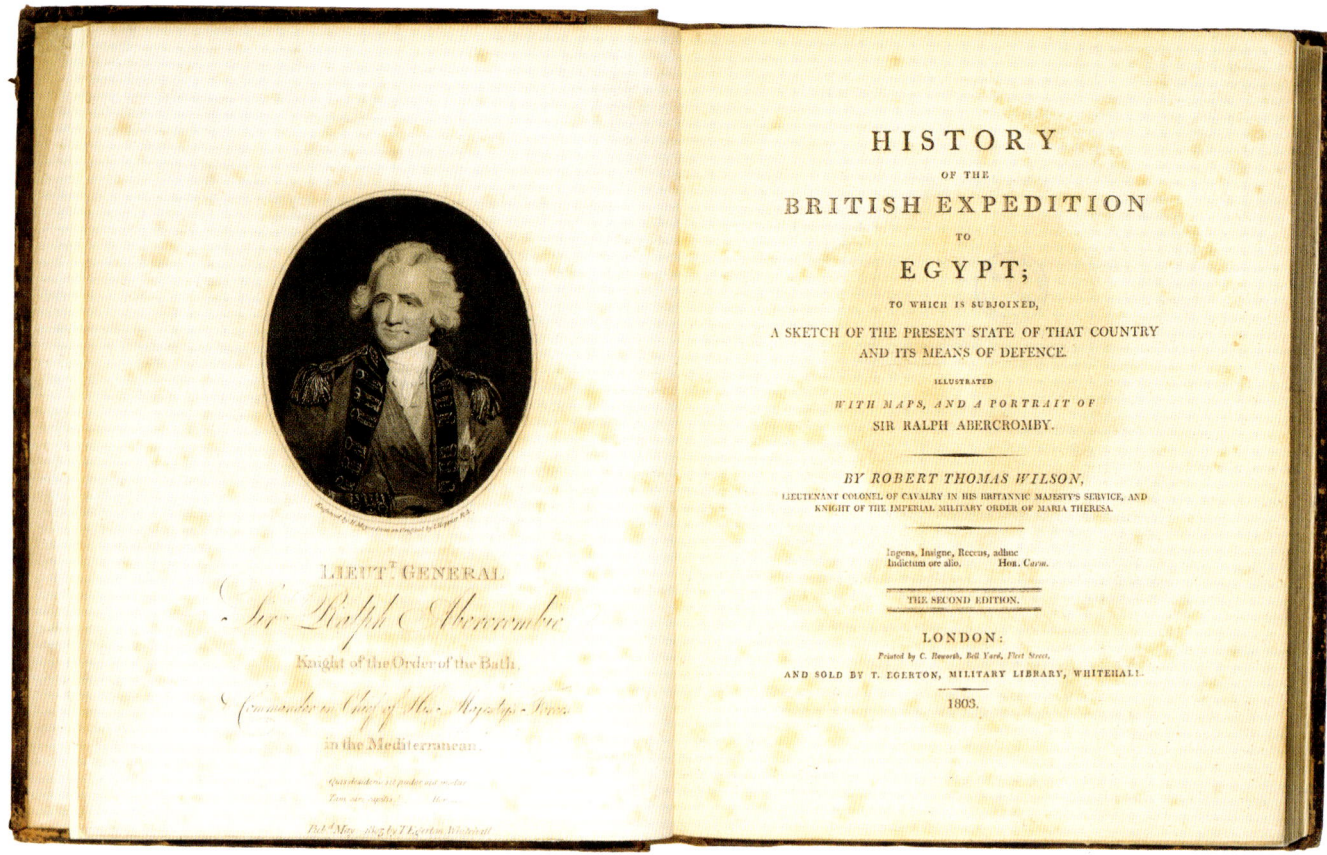

HISTORY

OF THE

BRITISH EXPEDITION

TO

EGYPT;

TO WHICH IS SUBJOINED,

A SKETCH OF THE PRESENT STATE OF THAT COUNTRY
AND ITS MEANS OF DEFENCE.

ILLUSTRATED

WITH MAPS, AND A PORTRAIT OF
SIR RALPH ABERCROMBY.

BY ROBERT THOMAS WILSON,
LIEUTENANT COLONEL OF CAVALRY IN HIS BRITANNIC MAJESTY'S SERVICE, AND
KNIGHT OF THE IMPERIAL MILITARY ORDER OF MARIA THERESA.

Ingens, Insigne, Recens, adhuc
Indictum ore alio.   Hor. Carm.

THE SECOND EDITION.

LONDON:
Printed by C. Roworth, Bell Yard, Fleet Street,
AND SOLD BY T. EGERTON, MILITARY LIBRARY, WHITEHALL.

1803.

76

Robert Thomas Wilson (1777–1849)

History of the British expedition to Egypt

(2nd ed., London: Printed by C. Roworth and sold by T. Egerton,
Military Library, Whitehall, 1803)
24676 d.45

Wilson served under General Sir Ralph Abercromby at
the Battle of Alexandria in March 1798, when
Abercromby was killed. His *History of the British
Expedition* quickly went through four editions,
including a French translation in 1803. Much attention
was paid to his descriptions of Napoleon's
mistreatment of soldiers and civilians during the
French expedition to Egypt.

Thomas Egerton's Military Library was also Jane
Austen's first publisher, producing *Sense and Sensibility*
in 1811.

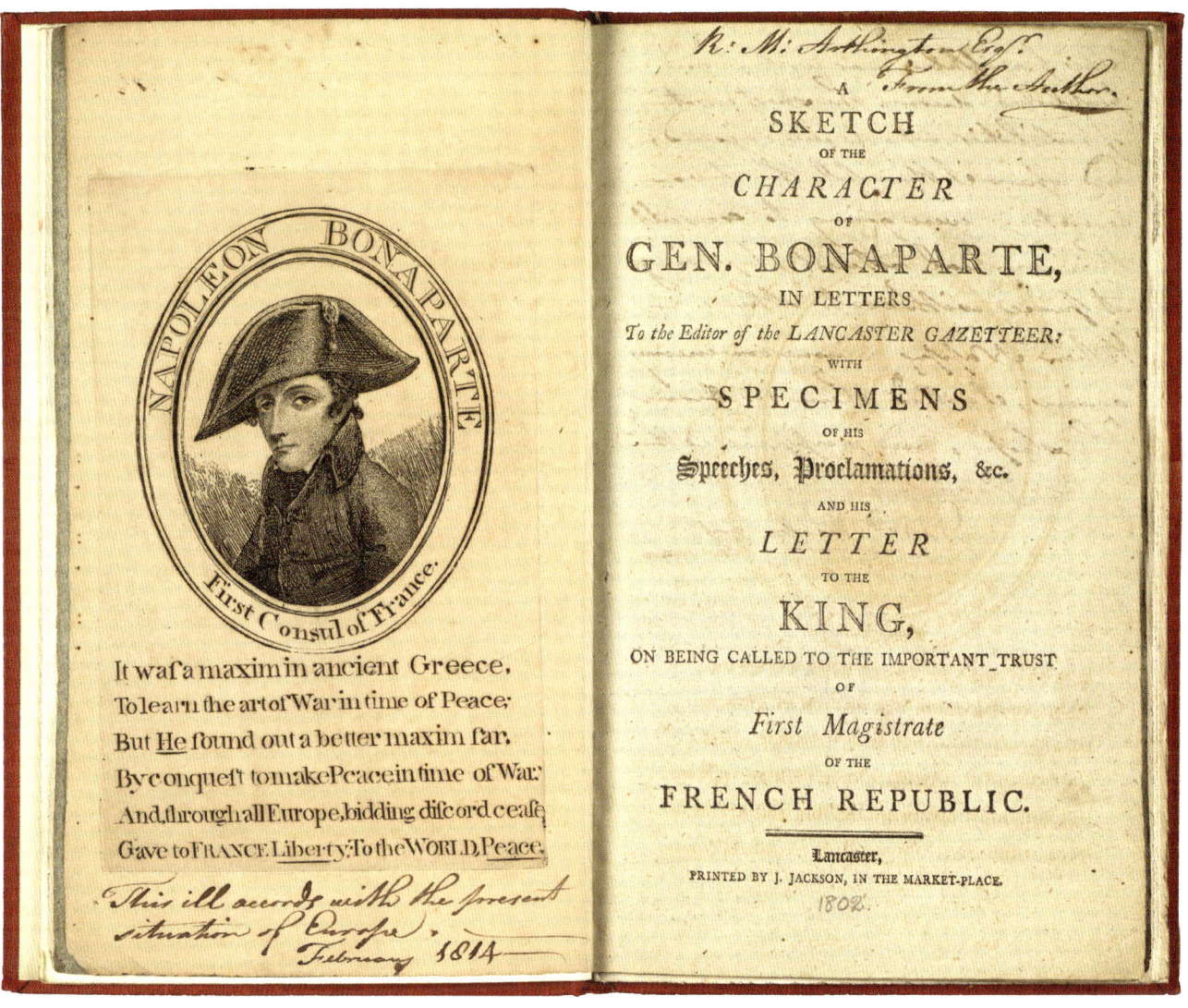

77

[D.B.P. Eccleston]
A sketch of the character of Gen. Bonaparte
Lancaster, J. Jackson [1802]
2376 e.433
With A. M. Broadley's bookplate

In these letters to a local newspaper in 1802, Eccleston attempted to defend Napoleon and to deny the charges incorporating the 'Black Legend'. The frontispiece and caption reflect the sympathetic view of Napoleon following the Peace of Amiens. This copy was part of

A. M. Broadley's collection before it was donated to the Bodleian Library by a later owner.

[MS. note by Eccleston on reverse of title page:]

This pamphlet was written and published during the short cessation of hostilities which we enjoyed, and when I thought the two countries were going to consult their mutual interest, by being at peace with each other. When Nappy became our enemy again, I called them in from the shop, and suppressed their sale.

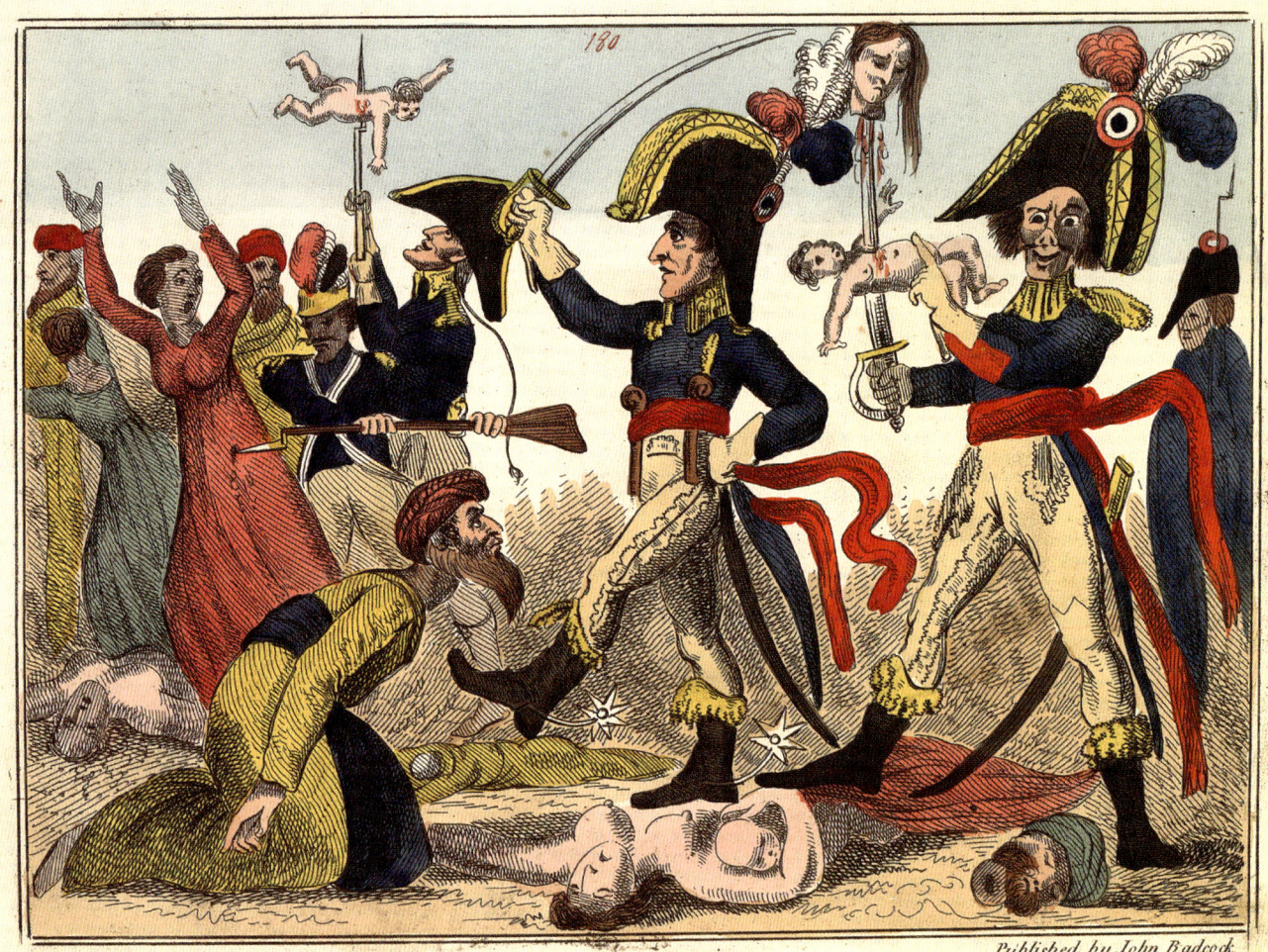

WHAT BRITONS, OUGHT TO AVOID.

The tender Mercies of Buonaparte in Egypt.

Published by John Badcock.
October 1803.

78

What Britons ought to avoid. The tender mercies of Buonaparte in Egypt

Hand-coloured etching, 19 x 24.3 cm (platemark)
Published [October 1803] by John Badcock
Curzon b.12(39)
Date added in MS.

79

James Gillray (1756–1815)

Maniac-raving's or Little Boney in a strong fit

Hand-coloured etching, 25.5 x 34.5 cm (subject)
Published 24 May 1803 by James Gillray
Curzon b.21(301)
BMC 9998

A satire on Napoleon's fury at reports in the British press which he believed were inspired by royalist French émigrés. He especially objected to the allegations of atrocities during the Egyptian campaign. Contained in Robert Wilson's *History of the British Expedition to Egypt* (1802).

This was one of several of Gillray's works reproduced in the German journal *London und Paris*, which began publication in Weimar in 1798. As the title suggested, the journal consisted of accounts of literary and social life in the two capitals of Europe. The 'war of pamphlets and caricatures' was a regular feature of *London und Paris*, but the editors attempted to uphold a standard of literary discourse and a political neutrality which Gillray's vicious caricatures sometimes violated. 'Maniac-Ravings' was revised for publication in the journal; the hopping figure of the First Consul was replaced by a winged sword, with Napoleon's head, and the plate was re-titled 'The Flying-Sword run mad'.[78]

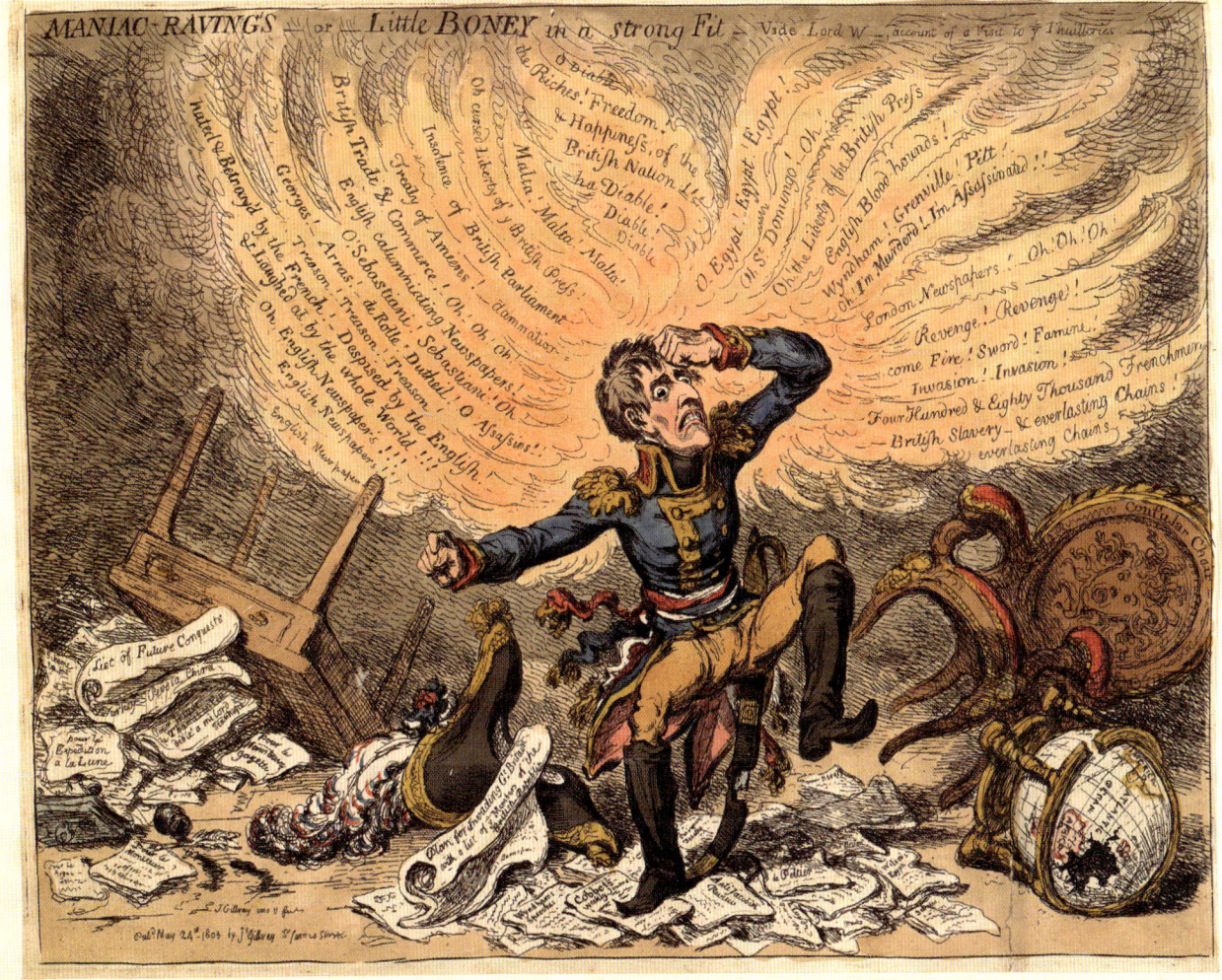

80

T. L.B.

A little man's night comforts, or Boney's visions

Hand-coloured etching and engraving, 24.1 x 32.9 cm (subject)
Published 14 July 1803
Curzon b.4(29)

Among the visions disturbing Napoleon's sleep are
ghosts of Turkish soldiers and the 'Infernal Machine',
or explosive used in an attempt to assassinate the First
Consul on Christmas Eve 1800. He clutches a map of
England, ready to invade. On the floor are products of
the British press which infuriated him; a caricature of
'Little Boney' and the title page of Robert Wilson's
History of the British Expedition to Egypt. Gillray also
produced a drawing on this theme, 'Troubled slumbers
of Bonaparte', which is held in the Curzon collection
(Curzon b.12(36)).

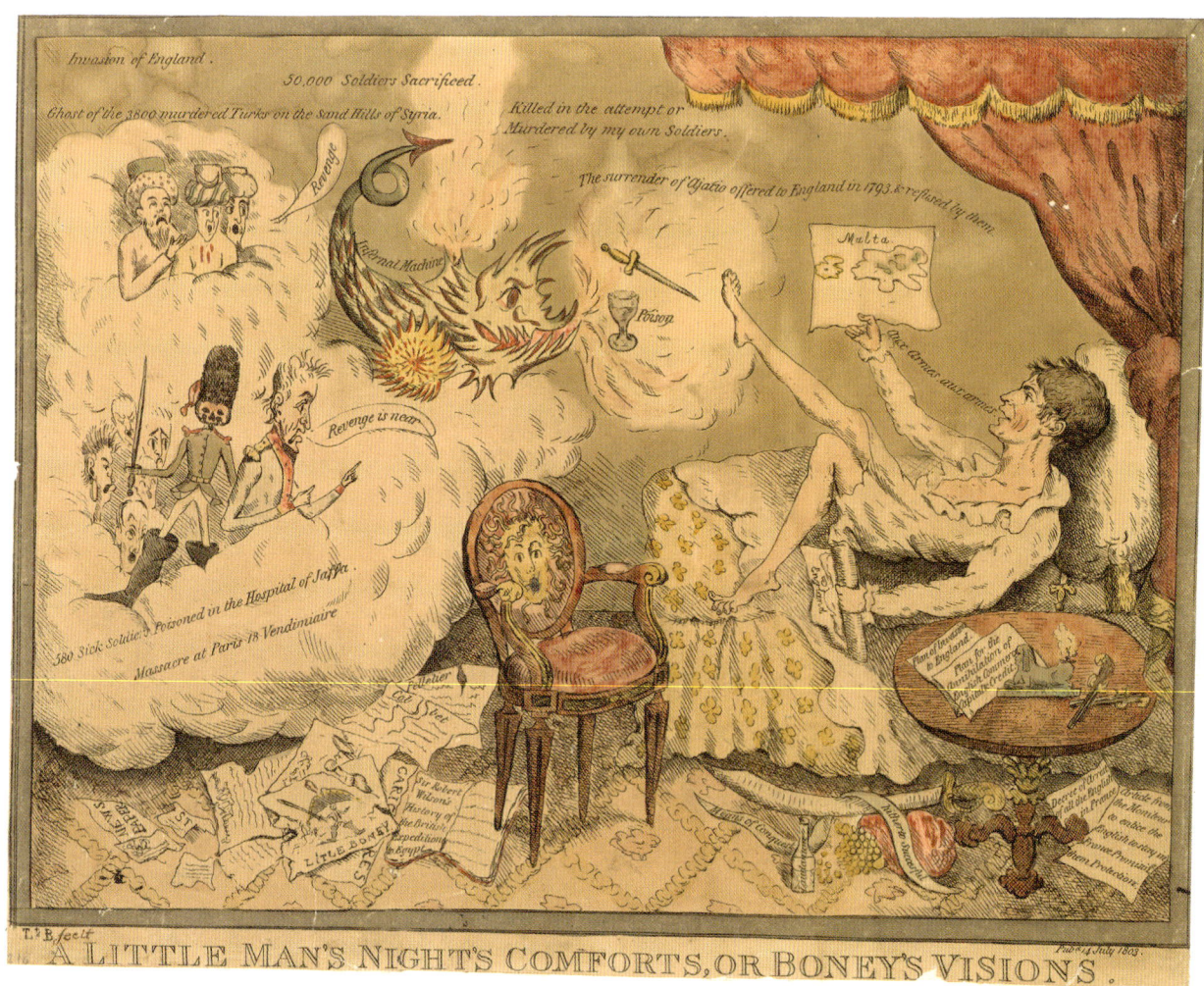

Napoleon's Career III

1805: Frustration

Napoleon's failure to leap the narrow
Channel with his troops was confirmed
by the Battle of Trafalgar, in October
1805. That British victory, which
claimed the life of Admiral Nelson,
cemented Nelson's fame and seemed to
confirm the dominance of Britain's
navy. Yet Napoleon remained a power
on the Continent, and ten more years
of land and sea warfare remained
ahead before his final defeat.

81

The man in the moon! or consular observations

Hand-coloured etching and aquatint, 35 x 24.8 cm (platemark)
Published September 1803 by William Holland
Curzon b.12(13)

The subtle colouring, with the night sky in aquatint,
gives an eerie look to this print, in which fears of a
royalist invasion of France are turned back on
Napoleon.

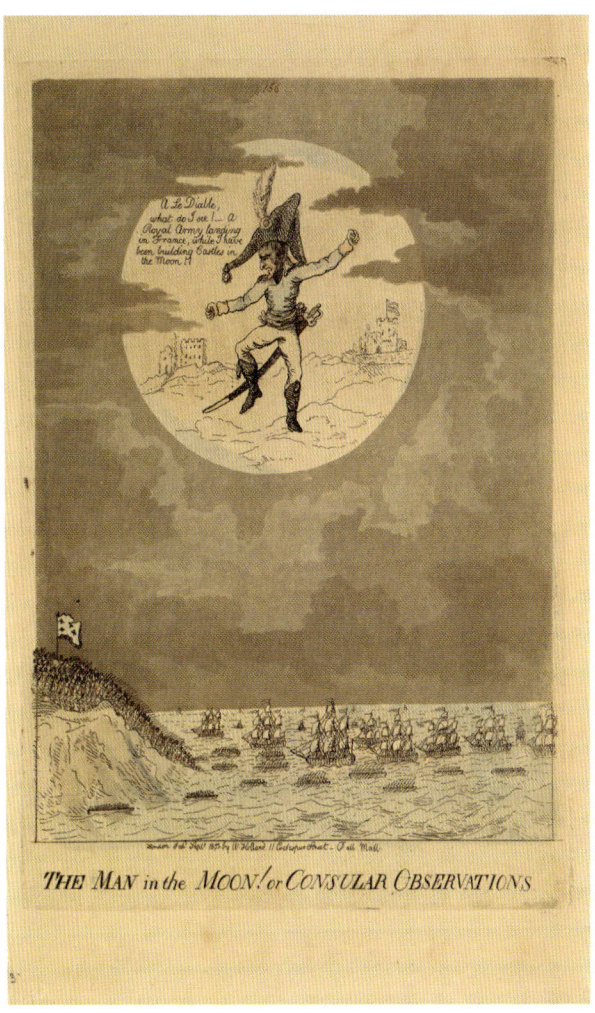

THE MAN in the MOON! or CONSULAR OBSERVATIONS

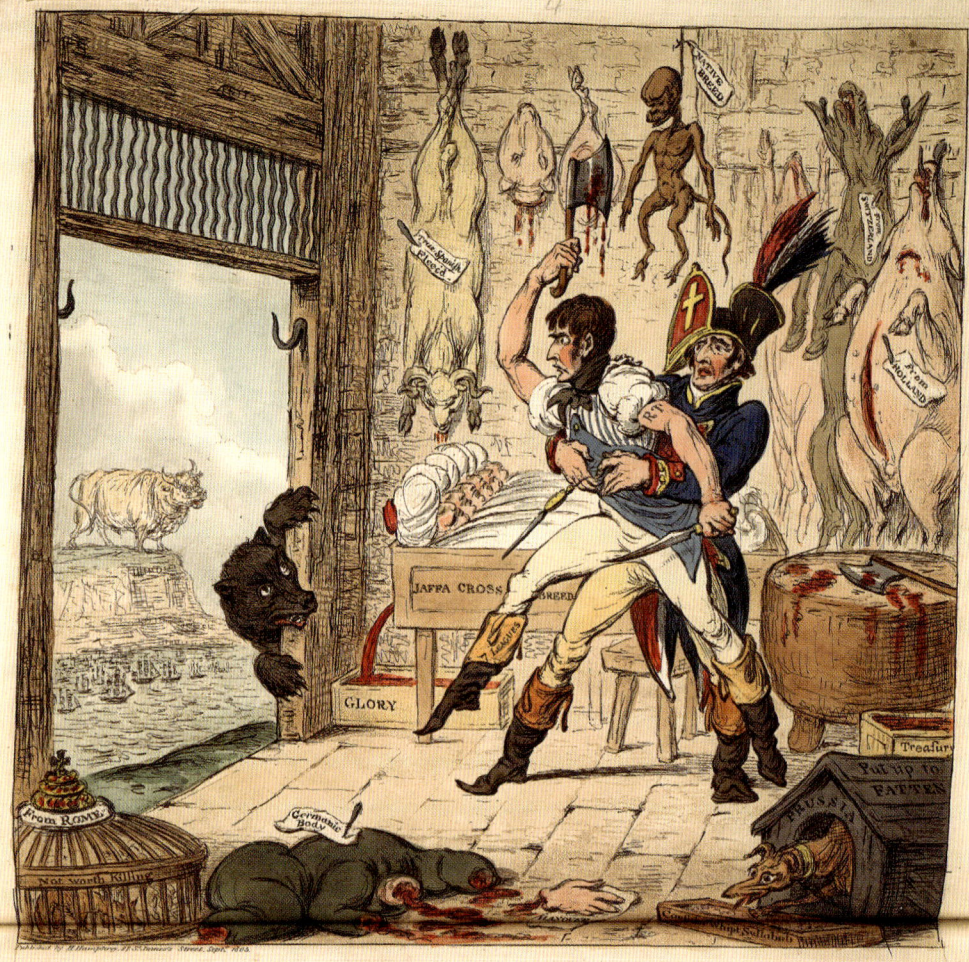

BONEY and TALLEY.

THE CORSICAN CARCASE-BUTCHER'S RECKONING DAY.

New Style---*No Quarter Day!*

Says Boney, the Butcher*, to Talley his man,
One settling-day, as they reckon'd,
 "Times are hard—'twere a sin
 "Not to keep our hand in—"
Talley guess'd at his thoughts in a second.

Then he reach'd the account-book, turn'd over awhile—
"I have it—see, here are the Dutch, Sir :"
 Boney cries, "It appears
 "That they're much in arrears—"
Quoth Talley, "*They don't owe us much, Sir !*"

"Here's Parma, Placentia ; there's Naples and Rome ;"
Talley smil'd—" They are nothing but bone, Sir !"
 "For the present pass Prussia ;
 "What think you of Russia?"
"*'Twere as good that we leave her alone, Sir !*"

"My ambition unsated, my fury unquench'd,
"Let Europe now shake to her bases ;
 "For, my banner unfurl'd,
 "I'll defy all the world,
"And *spit in th' ambassadors' faces.*"

Seeing raw-head and bloody-bones wondrous irate,
Talley turn'd o'er the leaf with his finger ;
 "Here's Hanover—if—"
 "If what?" in a tiff
Cries Boney, "Tell Mortier to bring her.

"Let her bleed till her life-strings are ready to burst,
"To drain her let Massena shew you ;
 "The job being done,
 "And all her fat run,
"We'll give up her trunk to—*you know who.*"

"This will do for a breakfast—read on :"—Talley read,
Each page they coun'd over and over ;
 "I can find nothing here ;"
 "We must stop, Sir, I fear :"
Boney scowl'd, *and then pointed to Dover.*

"Shall I want employ—whilst a breed there exists
"So sleek and so tempting to slaughter?
 "Reach my cleaver and steel,
 "I'll not sit at a meal—
"Till"—Talley cries,—"Think of *The Water.*"

"A soul such as mine, by the Koran I swear,
"Such childish impediment scorns, Sir ;
 "I will bait this great Bull,
 "And his crest I will pull :"—
Cries Talley—"*Remember his horns, Sir !*"

"Psha ! my mouth 'gins to water, and yearns for the feast,
"Such dainty, such delicate picking ;
 "By his horns will I seize him,
 "Goad, worry, and teaze him :"—
Quoth Talley—"*He's given to kicking.*"

"Let him kick, let him toss, and for mercy implore,
"Be mine the proud task to refuse it ;
 "The fates shall obey ;
 "I will have my way :"
Talley mutters—"*I hope you may'nt lose it !*"

"Sound the cleaver and marrow-bones," Boney exclaims,
"Strait this herd in my power shall be, Sir ;"
 "Should you once reach the shore,"
 (Talley said somewhat lower,)
"You'll soon *be at the top of the tree, Sir !*"

"Do'st jest with thy master, thou recreant knave !
"Am I, Sir, or am I, Sir, no king ?
 "By the Prophet I swear—"
 "Cry you mercy, forbear !"
Quoth Talley, "*I thought you were joking.*"

"Am I such a lover of jibes or of jests,
"Do I ever smile?" Boney cry'd, Sir ;
 "No, that I may say,
 "But to blast or betray ;"
(But this Talley uttered aside, Sir.)

He calls on Great Mahomet, swears by his beard,
The Lama he begs to be civil ;
 Now tells all his complaints
 To the Calendar Saints,
And now sends them all to the devil.

Thus prepared, he clasp'd firm the dread steel in his hand,
And wielded his cleaver on high, Sir :—
 "Oh, thou Bull, thou *Grand Bête !*
 "Oh, thou barb of my fate !
"This day thou most surely shalt die, Sir !"

Tho' artful and cunning some madmen appear,
The simplest expedient will turn 'em ;
 Talley saw what he meant ;
 On the schemes he was bent,
And fully resolv'd to adjourn 'em.

Now Boney grown wilder, his eyes seem'd to start,
And loudly began he to bellow ;
 When Talley seiz'd hold
 Of this hero so bold,
And pinion'd *the poor little fellow* †.

"Oh brave, great, and noble, magnanimous man !!!!!!
"To save thee thy servant is bound, Sir ;
 "The sea it is deep,
 "And the shores they are steep,
"*Most certainly you will be drown'd, Sir.*

"Think how precious your life is to France and to me,
"Obey then your fate, and don't mock it ;
 "Think what we shou'd do,
 "Mighty Sir, without you,
"With our *liberties* all in your pocket.

"Nay, *sweet, gentle* Sir !" (Boney kick'd with all might),
"Oh !—this chivalry's quite out of fashion !"
 Talley had his own way,
 Not a word did Bo say,
For speak he cou'd not for his passion.

"Dread Sir, your great project is worthy yourself,
"Your knife shall soon hit the bull's throat, Sir,
 "I'd only premise,
 "Were I fit to advise,
"*Twou'd be better to order a boat, Sir.*"

"A boat!—aye a boat! why there's reason in that,"
Boney cries with a scowl of delight, Sir ;
 For the truth must be told,
 He knew Talley of old,
And felt in a devilish fright, Sir.

Boney thought that the boat was a much safer plan,
He voted the counsel discreet, Sir ;
 Quoth Talley, "'Tis done,
 "And the day is your own,
"*Just—take—care—to avoid the fleet, Sir.*"

Talley cautiously then let the little man down,
When the little man softened his features ;
 Yet though little in size, Sir,
 His soul is as high, Sir,
As the cross at the top of St. Peter's.

Little Boney shook hands then with Talley the good ;
(*And thought how he best might dispatch him ;*)
 Whilst Talley, as meek,
 Kiss'd the Mussulman's cheek,
(*And swore in his heart to o'ermatch him.*)

They drank to their hopes,—hob-a-nobb'd to their scheme,
Which promis'd such royal diversion ;
 Thus cordial they sat,
 And, in *harmless chit-chat,*
Sketch'd the *plan of this water excursion.*

When the boat will be ready we none of us know,
Talley swears 'twill be here in a trice, Sir ;
 But it must be confess'd,
 Boney's not in such haste,
Since he thought of the business twice, Sir.

Then a health to the Butcher !—and life long enough,
That he once of the Bull may a view get,
 For whenever we meet,
 If he *skulk from the* FLEET,
We will find him head-quarters in NEWGATE.

* It is curious to observe how the natural bent and genius of a family glides in the same current for generations: it may be called *the bias of blood* in the present instance ; for the grandfather of our hero was himself a great proficient in the line which his descendant has carried to such perfection, and in which he has enjoyed such universal practice.

† This remedy has been most successfully employed on several occasions with the hero of our tale ; and he has too great a knowledge of the world, when he recovers his senses, to shew any resentment towards his keeper—because he could not do without him!

82

[James Gillray (1756–1815)]

Boney and Talley. The Corsican carcase butcher's reckoning day

Broadside with illustration, 60.4 x 43.5 cm; platemark of illustration 31.7 x 32.6 cm
[Published September 1803]
John Johnson Collection: French Wars and Revolutions folder 4 (11)
BMC 10091

With some difficulty, 'Talley' – Charles-Maurice de Talleyrand-Périgord – holds back Napoleon from an invasion of Britain. Other European nations are carcases – the turbaned corpses of Jaffa are also shown, continuing the 'Black Legend'.

The design may have been suggested by George Canning, a political disciple of William Pitt who arranged for Gillray's pension from the Pitt Government in 1797. It presents Britain's strong stand against Napoleon in the context of the capitulations of other European nations.

83

George M. Woodward (1760?–1809)

John Bull exchanging news with the continent

Hand-coloured etching, 23.8 x 36.2 cm (platemark)
[Etched by C. Williams]
Published 11 December 1805 by S. W. Fores
John Johnson Collection: French Wars and Revolutions folder 6 (4)
BMC 10441

A satire on the unreliability of French military bulletins: reports of the Battle of Trafalgar were kept out of French newspapers.

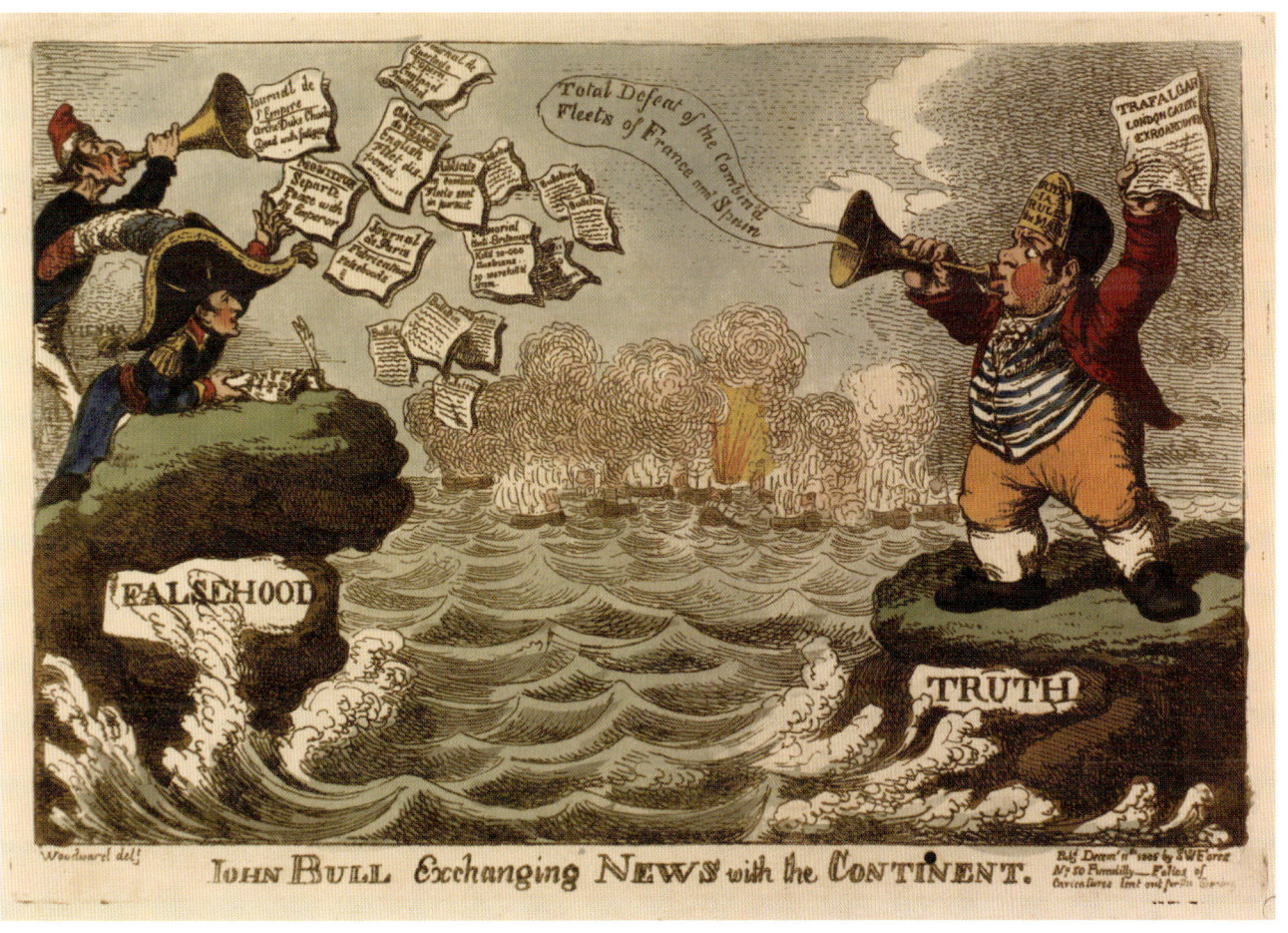

JOHN BULL Exchanging NEWS with the CONTINENT.

84

Medals commemorating the Battle of Trafalgar, October 21 1805

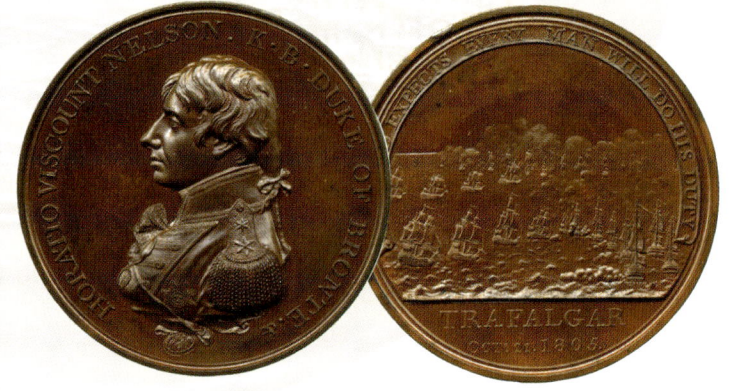

84a

C.K. Küchler, struck by M. Boulton

Obverse: Bust of Nelson, left profile: HORATIO VISCOUNT NELSON. K.B. DUKE OF BRONTE &. [Sign CHK on truncation]

Reverse: View of the Battle of Trafalgar: ENGLAND EXPECTS EVERY MAN WILL DO HIS DUTY

In exergue: TRAFALGAR OCT^R 21. 1805

Edge inscribed: TO THE HEROES OF TRAFALGAR FROM M. BOULTON

Bronze, 48mm

Ashmolean Museum (M. H. Grant)

84b

As 84a, but an earlier version of the Nelson portrait and no inscription around the edge.

Ashmolean Museum (M. H. Grant)

Boulton had this medal struck after careful consultation with the relatives of Nelson over the representation of the Admiral and distributed copies to over 14,000 people in commemoration of the battle. Number 84b is the earlier trial copy with a portrait of Nelson, fuller of face and with curlier hair, that was not approved.

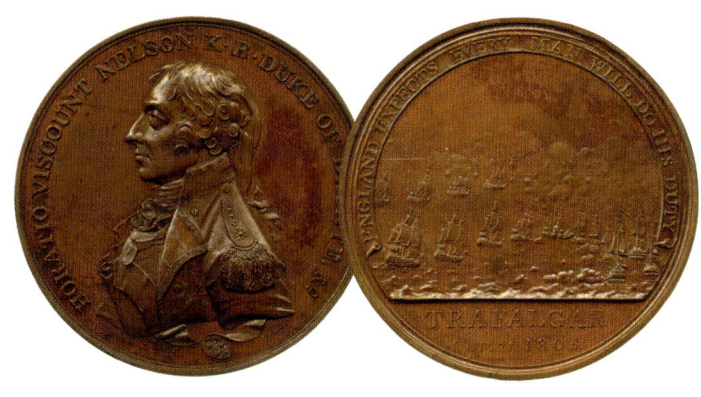

84c

T. Wyon Sr.

Obverse: Uniformed bust of Lord Nelson, left
profile: NELSON ET BRONTI. VICTOR
TRAFALGAR ET VICTIMA (Nelson and Bronte,
victor and victim of Trafalgar). Below: PERIIT
ET PERIIT. OCT 21 1805 (He passed through
and perished)

Reverse: View of the battle, clouds above, with
laurel wreath MEMORIAE CONSECRAVIT.
GUL. TURTON.M.D.F.L.S. (Dedicated By
William Turton, MD)

In exergue: ESTO PERPETUA (live forever)

Bronze, 44mm

Ashmolean Museum (M. H. Grant)

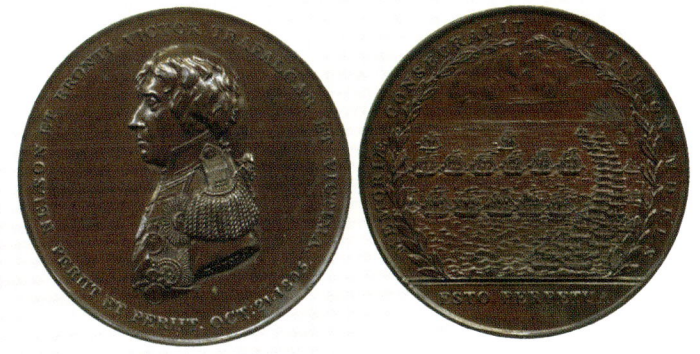

84d

P. Wyon

Obverse: Bust of Lord Nelson on a medallion, naval
crown above an obelisk with trophies of war;
seaman weeping at base, inscribed GALLANT
NELSON/DIED IN THE/ HOUR OF VICTORY/
21. OCT^R AD 1805

In exergue: TRAFALGAR

Reverse: Britannia seated weeping, Neptune
drawing veil over an urn inscribed HN. Plinth
below inscribed BASTIA/ABOVKIR/
COPENHAG[EN]. Surround, IN LIFE
VICTORIOUS IN DEATH TRIUMPHANT

In exergue: MDCCCV

Lead, 51 mm

Ashmolean Museum (M. H. Grant)

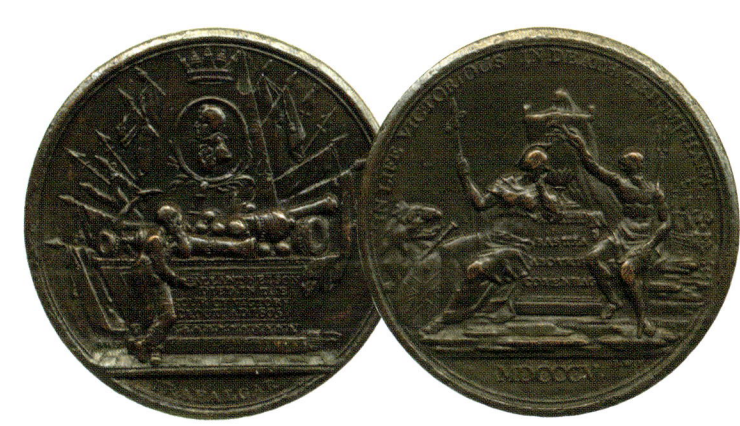

Caricaturists
Return to Satire

—————⛵—————

After the end of the invasion scare, cartoonists continued to appeal to the patriotic spirit of John Bull. But now their pens were directed again at domestic targets, and charges of corruption, weakening the nation in a time of war, found ample scope in the forced resignation of Lord Melville over embezzlement at the Navy Office, and later in the scandal over sales of commissions in the Army by the Duke of York's mistress. William Cobbett was prominent among those who prescribed political reform, including expansion of the franchise, as a cure for corruption in Government.

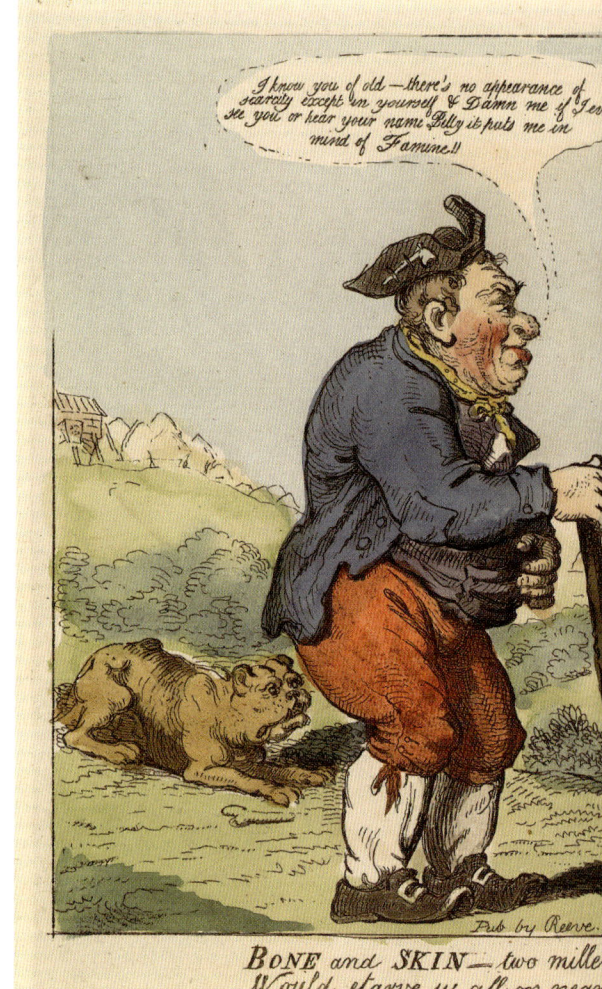

I know you of old — there's no appearance of scarcity except in yourself & Damn me if I ever see you or hear your name Billy it puts me in mind of Famine!!

Pub by Reeve.

BONE and SKIN — two mille.
Would starve us all or near

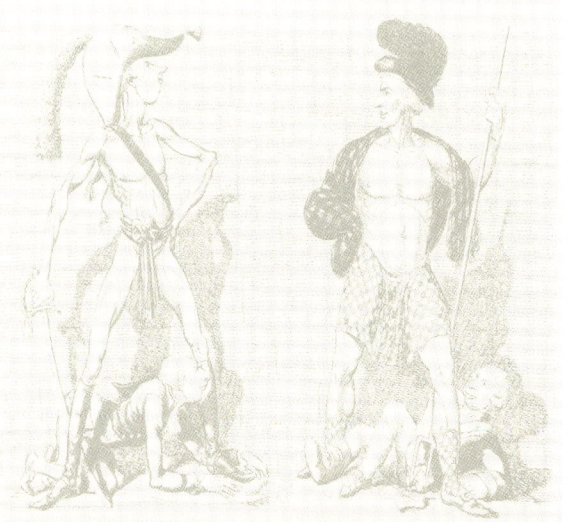

85

[C. Williams]

Giants – Triumphant

Hand-coloured etching, 24.8 x 35.2 cm (platemark)
Published 22 May 1804 by S. W. Fores
John Johnson Collection: Political Cartoons 1 (207)
BMC 10246

William Pitt and Henry Dundas (Lord Melville) are
the 'giants' overcoming Addington and Lord St
Vincent. The return of Pitt as Prime Minister and
Melville as First Lord of the Admiralty is hailed in
this cartoon as a restoration of Britain's warlike
resolve.

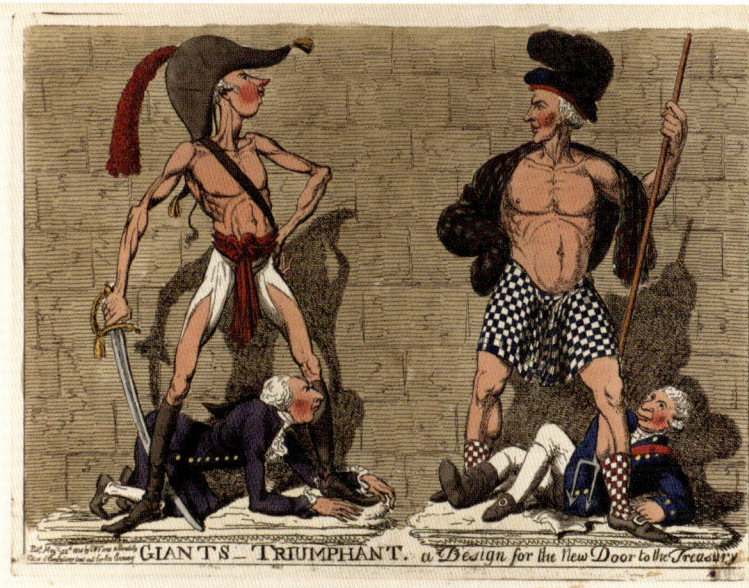

86

[Isaac Cruikshank (1764–1811?)]

Bone and skin

Hand-coloured etching and aquatint, 21.3 x 30.5 cm (subject)
Published 19 November 1804 by Reeve
Curzon b.12(15)
BMC 10282

This cartoon returns to the theme of high food prices.
A bad harvest in 1804 revived memories of 1799–1800.
Pitt's 1804 Corn Bill, a protectionist act intended to
make Britain self-sufficient in grain, was blamed for
keeping prices high. As in cartoons of 1797, Pitt and
Melville appear as parasites on the long-suffering John
Bull.

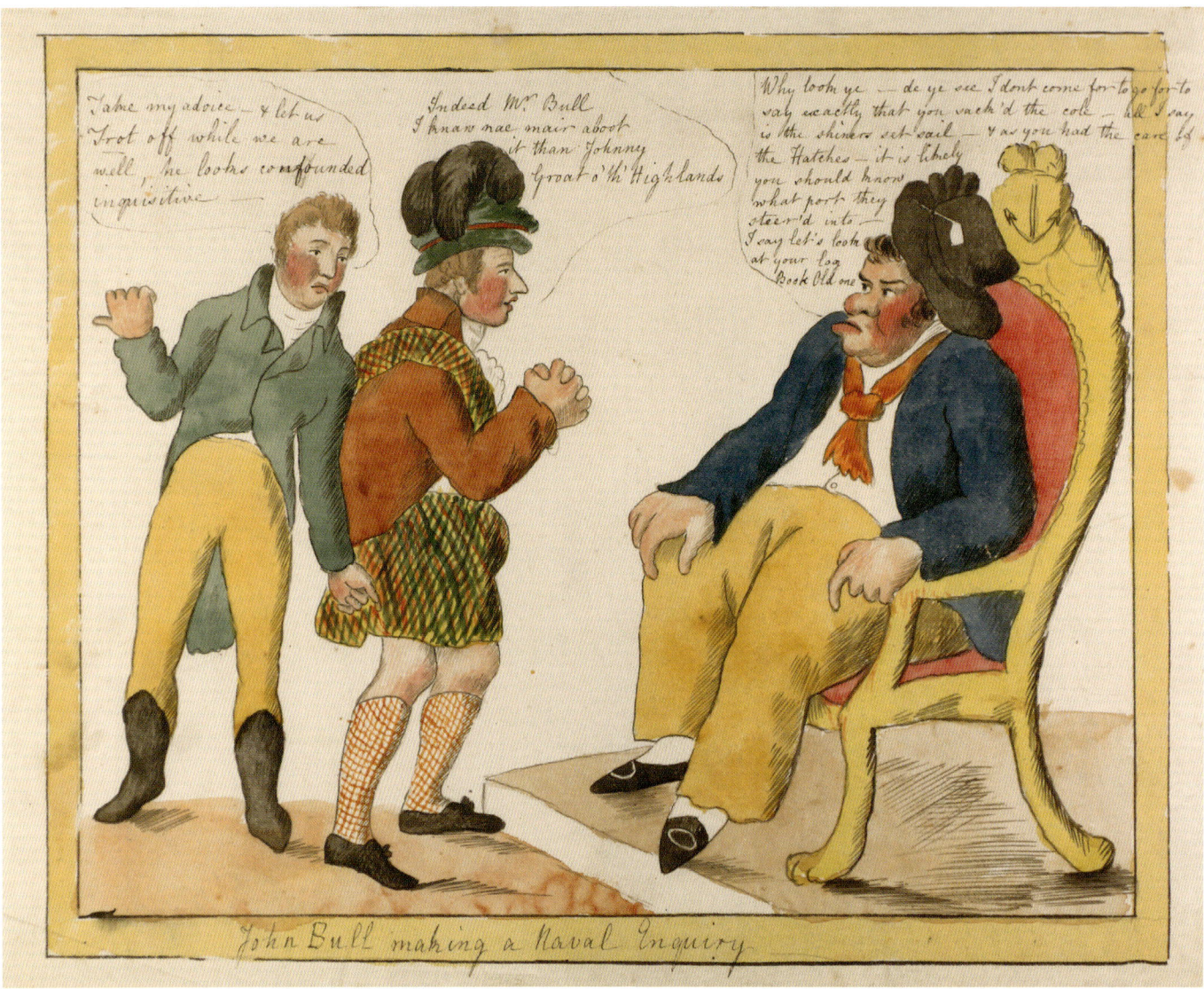

John Bull making a Naval Inquiry

87

[C. Williams]
John Bull making a naval inquiry
Hand-coloured etching, 26.1 x 41.8 cm (sheet)
[Published 1 April 1805 by S. W. Fores]
John Johnson Collection: Political Cartoons 2 (3)
BMC 10381

A report on Navy finances in March 1805 accused the Paymaster of the Navy of embezzlement of public funds. Here John Bull is a patriotic sailor, indignant at the misdeeds of his ministerial masters.

88

Johnny MacCree at confession. St Stephens Oratory
Hand-coloured etching, 35.8 x 25.2 cm (platemark)
Published 29 March 1805 by S. W. Fores
John Johnson Collection: Taxation folder 3 (5)
BMC 10378

Henry Dundas (Lord Melville), Pitt's long-time political ally, was forced to resign as First Lord of the Admiralty in April, 1805, over the embezzlement of money at the Navy Office. Pitt, a lifelong bachelor, is represented as a monk, attempting to proclaim his own innocence. His self-defensive speech draws a parallel between the theft of public funds and Pitt's imposition of taxes during his first administration.

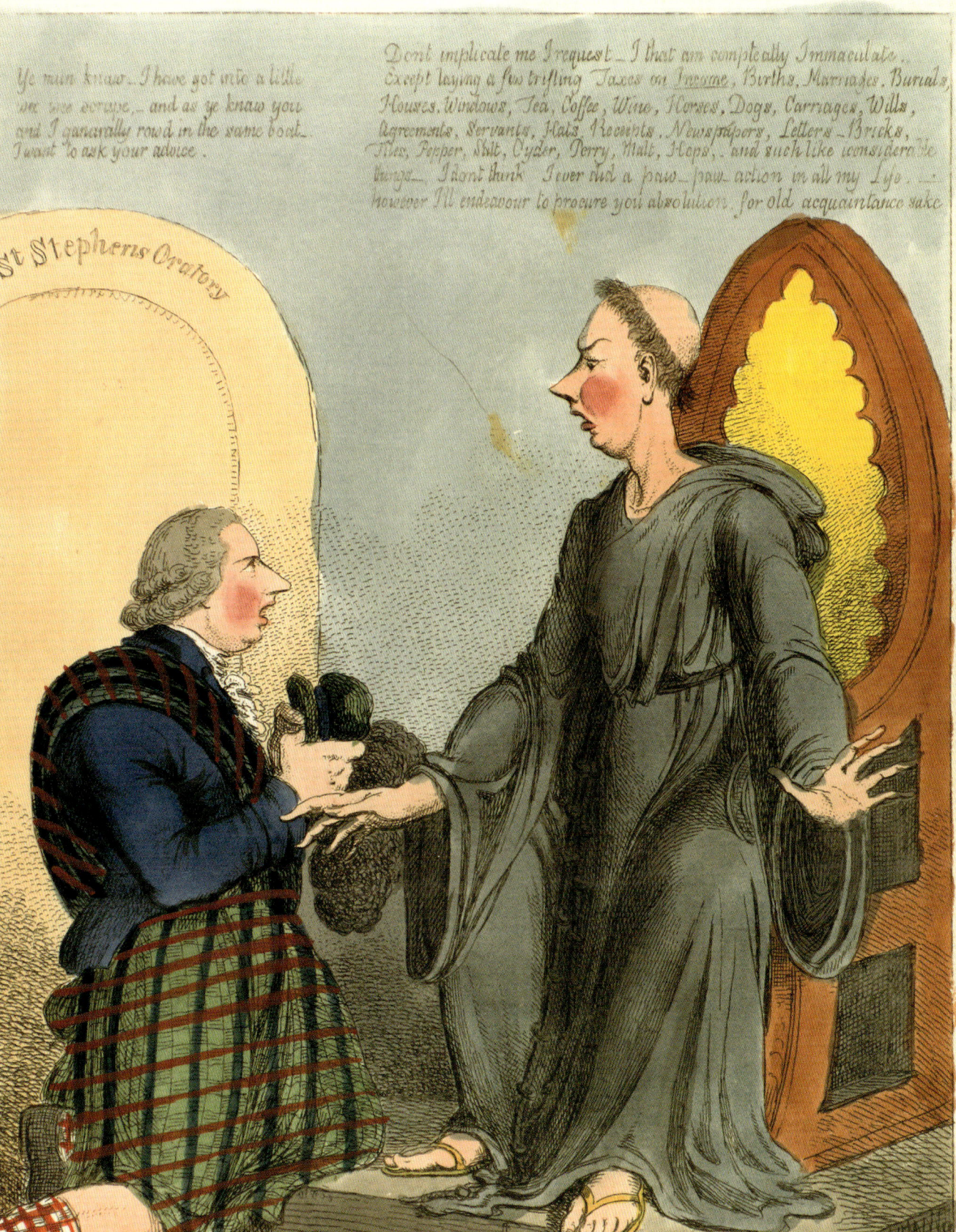

Ye mun knaw—I have got into a little
wee wee scrape,—and as ye knaw you
and I generally row'd in the same boat_
I want to ask your advice.

Dont implicate me I request_ I that am compleatly Immaculate_
Except laying a few trifling Taxes on Income, Births, Marriages, Burials,
Houses, Windows, Tea, Coffee, Wine, Horses, Dogs, Carriages, Wills,
Agreements, Servants, Hats, Receipts, Newspapers, Letters, Bricks,
Tiles, Pepper, Salt, Cyder, Perry, Malt, Hops,—and such like considerable
things_ I dont think I ever did a paw—paw action in all my Life_
however I'll endeavour to procure you absolution for old acquaintance sake

St Stephens Oratory

Pub.d March 19th 1805 by S W Fores 50 Piccadilly   Folios & Caricatures lent out for the Evening

IOHNNY Mac CREE at Confession.

Napoleon in British Memory

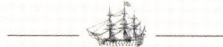

Even during the wars, Napoleon proved a popular subject of picture prints, his interesting face supposedly expressive of his inner drive and ambition. After 1815 a romantic image of Napoleon as an individual who had seized his own destiny prevailed in images and songs expressing admiration for Britain's former enemy.

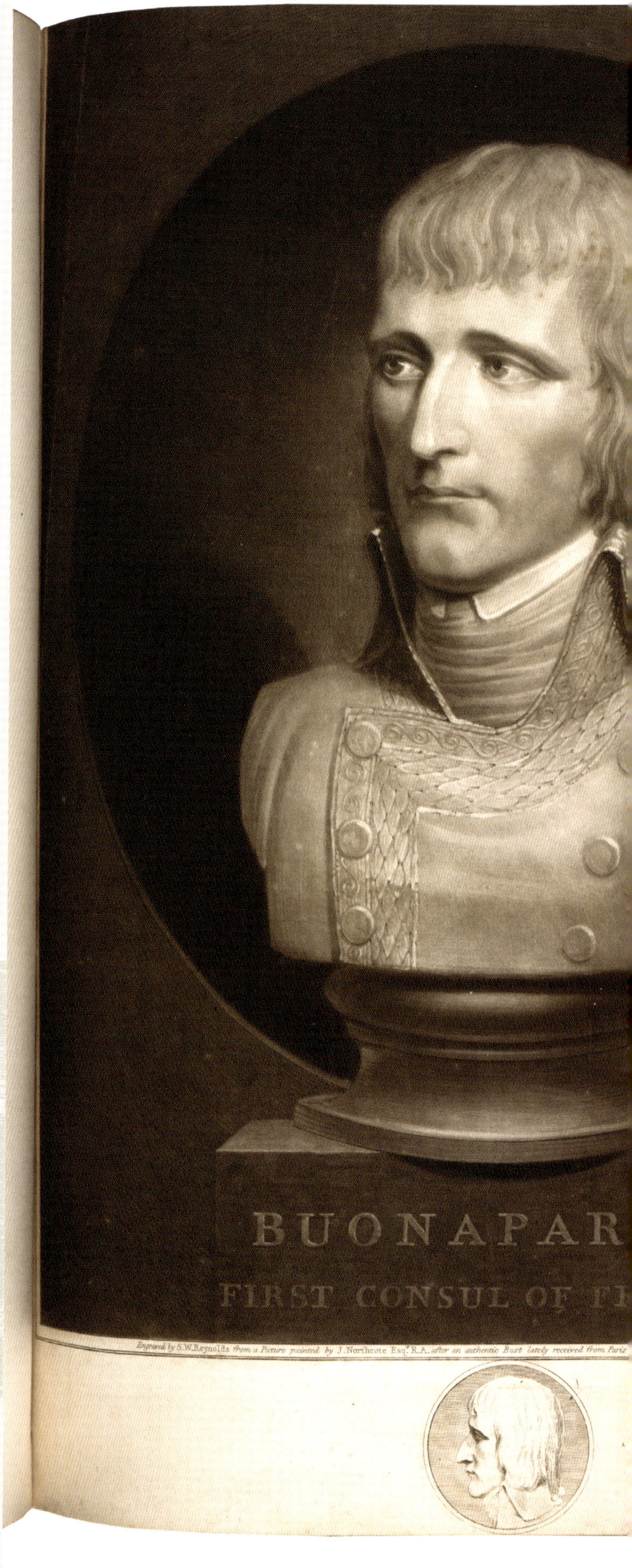

BUONAPAR

FIRST CONSUL OF F

Engraved by S.W.Reynolds from a Picture painted by J.Northcote Esq.^R.A. after an authentic Bust lately received from Paris

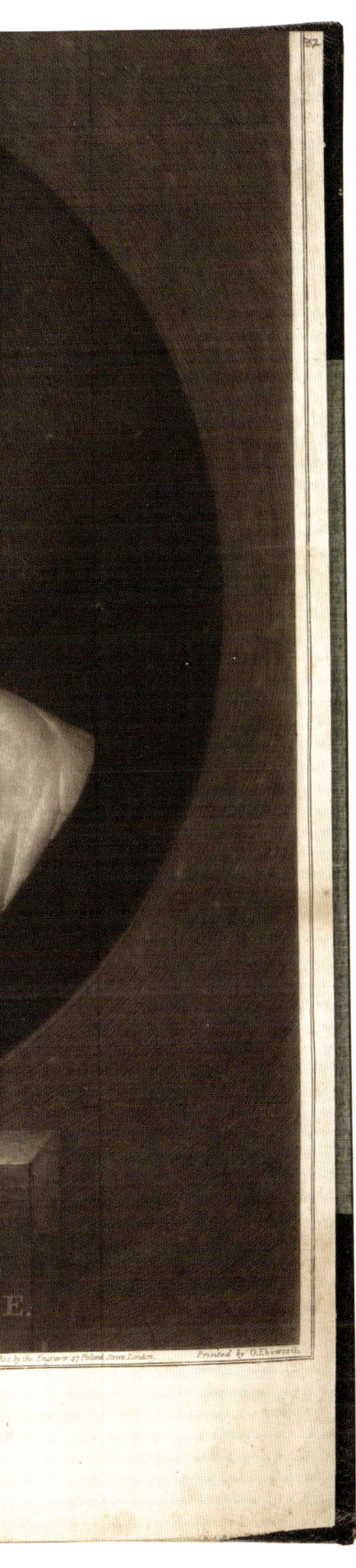

89

Buonaparte. First Consul of France.
Engraved by S. W. Reynolds from a picture
painted by J. Northcote, Esq. R.A. after an
authentic bust lately received from Paris
Mezzotint, 49 x 37 cm (sheet)
Published 20 August 1800 by S. W. Reynolds
Printed by G. Ebsworth
Curzon b.19(83)

British printsellers capitalized on public fascination
with the young General whose rise to political power in
France owed something to the strong marketing of his
portrait. The model depicted in this print most closely
resembles the first bust of Napoleon by Guiseppe
Ceracchi (1751-1801) which inspired other English
prints.[79]

90

[Leaf silhouette of Napoleon]
Curzon b.12(37)

Napoleon is shown in exile on St Helena, in an intricate
silhouette cut from a real leaf.

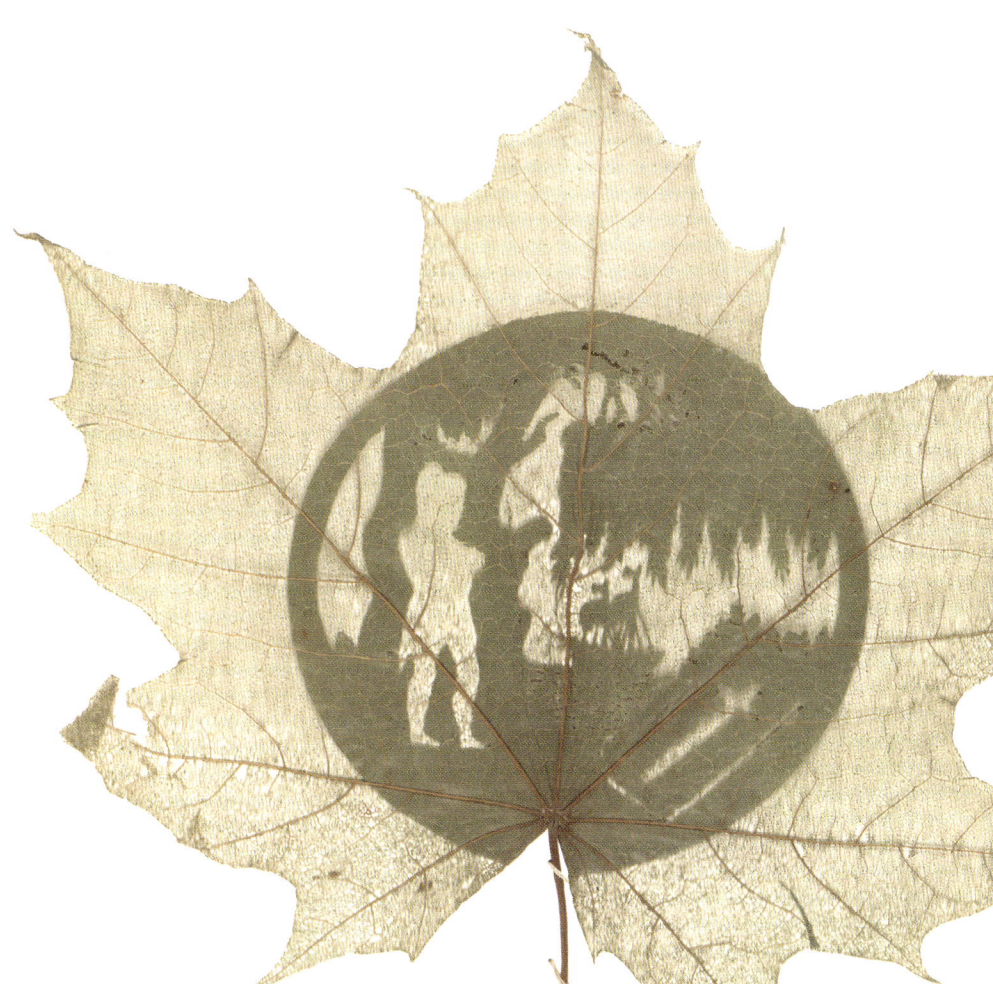

BONNY BUNCH OF
ROSES O.

By the dangers of the ocean,
  One morning in the month of June,
The feather'd warbling songster,
  Their charming notes so sweet did tune.
Here I espied a female,
  Seemingly in grief and woe,
And conversing with young Buonaparte,
  Concerning the bonny bunch of Roses O.

O then said young Napoleon,
  And grasp'd his mother by the hand,
Do mother pray have patience,
  Until I am able to command.
I will raise a terrible army,
  And through tremendous dangers go,
And in spite of all the universe,
  I will gain the bonny bunch of Roses O.

When first you saw great Buonaparte,
  You fell upon your bended knee,
And asked your father's life of him,
  He granted it most manfully.
Twas then he took an army,
  And o'er the frozen realms did go,
He said I'll conquer Moscow,
  Then go to the bonny bunch of Roses O,

He took three hundred thousand men,
  And likewise kings to join his throng
He was so well provided,
  Enough to sweep this world along.
But when he came to Moscow,
  Near overpower'd by driven snow,
All Moscow was a blazing,
  Then he lost the bonny bunch of Roses, O.

Now son ne'er speak so venturesome,
  For England is the heart of oak,
England, Ireland, and Scotland,
  Their unity has ne'er been broke.
And son look at your father,
  In St Helena my body lays low,
And you will follow after
  So beware of the bonny bunch of Roses O.

Oh! mother adieu for ever,
  Now I am on my dying bed,
If I had lived I should have been clever,
  But now I droop my youthful head,
But while our bones do moulder,
  And weeping willows round us grow.
The deeds of bold Napoleon,
  Will sting the bonny bunch of Roses, O.

[Cadman, Printer, Manchester.]

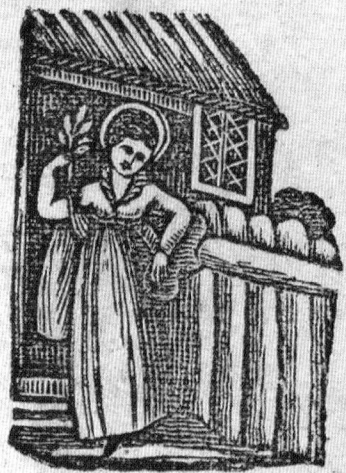

As I wandered by the brookside.

As I wandered by the brook side,
  I wandered by the mill,
I could not hear the brook,
  The noisy wheel was still?
There was no burr of grasshopper
  Nor chirp of any bird,
But the beating of my own heart,
  Was the only sound I heard.

I sat beneath the elm tree,
  I watch'd the long, long shade,
And as it grew still longer,
  I did not feel afraid,
For I listened for a foot fall,
  I listened for a word,
But the beating of my own heart,
  Were the only sound I heard,

He came not—ah! he came not,
  The night came on alone,
The little stars set one by one,
  Each on his golden throne,
The evening wind swept by me,
  The leaves above were stirred;
But the beatings of my own heart
  Were the only sound I heard.

Fast silent tears were flowing,
  When something stood behind,
A hand was on my shoulder,
  I knew its touch was kind,
It drew me nearer, nearer,
  We could not speak one word,
For the beating of our own hearts
  Were all the sounds we heard.

91

Bonny bunch of roses

Broadside ballad
Harding B 11(404)

This ballad recounts the story of Napoleon's march on
Moscow, in the words of the Empress Marie Louise to
her son, the Prince of Rome and partly in the voice of
Napoleon himself. The 'bonny bunch of roses' is the
British Isles, in the song envisioned as Napoleon's
intended conquest after Russia. Losing his army on the
retreat from Moscow, Napoleon 'lost the bonny bunch
of Roses O'.

He took three hundred thousand men,
And likewise kings to join this throng,
He was so well provided,
Enough to sweep this world along.
But when he came to Moscow,
Near overpower'd by driven snow,
All Moscow was a blazing,
Then he lost the bonny bunch of Roses O.

Now son ne'er speak so venturesome,
For England is the heart of oak,
England, Ireland, and Scotland,
Their unity has ne'er been broke.
And son look to your father,
In St. Helena my body lays low,
And you will follow after,
So beware of the bonny bunch of Roses O.

[verses 4 and 5]

92

The grand conversation on Napoleon

Broadside ballad
Harding B 11(1388)

While the songs from the war years are almost
uniformly hostile to Napoleon, a number of those
published after, or recorded by ballad collectors, such as
these, have a more nuanced and sympathetic character.
The illustration of this song expresses a romantic
admiration for Napoleon as an individual, while the
verses praise his lofty ambition.

It was over that wild beaten track, a friend of bold
    Buonaparte,
Did pace the sands and lofty rocks of St. Helena's shore,
The wind it blew a hurricane, the lightning's flash around did
    dart.
The sea gulls were shrieking and the waves around did roar;
Ah! hush, rude winds, the stranger cried, awhile I range the
    dreary spot,
Where last a gallant hero his envied eyes did close.
But while his valued limbs do rot, his name will never be
    forgot,
This grand conversation on Napoleon arose.

Ah England! he cried, did you persecute that hero bold,
Much better had you slain him on the plains of Waterloo;
Napoleon he was a friend to heroes all, both young and old,
He caus'd the money for to fly wherever he did go;
When plans were ranging night and day, the bold commander
    to betray,
He cried I'll go to Moscow, and then 'twill ease my woes.
If fortune shines without delay, then all the world shall me
    obey,
This grand conversation on Napoleon arose.

[verses 1 and 2]

Illustrated overleaf

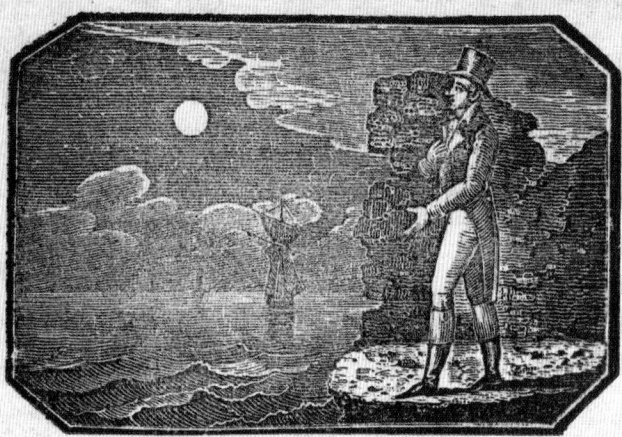

THE GRAND CONVERSATION OF
NAPOLEON.

It was over that wild beaten track, a friend of bold Buonaparte,
  Did pace the sands and lofty rocks of St. Helena's shore.
The wind it blew a hurricane, the lightning's flash around did
    dart,
  The sea gulls were shrieking and the waves around did roar ;
Ah ! hush, rude winds, the stranger cried, awhile I range the
    dreary spot,
  Where last a gallant hero his envied eyes did close,
But while his valued limbs do rot, his name will never be forgot,
  This grand conversation on Napoleon arose.

Ah England ! he cried, did you persecute that hero bold,
  Much better had you slain him on the plains of Waterloo ;
Napoleon he was a friend to heroes all, both young and old,
  He caus'd the money for to fly wherever he did go;
When plans were ranging night and day, the bold commander
    to betray,
  He cried I'll go to Moscow, and then 'twill ease my woes,
If fortune shines without delay, then all the world shall me obey,
  This grand conversation on Napoleon arose.

Thousands of men he then did rise, to conquer Moscow by
    surprise,
  He leads his men across the Alps oppressed by frost & snow,
But being near the Russian's land, he then began to ope his eyes,
  For Moscow was a burning and the men drove to and fro,
Napoleon dauntless viewed the flame, and wept in anguish for
    the same,
  He cried, retreat my gallant men, for time so swiftly goes ;
What, thousands died on that retreat, some forced their horses
    for to eat.
  This grand conversation on Napoleon arose.

At Waterloo his men they fought, commanded by great
    Buonaparte,
  Attended by field-marshall Ney, and he was bribed with gold,
When Blucher led the Russians in, it nearly broke Napoleon's
    heart,
  He cried my thirty thousand men are kill'd and I am sold ;
He view'd the plain and cried it's lost, he then his favourite
    charger cross'd.
  The plain was in confusion with blood and dying woes,
The bunch of roses did advance, and boldly entered into France,
  This grand conversation on Napoleon arose.

Then Buonaparte was plann'd to be a prisoner across the sea,
  The rocks of St. Helena, it was the fatal spot,
Doom'd as a prisoner there to be, till death did end his misery,
  His son soon followed to the tomb, it was an awful plot.
It's long enough have they been dead, the blast of war around
    is spread,
  And may our sapling float again to face the daring foes ;
And now my boys, when honour calls, we'll boldly mount the
    wooden walls,
  This grand conversation on Napoleon arose.

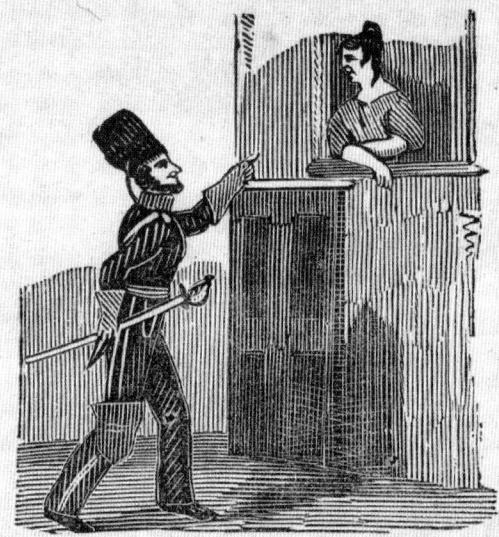

THE OPERA BOX

He. Miss Emily Chatter !
She.   Well, what is the matter ?
He. My heart in my bosom goes bumpity bump ;
    Whene'er you are near me, I feel so, oh, dear
      me,
  Right out of my skin I am ready to jump.
She. Then distant pray keep, sir, for fear you leap, sir ;
    Disappearing too sudden would make us all start,
  'Tis useless your trying by jumping or flying,
    You never will jump in a place in my heart.
He. Miss Emily Chatter, I don't wish to flatter,
    But beauties like thine are would captivate rocks
  I think them divine miss, and if they were mine
    miss,
  How well we should look in a *nopera* box.
SPOKEN.]—Have me Emily, and you shall have one—
  can you resist a *nopera* box.
Both.   Fal lal, &c

He. Mis Emily Chatter, why, I keep a *nunter !*
    And would'nt you like miss a horse of your own ?
  Then wed me instanter and off we will canter,
    To an house which I have seven miles out of
      town.
She. I pr'ythee give over—I don't want a love ;
    Then go with your hunter a different course :
  I'm not fond of sporting so take this for certain,
    I'm not to be caught with an 'ouse nor an 'orse.
He. Oh, Emily Chatter, my senses you'd scatter,
    Though fastened by one of the famed Bramah
      locks,
  Come say you will choose me—how can you
    refuse me,
  Who offers an 'orse and a *nopera* box.
SPOKEN.]—Can you resist a man what keeps a nunter ?
Both.   Fal lal, &c

George Walker, Jun., Printer, Durham.

Further reading

Boney: or, Napoleon through English eyes. Catalogue of a travelling exhibition prepared by Devon Library Services first shown at la Bibliothèque Municipale de Caen. September–October 1985 ([Exeter],1985).

David Alexander, *Richard Newton and English Caricature in the 1790s* (Manchester, 1998).

John Barrell, *Imagining The King's Death: Figurative Treason, Fantisies of Regicide, 1793–1796* (Oxford, 2000).

David Bindman, *The Shadow of The Guillotine: Britain and the French Revolution*; with contributions by Aileen Dawson and Mark Jones [Catalogue of an exhibition at the British Museum, 1989] (London, 1989).

J.E. Cookson, *The British Armed Nation, 1793–1815* (Oxford, 1997).

Diana Donald, *The Age of Caricature* (New Haven, Conn., 1996).

Pascal Dupuy, 'La caricature anglaise face à la France en révolution (1789–1802)', *Dix-Huitième Siècle*, 32 (2000), 307–20.

Austin Gee, *The British Volunteer Movement 1794–1815*, Oxford Historical Monographs (Oxford, 2003).

Richard Godfrey, *The Art of Caricature* (London, 2001).

Marilyn Morris, *The British Monarchy and the French Revolution* (New Haven, Conn., 1998).

Tom Pocock, *The Terror before Trafalgar: Nelson, Napoleon and the Secret War* (London, 2002).

Marcus Wood, *Radical Satire and Print Culture, 1791–1822* (Oxford, 1994).

Notes

[1] *Copy Book of Military Orders*, Eastern Military District, 1803–04, MS. Eng. Hist. c 263, ff. 1–2.

[2] Frank McLynn, *Napoleon: A Biography* (London, 1998), p. 322.

[3] Mclynn, *Napoleon*, p. 330.

[4] T. Bartlett, ed., *The Life of Theobald Wolfe Tone: Memoirs, Journals and Political Writings*, compiled and arranged by William T. W. Tone, 1826 (Dublin, 1998), p. 669.

[5] Cited in Marianne Elliot, *Partners in Revolution: The United Irishmen and France* (New Haven, Conn., 1982), p. 122.

[6] J. Holland Rose, *The Life of Napoleon I* (London, 1907), p. 176; Norman Longmate, *Island Fortress: The Defence of Great Britain 1603–1945* (London, 2001), p. 245.

[7] McLynn, *Napoleon*, p. 324.

[8] Gunther E. Rothenberg, *The Art of Warfare in the Age of Napoleon* (London, 1977), p. 31.

[9] Richard Price, *A Discourse on the Love of Our Country* (London, 1789).

[10] Charles François Dumouriez, *Thoughts on the French Invasion of England* (London, 1798), p. 5.

[11] Longmate, *Island Fortress*, pp. 278–9. See also Tom Pocock, *The Terror Before Trafalgar* (London, 2002).

[12] J. Ann Hone, *For the Cause of Truth: Radicalism in London 1796–1821* (Oxford, 1982), pp. 83–116.

[13] Dundas, writing in June 1798, cited in J. E. Cookson, *The British Armed Nation 1793–1815* (Oxford, 1997), p. 71.

[14] Sir George Sher, quoted in Cookson, *The British Armed Nation*, p. 76, n. 33.

[15] James Burney, *Plan of Defence against Invasion* (London, 1797), p. 7.

[16] Cookson, *The British Armed Nation*, Chapter 3.

[17] McLynn, *Napoleon*, p. 189.

[18] Robert Wilson, *History of the British expedition to Egypt* (London, 1803), pp. 74–6; also William Wittman, *Travels in Turkey, Asia-Minor, Syria, and across the desert into Egypt during the years 1799, 1800 and 1801, in company with the Turkish Army, and the British Military Mission* (London, 1802), pp. 128–9.

[19] William Cobbett, *Important Considerations* (London, 1803), p. 23.

[20] Diana Donald, *The Age of Caricature: Satirical Prints in the Reign of George III* (London, 1996), p. 2.

[21] H. T. Dickinson, *Caricatures and the Constitution 1760–1832* (Cambridge, 1986).

[22] David Alexander, *Richard Newton and English Caricature in the 1790s* (Manchester, 1998), p. 162.

[23] Draper Hill, *Mr. Gillray, The Caricaturist* (London, 1965), p. 46.

[24] John Brewer, *The Common People and Politics 1750–1790s* (Cambridge, 1986), pp. 41–3.

[25] M. Dorothy George, *Hogarth to Cruikshank: Social Change in Graphic Satire* (London, 1967, repr. 1968), pp. 21–5.

[26] Sir John Dalrymple, *Consequences of the French invasion* (London, 1798), description of No. IX, plate II.

[27] David Alexander, *Richard Newton and English Caricature in the 1790s* (Manchester, 1998), fig. 34, p. 52. Stella Cottrell draws our attention to the significance of the combinations of elements in prints, rather than the simple number of appearances of any single figure (Stella M. Cottrell, 'English views of France and the French, 1789–1815', D.Phil thesis, University of Oxford, 1990).

[28] Wayne Hanley, *The Genesis of Napoleonic Propaganda, 1796–1799* (gutenberg-e books, American Historical Association and Columbia University Press, <http://www.gutenberg-e.org/index.html>).

[29] M. Dorothy George, *English Political Caricature: a Study of Opinion and Propaganda* (London, 1959), p. 66.

[30] Many of these are also contained in the Curzon collection, in the volume Curzon b.10.

[31] Cottrell, 'English views of France and the French'.

[32] William Cobbett, *Important Considerations for the People of this Kingdom* (London, 1803).

[33] *Letters to the Right Honourable Lord Hawkesbury* (London, January 1802), pp. 27–8.

[34] Principal sources for details of the medals are: Laurence A. Brown, *A Catalogue of British Historical Medals 1760–1960*, vol. 1 (London, 1980); Ludwig Ernst Bramsen, Medailler *Napoléon le grand, ou Description dés medailles relatives aux affairs de la France pendant le Consulat et L'Empire* (Paris, 1904–13); J. G. Pollard 'Matthew Boulton and Conrad Heinrich Küchler', *The Numismatic Chronicle* seventh series, 10 (1970), 259–318; and H. F. B. Wheeler and A. M. Broadley, *Napoleon and the Invasion of England* (London, 1908), Chapter 21.

[35] Hemlow, quoted in Pocock, *The Terror before Trafalgar*, p. 61.

[36] A. M. Broadley and J. Rose, *Dumouriez and the Defence of England Against Napoleon* (London, 1909), p. xi.

[37] D. Gates, *The British Light Infantry Arm, c.1790–1815* (London, 1987), p. 129.

[38] Broadley and Rose, *Dumouriez*, p. 292.

[39] Ibid., p. 270.

[40] Ibid., p. 255.

[41] P.R.O., WO 30/72.

[42] Broadley and Rose, *Dumouriez*, p. 240.

[43] Ibid., p. 252.

[44] Dumouriez, *Memoirs on the defences of Great Britain and Ireland*, chapter entitled, 'Military Principles'.

[45] Broadley and Rose, *Dumouriez*, p. 256.

[46] Gates, *British Light Infantry Arm*, p. 130.

[47] Broadley and Rose, *Dumouriez*, p. 311.

[48] Bodleian Library, M.S. Eng. Hist. c.263, *Copy Book of Military Orders*, Eastern Military District, 1803–04.

[49] Broadley and Rose, *Dumouriez*, p. 255.

[50] P.R.O. 30/70/4/235, Dumouriez to Pitt, 20 May 1804.

[51] P.R.O. 30/8/131, Dumouriez to Pitt, 1 June 1804.

[52] Broadley and Rose, *Dumouriez*, p. 206.

[53] Ibid., p. 213.

[54] Dumouriez, *Memoirs*, chapter entitled 'Examination of Ports and Harbours'.

[55] Broadley and Rose, *Dumouriez*, p. 383.

[56] British Library, Add. MS. 31230 ff.167, pp. 351–90.

[57] Gates, *British Light Infantry Arm*, p. 133.

[58] WO 30/65, D. Dundas, *Papers connected with the Defence of Great Britain*, 1796–1804.

[59] J. E. Cookson, *The British Armed Nation, 1793–1815* (Oxford, 1997), pp. 45–6.

[60] WO 30/65, *Papers connected with the Defence of Great Britain*, 1796–1804.

[61] WO 30/100, *Defence of Eastern District, Lt. Gen. Craig to the Duke of York*, 23 June 1803.

[62] A. Saunders, *Fortress Britain* (Hants, 1989), p. 144.

[63] J. Burrows, *Essex Units in the War, 1914–19, vol. 3: Essex Yeomanry* (Southend, 1924), pp. 14, 20.

[64] WO 30/100, Defence of Eastern District, Lt. Gen. Craig to the Duke of York, 23 June 1803; WO 30/78, Craig, 'The Fortification of Eastern England,' 11 July 1804, in R. Glover, *Britain at Bay* (London, 1973), p. 198.

[65] P. Boynden, 'A System of Communication Throughout Each Country,' in A. J. Guy, ed., *The Road to Waterloo* (London, 1990), p. 129.

[66] Burrows, *Essex Yeomanry*, p. 33.

[67] J. Amphlett, *Invasion; a Descriptive and Satirical Poem* (Wolverhampton and London [1804]).

[68] *Returns of Yeomanry and Volunteer Corps Presented to the House of Lords, December 1803.*

[69] Abstract of the Census Return, 1801.

[70] J. Dunkin, *The History and Antiquities of Bicester* (London, 1816), p. 183.

[71] Oxfordshire R.O., QSD/L/36–7, Bicester Land Tax, 1802.

[72] *Jackson's Oxford Journal*, 11 February 1804.

[73] P.R.O. HO 50/82.

[74] P.R.O. WO 13/4489.

[75] *Victoria County History of the County of Oxford*, vol. 6 (London, 1907), p. 21; Bicester Land Tax.

[76] Dunkin, *The History and Antiquities of Bicester*, p. 16.

[77] *Memoirs and Correspondence of Francis Horner, MP* (London, 1853).

[78] Diana Donald and Christiane Banerji, *Gillray observed: the earliest account of his caricatures in* London und Paris (Cambridge, 1999), pp. 11–13.

[79] Gérard Hubert and Guy Ledoux-Lebard, *Napoléon: portraits contemporains bustes et statues* (Paris, 1999).

For cartoons listed in the British Museum Catalogue of Political and Personal Satires, the BMC number is noted.